THE NEW FOLGER LIBRARY
SHAKESPEARE

Designed to make Shakespeare's great plays available to all readers, the New Folger Library edition of Shakespeare's plays provides accurate texts in modern spelling and punctuation, as well as scene-by-scene action summaries, full explanatory notes, many pictures clarifying Shakespeare's language, and notes recording all significant departures from the early printed versions. Each play is prefaced by a brief introduction, by a guide to reading Shakespeare's language, and by accounts of his life and theater. Each play is followed by an annotated list of further readings and by a "Modern Perspective" written by an expert on that particular play.

Barbara A. Mowat is Director of Research *emerita* at the Folger Shakespeare Library, Consulting Editor of *Shakespeare Quarterly*, and author of *The Dramaturgy of Shakespeare's Romances* and of essays on Shakespeare's plays and their editing.

Paul Werstine is Professor of English in the Graduate School and at King's University College at Western University. He is a general editor of the New Variorum Shakespeare and author of *Early Modern Playhouse Manuscripts and the Editing of Shakespeare,* as well as many papers and essays on the printing and editing of Shakespeare's plays.

Folger Shakespeare Library

The Folger Shakespeare Library in Washington, D.C., is a privately funded research library dedicated to Shakespeare and the civilization of early modern Europe. It was founded in 1932 by Henry Clay and Emily Jordan Folger, and incorporated as part of Amherst College in Amherst, Massachusetts, one of the nation's oldest liberal arts colleges, from which Henry Folger had graduated in 1879. In addition to its role as the world's preeminent Shakespeare collection and its emergence as a leading center for Renaissance studies, the Folger Shakespeare Library offers a wide array of cultural and educational programs and services for the general public.

EDITORS

BARBARA A. MOWAT
Director of Research emerita
Folger Shakespeare Library

PAUL WERSTINE
Professor of English
King's University College at Western University, Canada

FOLGER SHAKESPEARE LIBRARY

Timon of Athens

By

WILLIAM SHAKESPEARE

EDITED BY BARBARA A. MOWAT
AND PAUL WERSTINE

SIMON & SCHUSTER PAPERBACKS
NEW YORK LONDON TORONTO SYDNEY NEW DELHI

Simon & Schuster Paperbacks
A Division of Simon & Schuster, Inc.
1230 Avenue of the Americas
New York, NY 10020

Copyright © 1992, 2013 by The Folger Shakespeare Library

This Simon & Schuster paperback edition November 2013

SIMON & SCHUSTER PAPERBACKS and colophon are registered trademarks of Simon & Schuster, Inc.

For information about special discounts for bulk purchases, please contact Simon & Schuster Special Sales at 1-866-506-1949 or business@simonandschuster.com

The Simon & Schuster Speakers Bureau can bring authors to your live event. For more information or to book an event contact the Simon & Schuster Speakers Bureau at 1-866-248-3049 or visit our website at www.simonspeakers.com.

Manufactured in the United States of America

10 9 8 7 6 5 4 3

ISBN 978-0-671-47955-8
ISBN 978-1-4516-8248-9 (ebook)

From the Director of the Folger Shakespeare Library

It is hard to imagine a world without Shakespeare. Since their composition four hundred years ago, Shakespeare's plays and poems have traveled the globe, inviting those who see and read his works to make them their own.

Readers of the New Folger Editions are part of this on-going process of "taking up Shakespeare," finding our own thoughts and feelings in language that strikes us as old or unusual and, for that very reason, new. We still struggle to keep up with a writer who could think a mile a minute, whose words paint pictures that shift like clouds. These expertly edited texts, presented here with accompanying explanatory notes and up-to-date critical essays, are distinctive because of what they do: they allow readers not simply to keep up, but to engage deeply with a writer whose works invite us to think, and think again.

These New Folger Editions of Shakespeare's plays are also special because of where they come from. The Folger Shakespeare Library in Washington, DC, where the Editions are produced, is the single greatest documentary source of Shakespeare's works. An unparalleled collection of early modern books, manuscripts, and artwork connected to Shakespeare, the Folger's holdings have been consulted extensively in the preparation of these texts. The Editions also reflect the expertise gained through the regular performance of Shakespeare's works in the Folger's Elizabethan Theater.

I want to express my deep thanks to editors Barbara Mowat and Paul Werstine for creating these indispensable editions of Shakespeare's works, which incorporate the best of textual scholarship with a richness of commentary that is both inspired and engaging. Readers who want to know more about Shakespeare and his plays can follow the paths these distinguished scholars have tread by visiting the Folger itself, where a range of physical and digital resources (available online) exist to supplement the material in these texts. I commend to you these words, and hope that they inspire.

Michael Witmore
Director, Folger Shakespeare Library

Contents

Contents

Editors' Preface

In recent years, ways of dealing with Shakespeare's texts and with the interpretation of his plays have been undergoing significant change. This edition, while retaining many of the features that have always made the Folger Shakespeare so attractive to the general reader, at the same time reflects these current ways of thinking about Shakespeare. For example, modern readers, actors, and teachers have become interested in the differences between, on the one hand, the early forms in which Shakespeare's plays were first published and, on the other hand, the forms in which editors through the centuries have presented them. In response to this interest, we have based our edition on what we consider the best early printed version of a particular play (explaining our rationale in a section called "An Introduction to This Text") and have marked our changes in the text—unobtrusively, we hope, but in such a way that the curious reader can be aware that a change has been made and can consult the "Textual Notes" to discover what appeared in the early printed version.

Current ways of looking at the plays are reflected in our brief prefaces, in many of the commentary notes, in the annotated lists of "Further Reading," and especially in each play's "Modern Perspective," an essay written by an outstanding scholar who brings to the reader his or her fresh assessment of the play in the light of today's interests and concerns.

As in the Folger Library General Reader's Shakespeare, which this edition replaces, we include explanatory notes designed to help make Shakespeare's language clearer to a modern reader, and we place the

notes on the page facing the text that they explain. We also follow the earlier edition in including illustrations—of objects, of clothing, of mythological figures—from books and manuscripts in the Folger Library collection. We provide fresh accounts of the life of Shakespeare, of the publishing of his plays, and of the theaters in which his plays were performed, as well as an introduction to the text itself. We also include a section called "Reading Shakespeare's Language," in which we try to help readers learn to "break the code" of Elizabethan poetic language.

For each section of each volume, we are indebted to a host of generous experts and fellow scholars. The "Reading Shakespeare's Language" sections, for example, could not have been written had not Arthur King, of Brigham Young University, and Randall Robinson, author of *Unlocking Shakespeare's Language*, led the way in untangling Shakespearean language puzzles and shared their insights and methodologies generously with us. "Shakespeare's Life" profited by the careful reading given it by the late S. Schoenbaum; "Shakespeare's Theater" was read and strengthened by Andrew Gurr, John Astington, and William Ingram; and "The Publication of Shakespeare's Plays" is indebted to the comments of Peter W. M. Blayney. We, as editors, take sole responsibility for any errors in our editions.

We are grateful to the authors of the "Modern Perspectives"; to Gail Kern Paster for her unfailing interest and advice; to Leeds Barroll and David Bevington for their generous encouragement; to the Huntington and Newberry Libraries for fellowship support; to King's College for the grants it has provided to Paul Werstine; to the Social Sciences and Humanities Research Council of Canada, which provided him with a Research Time Stipend for 1990–91; to R. J. Shroyer of the University of Western Ontario for essential computer support; to the

Folger Institute's Center for Shakespeare Studies for its sponsorship of a workshop on "Shakespeare's Texts for Students and Teachers" (funded by the National Endowment for the Humanities and led by Richard Knowles of the University of Wisconsin), a workshop from which we learned an enormous amount about what is wanted by college and high-school teachers of Shakespeare today; to Alice Falk for her expert copyediting; and especially to Steve Llano, our production editor at Pocket Books, whose expertise and attention to detail are essential to this project.

Our biggest debt is to the Folger Shakespeare Library—to Werner Gundersheimer, Director of the Library, who made possible our edition; to Deborah Curren-Aquino, who provides extensive editorial and production support; to Jean Miller, the Library's former Art Curator, who combs the Library holdings for illustrations, and to Julie Ainsworth, Head of the Photography Department, who carefully photographs them; to Peggy O'Brien, former Director of Education at the Folger and now Director of Education Programs at the Corporation for Public Broadcasting, who gave us expert advice about the needs being expressed by Shakespeare teachers and students (and to Martha Christian and other "master teachers" who used our texts in manuscript in their classrooms); to Allan Shnerson and Mary Bloodworth for their expert computer support; to the staff of the Academic Programs Division, especially Rachel Kunkle (whose help is crucial), Mary Tonkinson, Kathleen Lynch, Carol Brobeck, Toni Krieger, Liz Pohland, Owen Williams, and Lisa Meyers; and, finally, to the generously supportive staff of the Library's Reading Room.

Barbara A. Mowat and Paul Werstine

A map of ancient Greece.
Stephen Llano, based on Thucydides, . . . *De bello
peloponnesiaco libri octo* . . . (1696).

Shakespeare's *Timon of Athens*

The historical Timon lived in Athens in the fifth century BCE. He was thus a contemporary of Socrates, Pericles, and Alcibiades. Shakespeare presents him as a figure who suffers such profound disillusionment that he becomes a misanthrope, or man-hater, preferring the wilderness to any human community. He is thus a more interesting and more complex figure than the harshly condemned caricature that Timon had become to Shakespeare's contemporaries. Timon was so well known in Shakespeare's day that the word "Timonist" was a slang term for an unsociable man, and Shakespeare's contemporaries saw his misanthropy as the outward manifestation of the mortal sin of envy. George Whetstone, for example, in the mid-sixteenth-century *The English Myrror*, introduces Timon as an example of a man who "without envy cannot endure to behold the glory of the other. For which cause Timon of Athens was called dogged, because he grinned at the felicity of man: yea, if we well considered their effects, the actions of the envious may well be termed devilish in that they repine at the glory of God, and bend all their forces to suppress virtue and her followers."

In contrast to such writers as Whetstone, Shakespeare provides us with a far more compassionate representation of Timon. Shakespeare's play includes not just the disillusioned misanthrope that Timon ultimately becomes but also the wealthy, magnificent, and extravagantly generous figure of Timon before his transformation into misanthropy. When Timon first takes the stage, he is thronged by petitioners, artists, and merchants, as well as by those he calls his friends.

He lays out great sums to free a friend from debtors' prison, to provide for the marriage of a servant, and to patronize the arts, as well as to buy a jewel. While not exclusively altruistic in his pursuits, Timon nonetheless is presented as unique among the play's characters in furthering the good of others. His most extravagant generosity is to his friends, to whom he tirelessly offers gifts. Timon so idealizes friendship that he believes that it can replace the financial arrangements of credit and debt as the basis for the distribution of wealth in Athens. Through his bounty, Timon makes his wealth and property the property of his friends. His giving sometimes seems rivalrous insofar as he strives to give his friends greater gifts than they give him. Yet his understanding of friendship is ultimately cooperative, rather than competitive; he expects that, having received as gifts all that he owned, his friends will be equally generous to him.

Once Timon's creditors begin to clamor for repayment, Timon has the opportunity to discover if his friends share his understanding of friendship. Then he finds that his idealization of friendship has been an illusion. All his social relations proving to be baseless, Timon invites his friends once more to his formerly great house so that he can repudiate them bitterly and then abandon Athens and retreat to the woods. There in soliloquy and in interviews with his former fellow citizens, he expounds the misanthropy for which he was to remain notorious for thousands of years and eventually earn the severe judgment of so many of Shakespeare's contemporaries. Shakespeare's Timon, however, can never be altogether reduced to the stereotypically envious and devilish misanthrope, because he has been shown to have had the capacity for marvelously inclusive, if indiscriminate, friendship. His misanthropy,

according to Shakespeare, arises from the destruction of an admirable illusion, from which his subsequent hatred can never be entirely disentangled.

After you have read the play, we invite you to turn to the essay printed after it, *"Timon of Athens:* A Modern Perspective," by Professor Coppélia Kahn of Brown University.

Reading Shakespeare's Language: *Timon of Athens*

For many people today, reading Shakespeare's language can be a problem—but it is a problem that can be solved. Those who have studied Latin (or even French or German or Spanish), and those who are used to reading poetry, will have little difficulty understanding the language of Shakespeare's poetic drama. Others, though, need to develop the skills of untangling unusual sentence structures and of recognizing and understanding poetic compressions, omissions, and wordplay. And even those skilled in reading unusual sentence structures may have occasional trouble with Shakespeare's words. Four hundred years of "static" intervene between his speaking and our hearing. Most of his immense vocabulary is still in use, but a few of his words are not, and, worse, some of his words now have meanings quite different from those they had in the seventeenth century. In the theater, most of these difficulties are solved for us by actors who study the language and articulate it for us so that the essential meaning is heard—or, when combined with stage action, is at least *felt*. When reading on one's own, one

must do what each actor does: go over the lines (often with a dictionary close at hand) until the puzzles are solved and the lines yield up their poetry and the characters speak in words and phrases that are, suddenly, rewarding and wonderfully memorable.

Shakespeare's Words

As you begin to read the opening scenes of a play by Shakespeare, you may notice occasional unfamiliar words. Some are unfamiliar simply because we no longer use them. In the opening scenes of *Timon of Athens*, for example, you will find the words *untirable* (i.e., tireless), *continuate* (i.e., lasting), *anon* (i.e., soon), *unclew* (i.e., ruin), and *hungerly* (i.e., hungrily). Words of this kind are explained in notes to the text and will become familiar the more of Shakespeare's plays you read.

In *Timon of Athens*, as in all of Shakespeare's writing, more problematic are the words that we still use but that we use with a different meaning. In the opening scenes of *Timon of Athens*, for example, the word *happy* has the meaning of "fortunate," *record* is used where we would say "witness," *breathed* is used where we would say "animated, inspired," *meat* where we would say "food," and *harness* where we would say "armor." Such words will be explained in the notes to the text, but they, too, will become familiar as you continue to read Shakespeare's language.

Some words are strange not because of the "static" introduced by changes in language over the past centuries but because these are words that Shakespeare is using to build a dramatic world. *Timon* is, as its title declares, "of Athens," which is the setting for most of the play. For us, Athens is the cradle of democracy; in the

play, however, Athens does not function as a unified social entity, and it seems anything but ideally democratic in the profound divisions that separate its classes. At the top of Athens's social order are its aristocratic "Lords" and "Senators," an economic and political elite of "happy [i.e., fortunate] men," whose lives are filled not only with luxury but also with "ceremony" and "masques," through which the elite elaborately "gratulate" each other. Their style of life is built on the labor of a servant class, which has no social standing; to the elite, a servant is no more than a lord's "creature," "one which holds a trencher." Finally, beneath the servants come the dispossessed, represented in *Timon of Athens* by the Cynic philosopher Apemantus, who is usually addressed as "dog" by the elite. He, in turn, thinks no better of them; he accuses them of making "traffic" (i.e., trade, commerce, business) their "god," and refers to their "ceremony" as the "serving of becks and jutting-out of bums." Craving "no pelf," he prefers instead "a little oil and root." These unusual words and others that build the play's dramatic world will be explained in notes to the text.

Shakespeare's Sentences

In an English sentence, meaning is quite dependent on the place given each word. "The dog bit the boy" and "The boy bit the dog" mean very different things, even though the individual words are the same. Because English places such importance on the positions of words in sentences, on the way words are arranged, unusual arrangements can puzzle a reader. Shakespeare frequently shifts his sentences away from "normal" English arrangements—often to create the rhythm he seeks, sometimes to use a line's poetic rhythm to

emphasize a particular word, sometimes to give a character his or her own speech patterns or to allow the character to speak in a special way. When we attend a good performance of the play, the actors will have worked out the sentence structures and will articulate the sentences so that the meaning is clear. In reading for yourself, do as the actor does. That is, when you become puzzled by a character's speech, check to see if words are being presented in an unusual sequence.

Shakespeare often, for example, rearranges subjects and verbs (i.e., instead of "He goes" we find "Goes he"). In *Timon of Athens*, when Flavius says "Happier is he that has no friend to feed," he is using such a construction (1.2.214). So is Timon when he says "More welcome are you to my fortunes" (1.2.20). The "normal" order would be "he is happier" and "you are more welcome." Shakespeare also frequently places the object before the subject and verb (i.e., instead of "I hit him," we might find "Him I hit"). The Painter's declaration "A thousand moral paintings I can show" (1.1.105) is an example of such an inversion, as is the Messenger's "Your honorable letter he desires" (114). The "normal" order would be "I can show a thousand moral paintings" and "he desires your honorable letter."

Inversions are not the only unusual sentence structures in Shakespeare's language. Often in his sentences words that would normally appear together are separated from each other. As with inversions, this is often done to create a particular rhythm or to stress a particular word. Take, for example, the Poet's observation concerning Timon: "His large fortune, / Upon his good and gracious nature hanging, / Subdues and properties to his love and tendance / All sorts of hearts" (1.1.66–69). Here, the phrase "Upon his good and gracious nature hanging" separates subject ("His large for-

tune") from verb ("subdues and properties"). Or take the Poet's description of his own poem:

> You see how *all conditions,* how *all minds,*
> As well of glib and slipp'ry creatures as
> Of grave and austere quality, *tender down*
> *Their services* to Lord Timon.

(1.1.63–66)

In this sentence the nouns "conditions" and "minds" are separated from the verb "tender down" by descriptive phrases that make concrete the generalized "conditions." To create for yourself sentences that seem more like the English of everyday speech, you may wish to rearrange the words, putting together the word clusters ("You see how all conditions, how all minds, tender down their services to Lord Timon"). You will usually find that the sentence will gain in clarity but will lose its rhythm or shift its emphasis.

Sometimes, in addition to separating basic sentence elements, Shakespeare also holds them back, delaying them until other material to which he wants to give greater emphasis has been presented. Shakespeare puts this kind of construction in the mouth of the Poet:

> Amongst them all
> Whose eyes are on this sovereign lady fixed,
> One do I personate of Lord Timon's frame. . . .

(1.1.79–81)

Holding back the subject, verb, and object, the Poet begins the sentence with a subordinate clause ("Amongst them all whose eyes are on this sovereign lady fixed"). The effect is that the picture of the masses turning to look at Lady Fortune provides a context within which to set the individual representation of

Timon himself. When the Poet does provide the main clause ("One do I personate"), he inverts the elements and gives us object-verb-subject, creating a more interesting rhythm than the "normal" "I do personate one."

Finally, in many of Shakespeare's plays, sentences are sometimes complicated not because of unusual structures or interruptions but because Shakespeare omits words and parts of words that English sentences normally require. (In conversation, we, too, often omit words. We say, "Heard from him yet?" and our hearer supplies the missing "Have you.") Frequent reading of Shakespeare—and of other poets—trains us to supply the words missing from elliptical speeches. Ellipsis serves a number of different ends in *Timon of Athens*. The principal end seems to be creation of dialogue that sounds conversational. When, for example, the Jeweler announces "I have a jewel here," the Merchant replies "For the Lord Timon, sir?"—just as a speaker would in conversation, rather than using a complete and formal sentence: "Is it for Lord Timon, sir?" It is apparently with the same end that so often pronominal subjects are dropped before their verbs, though to the modern ear such ellipsis hardly seems to imitate informal speech. The following exchange, from a choice of many, provides (in line 301) one example in which Apemantus drops the pronoun *thou* before the verb "Shouldst":

SECOND LORD   Fare thee well, fare thee well.
APEMANTUS
 Thou art a fool to bid me farewell twice.
SECOND LORD   Why, Apemantus?
APEMANTUS
  Shouldst have kept one to thyself, for I mean to
    give thee none.
                                              (1.1.298–302)

Rather than capturing the informality of conversation, sometimes ellipsis can instead inform dialogue with a concise elegance that conveys the gravity and urgency of the topic being addressed by a speaker. Such is the case when the Messenger tells Timon of Ventidius's desperate need for help: "Five talents is his debt, / His means most short, his creditors most strait" (1.1.112–13). By omitting the needless repetition of the verb *are* from the clauses "His means most short" and "his creditors most strait," the Messenger artfully balances the clauses against each other, while at the same time in the very economy of his expression indicating the immediacy of Ventidius's needs.

Shakespearean Wordplay

Shakespeare plays with language so often and so variously that entire books are written on the topic. Here we will mention only two kinds of wordplay, puns and metaphors. Puns in *Timon of Athens* usually play on the multiple meanings of a single word. Timon employs a pun to adorn his emotional address to the friends he invites to dinner in 1.2:

> O, no doubt, my good friends, but the gods themselves have provided that I shall have much help from you. . . . I have told more of you to myself than you can with modesty speak in your own behalf.
>
> (90–96)

In this speech *told* means both "narrated" or "related" and "counted," the second meaning perhaps indicating Timon's awareness of the wealth of his friends, should he ever need monetary help from them. More often in

Timon of Athens, however, puns are to be found in Apemantus's savagely satiric speeches, where their multiple meanings expose the improvidence of Timon's gifts to his friends. "I doubt," says Apemantus, "whether their legs be worth the sums / That are given for 'em" (1.2.249–50). In this speech, *legs* means both "lower limbs" and "courtly bows." It will be a long time before Timon adopts Apemantus's viewpoint, but when he finally does, he too will pun crudely on the body parts of his so-called friends, calling them "mouth-friends" (3.6.91), a term that may mean both "those who only mouth their friendship" and "those who are friends only so long as one feasts them."

A metaphor is a play on words in which one object or idea is expressed as if it were something else, something with which it shares common features. For instance, in the Poet's statement "You see this confluence, this great flood of visitors" (1.1.51), the crowd that attends on Timon is translated through a metaphor into "confluence" or "flood," a seemingly endless stream of people (to continue the metaphor). At Timon's dinner for his friends in 1.2, he and Alcibiades bandy back and forth a metaphor in which a battlefield strewn with the bodies of fallen enemy soldiers is compared to a feast:

> TIMON Captain Alcibiades, your heart's in the field [i.e., battlefield] now.
> ALCIBIADES My heart is ever at your service, my lord.
> TIMON You had rather be at a breakfast of enemies than a dinner of friends.
> ALCIBIADES So they were bleeding new, my lord, there's no meat like 'em. I could wish my best friend at such a feast.
>
> (1.2.76–82)

Later Timon, at this point markedly attentive to his friends, transforms them in another metaphor into musical instruments:

> O you gods, think I, what need we have any friends if we should ne'er have need of 'em? They were the most needless creatures living, should we ne'er have use for 'em, and would most resemble sweet instruments hung up in cases, that keeps their sounds to themselves.

> (97–102)

Implied Stage Action

Finally, in reading Shakespeare's plays we should always remember that what we are reading is a performance script. The dialogue is written to be spoken by actors who, at the same time, are moving, gesturing, picking up objects, weeping, shaking their fists. Some stage action is described in what are called "stage directions"; some is suggested within the dialogue itself. We should always try to be alert to such signals as we stage the play in our imaginations.

Consider, for example, the stage action that is suggested in the exchange between Timon's servant Flaminius and the Lord Lucullus in 3.1. When Lucullus says to Flaminius "Here's three solidares for thee," it can reasonably be inferred that the speech is to be accompanied by the action of handing over money. This inference is confirmed by Flaminius's angry reply "Fly, damnèd baseness, / To him that worships thee!"— a speech that also seems to demand an action, the hurling of the solidares at Lucullus. Therefore we, as editors, have added stage directions, set in half-square

brackets to advise readers that they are editorial additions:

> LUCULLUS . . . Here's three solidares for thee. (⌜*Gives*
> *him money.*⌝) . . .
> FLAMINIUS   . . . Fly, damnèd baseness,
>   To him that worships thee!
>   ⌜*He throws the money back at Lucullus.*⌝
>   (45–51)

This is one of several places where the dialogue allows us to be reasonably confident about adding, in brackets, a stage direction suggesting the action.

On other occasions in *Timon of Athens*, the signals for stage action are not so clear. These occasions offer interpretive challenges in the absence of explicit stage directions in the Folio text. One such challenge arises with the sharply satiric commentary that Apemantus offers during the course of Timon's dinner in 1.2. Apemantus's commentary, which consists primarily of indictments of Timon's friends' flattery and of Timon's gullibility, elicits not a single reply or comment from either Timon or his friends. This commentary might then be considered as delivered "aside," a convention that allows dramatic characters to convey to the audience sentiments that, in the fiction, cannot be heard by the rest of the characters onstage. If Apemantus's speeches are asides, the modern convention is to have them marked as such by the editor. One problem, however, with having Apemantus speak aside is that he has already been established as a character with no interest in keeping his contempt for his fellow Athenians a secret from them; in 1.1 he reviled to their faces some of Timon's dinner guests (292–307). The convention of speaking aside therefore does not seem to fit Apeman-

tus's speeches. We appear to need another explanation why they go unregarded by the others at Timon's dinner. Such an explanation may be suggested in the dialogue between Timon and Apemantus that takes place before Apemantus begins his commentary. Arriving at the dinner, Apemantus declares to Timon an intention to be intolerably disagreeable on the occasion—"you shall not make me welcome. / I come to have thee thrust me out of doors." In response Timon arranges that Apemantus sit apart from the rest of the diners: "Go, let him have a table by himself" (25–31). It seems, then, that Apemantus's commentary is delivered from a site onstage that is to one side, or at a remove from the rest of the actors personating Timon and his guests. Therefore we, as editors, have marked his speeches as being delivered "apart," not "aside," and we leave it to our readers to decide for themselves whether Apemantus's speeches simply go unheard by the others, or the others deliberately ignore what Apemantus is saying. However, we have, as is our usual practice, placed in half-square brackets the directions for the speeches to be delivered "apart," as we have all the stage directions of our own creation, in order to make clear to readers that these are only our interpretations and thereby to encourage readers and directors to feel free to work out their own versions of the action.

It is immensely rewarding to work carefully with Shakespeare's language so that the words, the sentences, the wordplay, and the implied stage action all become clear—as readers for the past four centuries have discovered. It may be more pleasurable to attend a good performance of a play—though not everyone has thought so. But the joy of being able to stage one of Shakespeare's plays in one's imagination, to return to passages that continue to yield further meanings (or

further questions) the more one reads them—these are pleasures that, for many, rival (or at least augment) those of the performed text, and certainly make it worth considerable effort to "break the code" of Elizabethan poetic drama and let free the remarkable language that makes up a Shakespeare text.

Shakespeare's Life

Surviving documents that give us glimpses into the life of William Shakespeare show us a playwright, poet, and actor who grew up in the market town of Stratford-upon-Avon, spent his professional life in London, and returned to Stratford a wealthy landowner. He was born in April 1564, died in April 1616, and is buried inside the chancel of Holy Trinity Church in Stratford.

We wish we could know more about the life of the world's greatest dramatist. His plays and poems are testaments to his wide reading—especially to his knowledge of Virgil, Ovid, Plutarch, Holinshed's *Chronicles*, and the Bible—and to his mastery of the English language, but we can only speculate about his education. We know that the King's New School in Stratford-upon-Avon was considered excellent. The school was one of the English "grammar schools" established to educate young men, primarily in Latin grammar and literature. As in other schools of the time, students began their studies at the age of four or five in the attached "petty school," and there learned to read and write in English, studying primarily the catechism from the Book of Common Prayer. After two years in the petty school, students entered the lower form (grade) of the grammar

school, where they began the serious study of Latin grammar and Latin texts that would occupy most of the remainder of their school days. (Several Latin texts that Shakespeare used repeatedly in writing his plays and poems were texts that schoolboys memorized and recited.) Latin comedies were introduced early in the lower form; in the upper form, which the boys entered at age ten or eleven, students wrote their own Latin orations and declamations, studied Latin historians and rhetoricians, and began the study of Greek using the Greek New Testament.

Since the records of the Stratford "grammar school" do not survive, we cannot prove that William Shakespeare attended the school; however, every indication (his father's position as an alderman and bailiff of Stratford, the playwright's own knowledge of the Latin classics, scenes in the plays that recall grammar-school experiences—for example, *The Merry Wives of Windsor*, 4.1) suggests that he did. We also lack generally accepted documentation about Shakespeare's life after his schooling ended and his professional life in London began. His marriage in 1582 (at age eighteen) to Anne Hathaway and the subsequent births of his daughter Susanna (1583) and the twins Judith and Hamnet (1585) are recorded, but how he supported himself and where he lived are not known. Nor do we know when and why he left Stratford for the London theatrical world, nor how he rose to be the important figure in that world that he had become by the early 1590s.

We do know that by 1592 he had achieved some prominence in London as both an actor and a playwright. In that year was published a book by the playwright Robert Greene attacking an actor who had the audacity to write blank-verse drama and who was "in his own conceit [i.e., opinion] the only Shake-scene in a

country." Since Greene's attack includes a parody of a line from one of Shakespeare's early plays, there is little doubt that it is Shakespeare to whom he refers, a "Shake-scene" who had aroused Greene's fury by successfully competing with university-educated dramatists like Greene himself. It was in 1593 that Shakespeare became a published poet. In that year he published his long narrative poem *Venus and Adonis;* in 1594, he followed it with *The Rape of Lucrece*. Both poems were dedicated to the young earl of Southampton (Henry Wriothesley), who may have become Shakespeare's patron.

It seems no coincidence that Shakespeare wrote these narrative poems at a time when the theaters were closed because of the plague, a contagious epidemic disease that devastated the population of London. When the theaters reopened in 1594, Shakespeare apparently resumed his double career of actor and playwright and began his long (and seemingly profitable) service as an acting-company shareholder. Records for December of 1594 show him to be a leading member of the Lord Chamberlain's Men. It was this company of actors, later named the King's Men, for whom he would be a principal actor, dramatist, and shareholder for the rest of his career.

So far as we can tell, that career spanned about twenty years. In the 1590s, he wrote his plays on English history as well as several comedies and at least two tragedies (*Titus Andronicus* and *Romeo and Juliet*). These histories, comedies, and tragedies are the plays credited to him in 1598 in a work, *Palladis Tamia*, that in one chapter compares English writers with "Greek, Latin, and Italian Poets." There the author, Francis Meres, claims that Shakespeare is comparable to the Latin dramatists Seneca for tragedy and Plautus for comedy, and calls him "the most excellent in both

kinds for the stage." He also names him "Mellifluous and honey-tongued Shakespeare": "I say," writes Meres, "that the Muses would speak with Shakespeare's fine filed phrase, if they would speak English." Since Meres also mentions Shakespeare's "sugared sonnets among his private friends," it is assumed that many of Shakespeare's sonnets (not published until 1609) were also written in the 1590s.

In 1599, Shakespeare's company built a theater for themselves across the river from London, naming it the Globe. The plays that are considered by many to be Shakespeare's major tragedies (*Hamlet*, *Othello*, *King Lear*, and *Macbeth*) were written while the company was resident in this theater, as were such comedies as *Twelfth Night* and *Measure for Measure*. Many of Shakespeare's plays were performed at court (both for Queen Elizabeth I and, after her death in 1603, for King James I), some were presented at the Inns of Court (the residences of London's legal societies), and some were doubtless performed in other towns, at the universities, and at great houses when the King's Men went on tour; otherwise, his plays from 1599 to 1608 were, so far as we know, performed only at the Globe. Between 1608 and 1612, Shakespeare wrote several plays—among them *The Winter's Tale* and *The Tempest*—presumably for the company's new indoor Blackfriars theater, though the plays seem to have been performed also at the Globe and at court. Surviving documents describe a performance of *The Winter's Tale* in 1611 at the Globe, for example, and performances of *The Tempest* in 1611 and 1613 at the royal palace of Whitehall.

Shakespeare wrote very little after 1612, the year in which he probably wrote *King Henry VIII*. (It was at a performance of *Henry VIII* in 1613 that the Globe caught fire and burned to the ground.) Sometime

between 1610 and 1613 he seems to have returned to live in Stratford-upon-Avon, where he owned a large house and considerable property, and where his wife and his two daughters and their husbands lived. (His son Hamnet had died in 1596.) During his professional years in London, Shakespeare had presumably derived income from the acting company's profits as well as from his own career as an actor, from the sale of his play manuscripts to the acting company, and, after 1599, from his shares as an owner of the Globe. It was presumably that income, carefully invested in land and other property, which made him the wealthy man that surviving documents show him to have become. It is also assumed that William Shakespeare's growing wealth and reputation played some part in inclining the crown, in 1596, to grant John Shakespeare, William's father, the coat of arms that he had so long sought. William Shakespeare died in Stratford on April 23, 1616 (according to the epitaph carved under his bust in Holy Trinity Church) and was buried on April 25. Seven years after his death, his collected plays were published as *Mr. William Shakespeares Comedies, Histories, & Tragedies* (the work now known as the First Folio).

The years in which Shakespeare wrote were among the most exciting in English history. Intellectually, the discovery, translation, and printing of Greek and Roman classics were making available a set of works and worldviews that interacted complexly with Christian texts and beliefs. The result was a questioning, a vital intellectual ferment, that provided energy for the period's amazing dramatic and literary output and that fed directly into Shakespeare's plays. The Ghost in *Hamlet*, for example, is wonderfully complicated in part because he is a figure from Roman tragedy—the spirit of the dead returning to seek revenge—who at

A stylized representation of the Globe theater.
From Claes Jansz Visscher, *Londinum florentissima Britanniae urbs* . . . [c. 1625].

the same time inhabits a Christian hell (or purgatory); Hamlet's description of humankind reflects at one moment the Neoplatonic wonderment at mankind ("What a piece of work is a man!") and, at the next, the Christian disparagement of human sinners ("And yet, to me, what is this quintessence of dust?").

As intellectual horizons expanded, so also did geographical and cosmological horizons. New worlds—both North and South America—were explored, and in them were found human beings who lived and worshiped in ways radically different from those of Renaissance Europeans and Englishmen. The universe during these years also seemed to shift and expand. Copernicus had earlier theorized that the earth was not the center of the cosmos but revolved as a planet around the sun. Galileo's telescope, created in 1609, allowed scientists to see that Copernicus had been correct; the universe was not organized with the earth at the center, nor was it so nicely circumscribed as people had, until that time, thought. In terms of expanding horizons, the impact of these discoveries on people's beliefs—religious, scientific, and philosophical—cannot be overstated.

London, too, rapidly expanded and changed during the years (from the early 1590s to around 1610) that Shakespeare lived there. London—the center of England's government, its economy, its royal court, its overseas trade—was, during these years, becoming an exciting metropolis, drawing to it thousands of new citizens every year. Troubled by overcrowding, by poverty, by recurring epidemics of the plague, London was also a mecca for the wealthy and the aristocratic, and for those who sought advancement at court, or power in government or finance or trade. One hears in Shakespeare's plays the voices of London—the struggles for power, the fear of venereal disease, the language of buy-

ing and selling. One hears as well the voices of Stratford-upon-Avon—references to the nearby Forest of Arden, to sheepherding, to small-town gossip, to village fairs and markets. Part of the richness of Shakespeare's work is the influence felt there of the various worlds in which he lived: the world of metropolitan London, the world of small-town and rural England, the world of the theater, and the worlds of craftsmen and shepherds.

That Shakespeare inhabited such worlds we know from surviving London and Stratford documents, as well as from the evidence of the plays and poems themselves. From such records we can sketch the dramatist's life. We know from his works that he was a voracious reader. We know from legal and business documents that he was a multifaceted theater man who became a wealthy landowner. We know a bit about his family life and a fair amount about his legal and financial dealings. Most scholars today depend upon such evidence as they draw their picture of the world's greatest playwright. Such, however, has not always been the case. Until the late eighteenth century, the William Shakespeare who lived in most biographies was the creation of legend and tradition. This was the Shakespeare who was supposedly caught poaching deer at Charlecote, the estate of Sir Thomas Lucy close by Stratford; this was the Shakespeare who fled from Sir Thomas's vengeance and made his way in London by taking care of horses outside a playhouse; this was the Shakespeare who reportedly could barely read but whose natural gifts were extraordinary, whose father was a butcher who allowed his gifted son sometimes to help in the butcher shop, where William supposedly killed calves "in a high style," making a speech for the occasion. It was this legendary William Shakespeare whose Falstaff (in *1* and *2 Henry IV*) so pleased Queen Elizabeth that

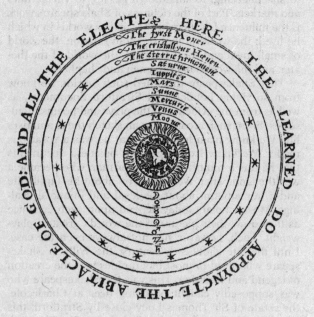

The fyrst Mouer
The cristallyne Heuen
The sterrie firmament
Saturne
Iuppiter
Mars
Sunne
Mercurie
Venus
Moone

HERE
THE
LEARNED
DO
APPOYNCTE
THE
ABITACLE OF
GOD: AND ALL THE
ELECTE

Ptolemaic universe.
From Leonard Digges, *A prognostication . . .* [1556].

she demanded a play about Falstaff in love, and demanded that it be written in fourteen days (hence the existence of *The Merry Wives of Windsor*). It was this legendary Shakespeare who reached the top of his acting career in the roles of the Ghost in *Hamlet* and old Adam in *As You Like It*—and who died of a fever contracted by drinking too hard at "a merry meeting" with the poets Michael Drayton and Ben Jonson. This legendary Shakespeare is a rambunctious, undisciplined man, as attractively "wild" as his plays were seen by earlier generations to be. Unfortunately, there is no trace of evidence to support these wonderful stories.

Perhaps in response to the disreputable Shakespeare of legend—or perhaps in response to the fragmentary and, for some, all-too-ordinary Shakespeare documented by surviving records—some people since the mid–nineteenth century have argued that William Shakespeare could not have written the plays that bear his name. These persons have put forward some dozen names as more likely authors, among them Queen Elizabeth, Sir Francis Bacon, Edward de Vere (earl of Oxford), and Christopher Marlowe. Such attempts to find what for these people is a more believable author of the plays is a tribute to the regard in which the plays are held. Unfortunately for their claims, the documents that exist that provide evidence for the facts of Shakespeare's life tie him inextricably to the body of plays and poems that bear his name. Unlikely as it seems to those who want the works to have been written by an aristocrat, a university graduate, or an "important" person, the plays and poems seem clearly to have been produced by a man from Stratford-upon-Avon with a very good "grammar-school" education and a life of experience in London and in the world of the London theater. How this particular man produced the works that dom-

inate the cultures of much of the world almost four hundred years after his death is one of life's mysteries— and one that will continue to tease our imaginations as we continue to delight in his plays and poems.

Shakespeare's Theater

The actors of Shakespeare's time performed plays in a great variety of locations. They played at court (that is, in the great halls of such royal residences as Whitehall, Hampton Court, and Greenwich); they played in halls at the universities of Oxford and Cambridge, and at the Inns of Court (the residences in London of the legal societies); and they also played in the private houses of great lords and civic officials. Sometimes acting companies went on tour from London into the provinces, often (but not only) when outbreaks of bubonic plague in the capital forced the closing of theaters to reduce the possibility of contagion in crowded audiences. In the provinces the actors usually staged their plays in churches (until around 1600) or in guildhalls. While surviving records show only a handful of occasions when actors played at inns while on tour, London inns were important playing places up until the 1590s.

The building of theaters in London had begun only shortly before Shakespeare wrote his first plays in the 1590s. These theaters were of two kinds: outdoor or public playhouses that could accommodate large numbers of playgoers, and indoor or private theaters for much smaller audiences. What is usually regarded as the first London outdoor public playhouse was called simply the Theatre. James Burbage—the father of Richard

Burbage, who was perhaps the most famous actor in Shakespeare's company—built it in 1576 in an area north of the city of London called Shoreditch. Among the more famous of the other public playhouses that capitalized on the new fashion were the Curtain and the Fortune (both also built north of the city), the Rose, the Swan, the Globe, and the Hope (all located on the Bankside, a region just across the Thames south of the city of London). All these playhouses had to be built outside the jurisdiction of the city of London because many civic officials were hostile to the performance of drama and repeatedly petitioned the royal council to abolish it.

The theaters erected on the Bankside (a region under the authority of the Church of England, whose head was the monarch) shared the neighborhood with houses of prostitution and with the Paris Garden, where the blood sports of bearbaiting and bullbaiting were carried on. There may have been no clear distinction between playhouses and buildings for such sports, for the Hope was used for both plays and baiting, and Philip Henslowe, owner of the Rose and, later, partner in the ownership of the Fortune, was also a partner in a monopoly on baiting. All these forms of entertainment were easily accessible to Londoners by boat across the Thames or over London Bridge.

Evidently Shakespeare's company prospered on the Bankside. They moved there in 1599. Threatened by difficulties in renewing the lease on the land where their first playhouse (the Theatre) had been built, Shakespeare's company took advantage of the Christmas holiday in 1598 to dismantle the Theatre and transport its timbers across the Thames to the Bankside, where, in 1599, these timbers were used in the building of the Globe. The weather in late December 1598 is recorded as having been especially harsh. It was so cold that the

Thames was "nigh [nearly] frozen," and there was heavy snow. Perhaps the weather aided Shakespeare's company in eluding their landlord, the snow hiding their activity and the freezing of the Thames allowing them to slide the timbers across to the Bankside without paying tolls for repeated trips over London Bridge. Attractive as this narrative is, it remains just as likely that the heavy snow hampered transport of the timbers in wagons through the London streets to the river. It also must be remembered that the Thames was, according to report, only "nigh frozen" and therefore as impassable as it ever was. Whatever the precise circumstances of this fascinating event in English theater history, Shakespeare's company was able to begin playing at their new Globe theater on the Bankside in 1599. After the first Globe burned down in 1613 during the staging of Shakespeare's *Henry VIII* (its thatch roof was set alight by cannon fire called for by the performance), Shakespeare's company immediately rebuilt on the same location. The second Globe seems to have been a grander structure than its predecessor. It remained in use until the beginning of the English Civil War in 1642, when Parliament officially closed the theaters. Soon thereafter it was pulled down.

The public theaters of Shakespeare's time were very different buildings from our theaters today. First of all, they were open-air playhouses. As recent excavations of the Rose and the Globe confirm, some were polygonal or roughly circular in shape; the Fortune, however, was square. The most recent estimates of their size put the diameter of these buildings at 72 feet (the Rose) to 100 feet (the Globe), but they were said to hold vast audiences of two or three thousand, who must have been squeezed together quite tightly. Some of these spectators paid extra to sit or stand in the two or three levels of roofed galleries that extended, on the upper levels, all

A stage play.
From [William Alabaster,] *Roxana tragœdia* . . . (1632).

the way around the theater and surrounded an open
space. In this space were the stage and, perhaps, the tiring house (what we would call dressing rooms), as well
as the so-called yard. In the yard stood the spectators
who chose to pay less, the ones whom Hamlet contemp-
tuously called "groundlings." For a roof they had only
the sky, and so they were exposed to all kinds of weather.
They stood on a floor that was sometimes made of mortar and sometimes of ash mixed with the shells of hazelnuts. The latter provided a porous and therefore dry
footing for the crowd, and the shells may have been
more comfortable to stand on because they were not as
hard as mortar. Availability of shells may not have been a
problem if hazelnuts were a favorite food for Shakespeare's audiences to munch on as they watched his
plays. Archaeologists who are today unearthing the
remains of theaters from this period have discovered
quantities of these nutshells on theater sites.

Unlike the yard, the stage itself was covered by a
roof. Its ceiling, called "the heavens," is thought to have
been elaborately painted to depict the sun, moon, stars,
and planets. Just how big the stage was remains hard
to determine. We have a single sketch of part of the
interior of the Swan. A Dutchman named Johannes de
Witt visited this theater around 1596 and sent a sketch
of it back to his friend, Arend van Buchel. Because van
Buchel found de Witt's letter and sketch of interest,
he copied both into a book. It is van Buchel's copy,
adapted, it seems, to the shape and size of the page in
his book, that survives. In this sketch, the stage appears
to be a large rectangular platform that thrusts far out
into the yard, perhaps even as far as the center of the
circle formed by the surrounding galleries. This drawing, combined with the specifications for the size of the
stage in the building contract for the Fortune, has led

scholars to conjecture that the stage on which Shakespeare's plays were performed must have measured approximately 43 feet in width and 27 feet in depth, a vast acting area. But the digging up of a large part of the Rose by archaeologists has provided evidence of a quite different stage design. The Rose stage was a platform tapered at the corners and much shallower than what seems to be depicted in the van Buchel sketch. Indeed, its measurements seem to be about 37.5 feet across at its widest point and only 15.5 feet deep. Because the surviving indications of stage size and design differ from each other so much, it is possible that the stages in other playhouses, like the Theatre, the Curtain, and the Globe (the outdoor playhouses where Shakespeare's plays were performed), were different from those at both the Swan and the Rose.

After about 1608 Shakespeare's plays were staged not only at the Globe but also at an indoor or private playhouse in Blackfriars. This theater had been constructed in 1596 by James Burbage in an upper hall of a former Dominican priory or monastic house. Although Henry VIII had dissolved all English monasteries in the 1530s (shortly after he had founded the Church of England), the area remained under church, rather than hostile civic, control. The hall that Burbage had purchased and renovated was a large one in which Parliament had once met. In the private theater that he constructed, the stage, lit by candles, was built across the narrow end of the hall, with boxes flanking it. The rest of the hall offered seating room only. Because there was no provision for standing room, the largest audience it could hold was less than a thousand, or about a quarter of what the Globe could accommodate. Admission to Blackfriars was correspondingly more expensive. Instead of a penny to stand in the yard at

the Globe, it cost a minimum of sixpence to get into Blackfriars. The best seats at the Globe (in the Lords' Room in the gallery above and behind the stage) cost sixpence; but the boxes flanking the stage at Blackfriars were half a crown, or five times sixpence. Some spectators who were particularly interested in displaying themselves paid even more to sit on stools on the Blackfriars stage.

Whether in the outdoor or indoor playhouses, the stages of Shakespeare's time were different from ours. They were not separated from the audience by the dropping of a curtain between acts and scenes. Therefore the playwrights of the time had to find other ways of signaling to the audience that one scene (to be imagined as occurring in one location at a given time) had ended and the next (to be imagined at perhaps a different location at a later time) had begun. The customary way used by Shakespeare and many of his contemporaries was to have everyone onstage exit at the end of one scene and have one or more different characters enter to begin the next. In a few cases, where characters remain onstage from one scene to another, the dialogue or stage action makes the change of location clear, and the characters are generally to be imagined as having moved from one place to another. For example, in *Romeo and Juliet*, Romeo and his friends remain onstage in Act 1 from scene 4 to scene 5, but they are represented as having moved between scenes from the street that leads to Capulet's house into Capulet's house itself. The new location is signaled in part by the appearance onstage of Capulet's servingmen carrying napkins, something they would not take into the streets. Playwrights had to be quite resourceful in the use of hand properties, like the napkin, or in the use of dialogue to specify where the action was taking place in

their plays because, in contrast to most of today's theaters, the playhouses of Shakespeare's time did not use movable scenery to dress the stage and make the setting precise. As another consequence of this difference, however, the playwrights of Shakespeare's time did not have to specify exactly where the action of their plays was set when they did not choose to do so, and much of the action of their plays is tied to no specific place.

Usually Shakespeare's stage is referred to as a "bare stage," to distinguish it from the stages of the last two or three centuries with their elaborate sets. But the stage in Shakespeare's time was not completely bare. Philip Henslowe, owner of the Rose, lists in his inventory of stage properties a rock, three tombs, and two mossy banks. Stage directions in plays of the time also call for such things as thrones (or "states"), banquets (presumably tables with plaster replicas of food on them), and beds and tombs to be pushed onto the stage. Thus the stage often held more than the actors.

The actors did not limit their performing to the stage alone. Occasionally they went beneath the stage, as the Ghost appears to do in the first act of *Hamlet*. From there they could emerge onto the stage through a trapdoor. They could retire behind the hangings across the back of the stage (or the front of the tiring house), as, for example, the actor playing Polonius does when he hides behind the arras. Sometimes the hangings could be drawn back during a performance to "discover" one or more actors behind them. When performance required that an actor appear "above," as when Juliet is imagined to stand at the window of her chamber in the famous and misnamed "balcony scene," then the actor probably climbed the stairs to the gallery over the back of the stage and temporarily shared it with some of the spectators. The stage was also provided with ropes and

winches so that actors could descend from, and reascend to, the "heavens."

Perhaps the greatest difference between dramatic performances in Shakespeare's time and ours was that in Shakespeare's England the roles of women were played by boys. (Some of these boys grew up to take male roles in their maturity.) There were no women in the acting companies, only in the audience. It had not always been so in the history of the English stage. There are records of women on English stages in the thirteenth and fourteenth centuries, two hundred years before Shakespeare's plays were performed. After the accession of James I in 1603, the queen of England and her ladies took part in entertainments at court called masques, and with the reopening of the theaters in 1660 at the restoration of Charles II, women again took their place on the public stage.

The chief competitors for the companies of adult actors such as the one to which Shakespeare belonged and for which he wrote were companies of exclusively boy actors. The competition was most intense in the early 1600s. There were then two principal children's companies: the Children of Paul's (the choirboys from St. Paul's Cathedral, whose private playhouse was near the cathedral); and the Children of the Chapel Royal (the choirboys from the monarch's private chapel, who performed at the Blackfriars theater built by Burbage in 1596, which Shakespeare's company had been stopped from using by local residents who objected to crowds). In *Hamlet* Shakespeare writes of "an aerie [nest] of children, little eyases [hawks], that cry out on the top of question and are most tyrannically clapped for 't. These are now the fashion and . . . berattle the common stages [attack the public theaters]." In the long run, the adult actors prevailed. The Children of Paul's dissolved

around 1606. By about 1608 the Children of the Chapel Royal had been forced to stop playing at the Blackfriars theater, which was then taken over by the King's company of players, Shakespeare's own troupe.

Acting companies and theaters of Shakespeare's time were organized in different ways. For example, Philip Henslowe owned the Rose and leased it to companies of actors, who paid him from their takings. Henslowe would act as manager of these companies, initially paying playwrights for their plays and buying properties, recovering his outlay from the actors. With the building of the Globe, Shakespeare's company, however, managed itself, with the principal actors, Shakespeare among them, having the status of "sharers" and the right to a share in the takings, as well as the responsibility for a part of the expenses. Five of the sharers, including Shakespeare, owned the Globe. As actor, as sharer in an acting company and in ownership of theaters, and as playwright, Shakespeare was about as involved in the theatrical industry as one could imagine. Although Shakespeare and his fellows prospered, their status under the law was conditional upon the protection of powerful patrons. "Common players"—those who did not have patrons or masters—were classed in the language of the law with "vagabonds and sturdy beggars." So the actors had to secure for themselves the official rank of servants of patrons. Among the patrons under whose protection Shakespeare's company worked were the lord chamberlain and, after the accession of King James in 1603, the king himself.

We are now perhaps on the verge of learning a great deal more about the theaters in which Shakespeare and his contemporaries performed—or at least of opening up new questions about them. Already about 70 percent of the Rose has been excavated, as has

about 10 percent of the second Globe, the one built in
1614. It is to be hoped that soon more will be available
for study. These are exciting times for students of
Shakespeare's stage.

The Publication of
Shakespeare's Plays

Eighteen of Shakespeare's plays found their way into
print during the playwright's lifetime, but there is nothing to suggest that he took any interest in their publication. These eighteen appeared separately in editions
called quartos. Their pages were not much larger than
the one you are now reading, and these little books were
sold unbound for a few pence. The earliest of the quartos that still survive were printed in 1594, the year that
both *Titus Andronicus* and a version of the play now
called *2 King Henry VI* became available. While almost
every one of these early quartos displays on its title page
the name of the acting company that performed the
play, only about half provide the name of the playwright,
Shakespeare. The first quarto edition to bear the name
Shakespeare on its title page is *Love's Labor's Lost* of
1598. A few of these quartos were popular with the
book-buying public of Shakespeare's lifetime; for example, quarto *Richard II* went through five editions
between 1597 and 1615. But most of the quartos were
far from best-sellers; *Love's Labor's Lost* (1598), for
instance, was not reprinted in quarto until 1631. After
Shakespeare's death, two more of his plays appeared in
quarto format: *Othello* in 1622 and *The Two Noble Kins-
men,* coauthored with John Fletcher, in 1634.

In 1623, seven years after Shakespeare's death, *Mr. William Shakespeares Comedies, Histories, & Tragedies* was published. This printing offered readers in a single book thirty-six of the thirty-eight plays now thought to have been written by Shakespeare, including eighteen that had never been printed before. And it offered them in a style that was then reserved for serious literature and scholarship. The plays were arranged in double columns on pages nearly a foot high. This large page size is called "folio," as opposed to the smaller "quarto," and the 1623 volume is usually called the Shakespeare First Folio. It is reputed to have sold for the lordly price of a pound. (One copy at the Folger Library is marked fifteen shillings—that is, three-quarters of a pound.)

In a preface to the First Folio entitled "To the great Variety of Readers," two of Shakespeare's former fellow actors in the King's Men, John Heminge and Henry Condell, wrote that they themselves had collected their dead companion's plays. They suggested that they had seen his own papers: "we have scarce received from him a blot in his papers." The title page of the Folio declared that the plays within it had been printed "according to the True Original Copies." Comparing the Folio to the quartos, Heminge and Condell disparaged the quartos, advising their readers that "before you were abused with divers stolen and surreptitious copies, maimed, and deformed by the frauds and stealths of injurious impostors." Many Shakespeareans of the eighteenth and nineteenth centuries believed Heminge and Condell and regarded the Folio plays as superior to anything in the quartos.

Once we begin to examine the Folio plays in detail, it becomes less easy to take at face value the word of Heminge and Condell about the superiority of the

Folio texts. For example, of the first nine plays in the Folio (one-quarter of the entire collection), four were essentially reprinted from earlier quarto printings that Heminge and Condell had disparaged; and four have now been identified as printed from copies written in the hand of a professional scribe of the 1620s named Ralph Crane; the ninth, *The Comedy of Errors*, was apparently also printed from a manuscript, but one whose origin cannot be readily identified. Evidently then, eight of the first nine plays in the First Folio were not printed, in spite of what the Folio title page announces, "according to the True Original Copies," or Shakespeare's own papers, and the source of the ninth is unknown. Since today's editors have been forced to treat Heminge and Condell's pronouncements with skepticism, they must choose whether to base their own editions upon quartos or the Folio on grounds other than Heminge and Condell's story of where the quarto and Folio versions originated.

Editors have often fashioned their own narratives to explain what lies behind the quartos and Folio. They have said that Heminge and Condell meant to criticize only a few of the early quartos, the ones that offer much shorter and sometimes quite different, often garbled, versions of plays. Among the examples of these are the 1600 quarto of *Henry V* (the Folio offers a much fuller version) or the 1603 *Hamlet* quarto (in 1604 a different, much longer form of the play got into print as a quarto). Early-twentieth-century editors speculated that these questionable texts were produced when someone in the audience took notes from the plays' dialogue during performances and then employed "hack poets" to fill out the notes. The poor results were then sold to a publisher and presented in print as Shakespeare's plays. More recently this story has given way to another in which the shorter versions are said

to be re-creations from memory of Shakespeare's plays by actors who wanted to stage them in the provinces but lacked manuscript copies. Most of the quartos offer much better texts than these so-called bad quartos. Indeed, in most of the quartos we find texts that are at least equal to or better than what is printed in the Folio. Many Shakespeare enthusiasts persuaded themselves that most of the quartos were set into type directly from Shakespeare's own papers, although there is nothing on which to base this conclusion except the desire for it to be true. Thus speculation continues about how the Shakespeare plays got to be printed. All that we have are the printed texts.

The book collector who was most successful in bringing together copies of the quartos and the First Folio was Henry Clay Folger, founder of the Folger Shakespeare Library in Washington, D.C. While it is estimated that there survive around the world only about 230 copies of the First Folio, Mr. Folger was able to acquire more than seventy-five copies, as well as a large number of fragments, for the library that bears his name. He also amassed a substantial number of quartos. For example, only fourteen copies of the First Quarto of *Love's Labor's Lost* are known to exist, and three are at the Folger Shakespeare Library. As a consequence of Mr. Folger's labors, scholars visiting the Folger Library have been able to learn a great deal about sixteenth- and seventeenth-century printing and, particularly, about the printing of Shakespeare's plays. And Mr. Folger did not stop at the First Folio, but collected many copies of later editions of Shakespeare, beginning with the Second Folio (1632), the Third (1663–64), and the Fourth (1685). Each of these later folios was based on its immediate predecessor and was edited anonymously. The first editor of Shakespeare whose name we know was Nicholas Rowe, whose first

edition came out in 1709. Mr. Folger collected this edition and many, many more by Rowe's successors.

An Introduction to This Text

Timon of Athens was first printed in the 1623 collection
of Shakespeare's plays now known as the First Folio. The
present edition is based directly upon that printing.* For
the convenience of the reader, we have modernized the
punctuation and the spelling of the Folio. Sometimes we
go so far as to modernize certain old forms of words; for
example, usually when *a* means *he*, we change it to *he;*
we change *mo* to *more*, and *ye* to *you*. But it is not our
practice in editing any of the plays to modernize words
that sound distinctly different from modern forms. For
example, when the early printed texts read *sith* or *apri-
cocks* or *porpentine*, we have not modernized to *since*,
apricots, *porcupine*. When the forms *an*, *and*, or *and if*
appear instead of the modern form *if*, we have reduced
and to *an* but have not changed any of these forms to
their modern equivalent, *if*. We also modernize and,
where necessary, correct passages in foreign languages,
unless an error in the early printed text can be reasonably explained as a joke.

Whenever we change the wording of the First Folio or
add anything to its stage directions, we mark the change
by enclosing it in superior half-brackets (⌐⌐). We want
our readers to be immediately aware when we have
intervened. (Only when we correct an obvious typo-

---

*We have also consulted the computerized text of the First Folio
provided by the Text Archive of the Oxford University Computing
Centre, to which we are grateful.

graphical error in the First Folio does the change not get marked.) Whenever we change either the First Folio's wording or its punctuation so that meaning changes, we list the change in the textual notes at the back of the book, even if all we have done is fix an obvious error.

We regularize spellings of a number of the proper names, as is the usual practice in editions of the play. For example, the Folio sometimes calls Apemantus "Apermantus" and sometimes calls Ventidius "Ventigius," "Ventiddius," or "Ventidgius," but we use the spellings "Apemantus" and "Ventidius" throughout the text.

This edition differs from many earlier ones in its efforts to aid the reader in imagining the play as a performance rather than as a series of actual events. Thus we as editors refrain from adding stage directions calling for action that is unlikely to have been performed or unlikely to be performed today onstage—no matter how helpful such stage directions may be to the reader in imagining the events that constitute the plot of the play. For example, when the anonymous soldier finds Timon's epitaphs in 5.3 and, unable to read one of them, resolves "the character [to] take with wax," some editors choose to help their readers visualize the soldier's intention by adding the stage direction "He makes a wax impression." Since it is unlikely that in performance an actor would actually do such a thing onstage, we have not added this direction or others of its kind. Nevertheless, whenever it is reasonably certain, in our view, that a speech is accompanied by a particular action, we provide a stage direction describing the action, setting the added direction in brackets to signal that it is not found in the Folio. (Occasional exceptions to this rule occur when the action is so obvious that to add a stage direction would insult the reader). Stage directions for the entrance of a character in mid-scene are, with rare exceptions, placed so

that they immediately precede the character's participation in the scene, even though these entrances may
appear somewhat earlier in the early printed texts.
Whenever we move a stage direction, we record this
change in the textual notes. Latin stage directions (e.g.,
Exeunt) are translated into English (e.g., *They exit*).

We expand the often severely abbreviated forms of
names used as speech headings in early printed texts
into the full names of the characters. We also regularize the speakers' names in speech headings, using only
a single designation for each character, even though
the early printed texts sometimes use a variety of desig-
nations. Variations in the speech headings of the early
printed texts are recorded in the textual notes.

In the present edition, as well, we mark with a dash
any change of address within a speech, unless a stage
direction intervenes. When the *-ed* ending of a word is
to be pronounced, we mark it with an accent. Like editors for the past two centuries, we print metrically
linked lines in the following way:

PAINTER
  It wears, sir, as it grows.
POET   Ay, that's well known.
                                              (1.1.4–5)

However, when there are a number of short verse-lines
that can be linked in more than one way, we do not,
with rare exceptions, indent any of them.

The Explanatory Notes

The notes that appear on the pages facing the text are
designed to provide readers with the help that they may
need to enjoy the play. Whenever the meaning of a word

in the text is not readily accessible in a good contemporary dictionary, we offer the meaning in a note. Sometimes we provide a note even when the relevant meaning is to be found in the dictionary but when the word has acquired since Shakespeare's time other potentially confusing meanings. In our notes, we try to offer modern synonyms for Shakespeare's words. We also try to indicate to the reader the connection between the word in the play and the modern synonym. For example, Shakespeare sometimes uses the word *head* to mean *source*, but, for modern readers, there may be no connection evident between these two words. We provide the connection by explaining Shakespeare's usage as follows: "**head:** fountainhead, source." On some occasions, a whole phrase or clause needs explanation. Then, if space allows, we rephrase in our own words the difficult passage, and add at the end synonyms for individual words in the passage. When scholars have been unable to determine the meaning of a word or phrase, we acknowledge the uncertainty.

Authorship of *Timon of Athens*

Since *Timon of Athens* was published in the 1623 collection of Shakespeare's plays that we now call the First Folio, it has as good a claim to being Shakespeare's as most of the plays now attributed to him and a better claim than some currently being put forward (e.g., *Edward III*). Nonetheless, there has long been dissatisfaction with passages and scenes in *Timon*, and this has led to the opinion that Shakespeare must have worked with one or more collaborators in writing the play. The tradition that *Timon* is not all Shakespeare's can be traced as far back as the great Romantic poet Samuel Taylor Coleridge, who claimed to be able to distinguish

on stylistic grounds Shakespeare's work from others'
line by line as he read the plays. Coleridge did not work
out in detail his conviction that parts of *Timon* (and of
other plays) were written by other dramatists, but he
inspired a host of Shakespeare scholars and enthusiasts
throughout much of the nineteenth century and well
into the twentieth in their attempts to identify Shakespeare's alleged collaborator and to assign to him those
parts of *Timon* judged to be not Shakespearean (which
usually meant that the parts were deemed somehow
"unworthy" of the Bard). So many different candidates
for the role of collaborator were proposed during those
years that the whole enterprise became easy for its
scholarly opponents to discredit.

By the middle of the twentieth century, the whole
practice of reattributing parts of *Timon* (and other
plays) to other dramatists became stigmatized by the
name *disintegrationism* and fell from scholarly favor.
Recently, however, some attribution scholars have
returned to the issue, adopting a disinterested, quasi-
scientific position that the individual styles of dramatists, Shakespeare among them, are neither inferior
nor superior to each other but are simply different.
What's more, they argue, these stylistic differences can
be quantified and subjected to statistical analysis.
Recent investigations of *Timon*'s authorship by such
methods have not, however, produced conclusive
results. Some attribution scholars have identified
Thomas Middleton as Shakespeare's collaborator on
the play, but others, equally expert in this narrow field
of study, have rejected this claim. Whether *Timon* is
Shakespeare's alone or not is still being rather hotly
debated. Among the evidence being advanced for dual
authorship are differences in the value of the talent
that, some scholars allege, occur between different
parts of the play. On this issue, see "Talents," page 208.

THE
ACTORS
NAMES.

 TYMON of *Athens.*
    Lucius, And
        Lucullus, two Flattering Lords.
Appemantus, a *Churlish Philosopher.*
Sempronius another *flattering Lord.*
Alcibiades, an *Athenian Captaine.*
Poet.
Painter.
Ieweller.
Merchant.
Certaine Senatours.
Certaine Maskers.
Certaine Theeues.

Flaminius, one of *Tymons Seruants.*
Seruilius, another.
Caphis.
Varro.
Philo.   *Seuerall Seruants to Vsurers.*
Titus.
Lucius.
Hortensis
Ventigius, one of *Tymons false Friends.*
Cupid.
Sempronius.
With diuers other Seruants,
And Attendants.

From the 1623 First Folio.

TIMON
OF
ATHENS

Characters in the Play

TIMON, a noble Athenian
FLAVIUS, his steward
LUCILIUS
FLAMINIUS } *servants of Timon*
SERVILIUS
Other SERVANTS of Timon

APEMANTUS, a Cynic philosopher

ALCIBIADES, an Athenian Captain
PHRYNIA } *his concubines*
TIMANDRA
SOLDIER of Alcibiades

SENATORS and LORDS of Athens
LUCIUS
LUCULLUS
SEMPRONIUS } *friends of Timon*
VENTIDIUS
Other FRIENDS of Timon

CAPHIS, servant to a Senator
ISIDORE'S MAN
VARRO'S two MEN
TITUS } *servants of Timon's creditors*
LUCIUS' MAN
HORTENSIUS
PHILOTUS

A POET
A PAINTER
A JEWELER
A MERCHANT
An OLD ATHENIAN

3

FOOL
PAGE

Three STRANGERS, one called HOSTILIUS

BANDITTI, thieves

"CUPID" and other Maskers (as Amazons)

Soldiers, Servants, Messengers, Attendants, Musicians

TIMON

OF

ATHENS

ACT 1

1.1 The stage fills with suitors to and admirers of Lord Timon. When he arrives, he spends lavishly in freeing a friend from prison, financing the marriage of one of his servants, patronizing artists, and buying a jewel. He also invites many in the crowd to dinner at his house, including Alcibiades and the Cynic philosopher Apemantus, who reviles Timon's other guests.

---

0 SD. **Enter . . . doors:** The Folio stage direction, which includes a "Mercer" who never speaks or is referred to in the scene, is inconsistent with the dialogue that follows. According to the dialogue, besides the Poet and Painter there are only two others—the Merchant and the Jeweler—onstage. ("I know them both," says the Painter, line 10.)   **several:** separate

3. **long:** i.e., for a **long** time; **How . . . world:** Proverbial for "How are you?" (In line 4, the Painter responds to the question's literal meaning.)

4. **wears:** wastes away; **grows:** grows old

6. **strange:** i.e., event not experienced before

7. **manifold record not matches:** i.e., is unmatched according to numerous and varied witnesses   **record:** accent on second syllable

8. **Magic of bounty:** i.e., Timon, whose generosity acts like a conjuror summoning **spirits**

12. **fixed:** securely established

13. **breathed:** animated, inspired

14. **untirable:** tireless; **continuate:** long-continued, lasting

15. **passes:** surpasses, excels

ACT 1

Scene 1

Enter Poet, Painter, Jeweler, ⌈and⌉ Merchant, at several doors.

POET   Good day, sir.

PAINTER   I am glad you're well.

POET
I have not seen you long. How goes the world?

PAINTER
It wears, sir, as it grows.

POET   Ay, that's well known.   5
But what particular rarity, what strange,
Which manifold record not matches? See,
Magic of bounty, all these spirits thy power
Hath conjured to attend. I know the merchant.

PAINTER   I know them both. Th' other's a jeweler.   10

MERCHANT, ⌈*to Jeweler*⌉
O, 'tis a worthy lord!

JEWELER   Nay, that's most fixed.

MERCHANT
A most incomparable man, breathed, as it were,
To an untirable and continuate goodness.
He passes.   15

JEWELER   I have a jewel here—

MERCHANT
O, pray, let's see 't. For the Lord Timon, sir?

7

18. **touch the estimate:** i.e., go as far as the attributed value

21. **sings:** i.e., **sings** of

22. **form:** kind; shape; quality

23. **water:** luster

24. **dedication:** i.e., **dedication** of a poem (**work**) to a patron

27–28. **gum . . . nourished:** This figure of speech perhaps refers to the sap secreted by trees and shrubs.

29. **it:** i.e., the **flint**

30. **Provokes itself:** i.e., calls **itself** forth (unlike the **flint** that must be **struck** before **flame** appears)

30–31. **flies each bound it chases:** i.e., seeks escape from its limits (literally, rebounds from each bank it flows toward)

33. **my presentment:** **my** offering it for acceptance and consideration (to Timon)

37. **Indifferent:** i.e., reasonably well

40. **big:** i.e., forcefully

41–42. **To . . . interpret:** i.e., **one might** use words to give meaning to the mute gestures

43. **mocking:** imitation

44. **touch:** detail, stroke or dash of color

JEWELER
    If he will touch the estimate. But for that—
POET, ⌜*to Painter*⌝
    When we for recompense have praised the vile,
    It stains the glory in that happy verse   20
    Which aptly sings the good.
MERCHANT, ⌜*looking at the jewel*⌝
    'Tis a good form.
JEWELER   And rich. Here is a water, look ye.
PAINTER, ⌜*to Poet*⌝
    You are rapt, sir, in some work, some dedication
    To the great lord.   25
POET   A thing slipped idly from me.
    Our poesy is as a ⌜gum⌝ which ⌜oozes⌝
    From whence 'tis nourished. The fire i' th' flint
    Shows not till it be struck; our gentle flame
    Provokes itself and, like the current, flies   30
    Each bound it chases. What have you there?
PAINTER
    A picture, sir. When comes your book forth?
POET
    Upon the heels of my presentment, sir.
    Let's see your piece.
PAINTER   'Tis a good piece.   35
POET
    So 'tis. This comes off well and excellent.
PAINTER
    Indifferent.
POET   Admirable! How this grace
    Speaks his own standing! What a mental power
    This eye shoots forth! How big imagination   40
    Moves in this lip! To th' dumbness of the gesture
    One might interpret.
PAINTER
    It is a pretty mocking of the life.
    Here is a touch. Is 't good?

46. **Artificial strife:** perhaps, the strong effort of art; perhaps, according to many editors, art striving to rival or emulate **nature**

47 SD. **Senators:** See "The Athenian Senate" in "Historical Background," page 207.

48. **followed:** i.e., sought after by admirers

49. **happy:** fortunate

53. **shaped out:** formed

54. **this beneath world:** i.e., the sublunary **world** (where Fortune rules)

55. **entertainment:** hospitality; support

55–60. **My free . . . behind:** i.e., I attack no single individual but rise far above the particular **Halts not particularly:** i.e., is not crippled by attention to any particular **wide sea of wax:** See longer note, page 191. **leveled malice:** i.e., **malice** aimed at someone, as if it were a gun **flies:** i.e., my **course flies forth on:** directly on, without interruption **tract:** trace, track

62. **unbolt:** unfold, explain

63. **all conditions:** i.e., people of **all** social **conditions**

65. **quality:** disposition; **tender down:** lay **down** in payment

68. **properties:** appropriates; **tendance:** attention, care

69. **glass-faced flatterer:** i.e., one who reflects, like a mirror, the looks of those he flatters

72. **returns:** turns away, retires

POET   I will say of it,   45
  It tutors nature. Artificial strife
  Lives in these touches livelier than life.

              Enter certain Senators.

PAINTER   How this lord is followed.
POET
  The senators of Athens, happy men.
PAINTER   Look, more.   50
POET
  You see this confluence, this great flood of visitors.
  (⌜*Indicating his poem.*⌝) I have in this rough work
    shaped out a man
  Whom this beneath world doth embrace and hug
  With amplest entertainment. My free drift   55
  Halts not particularly but moves itself
  In a wide sea of wax. No leveled malice
  Infects one comma in the course I hold,
  But flies an eagle flight, bold and forth on,
  Leaving no tract behind.   60
PAINTER   How shall I understand you?
POET   I will unbolt to you.
  You see how all conditions, how all minds,
  As well of glib and slipp'ry creatures as
  Of grave and austere quality, tender down   65
  Their services to Lord Timon. His large fortune,
  Upon his good and gracious nature hanging,
  Subdues and properties to his love and tendance
  All sorts of hearts—yea, from the glass-faced flatterer
  To Apemantus, that few things loves better   70
  Than to abhor himself; even he drops down
  The knee before him and returns in peace
  Most rich in Timon's nod.
PAINTER   I saw them speak together.
POET
  Sir, I have upon a high and pleasant hill   75

76. **Feigned:** represented in fiction; **Fortune:** the goddess Fortuna, who whimsically awards success or failure to individuals (See picture, page 88.)

77. **ranked with all deserts:** i.e., surrounded by rows of people of every kind of worthiness

79. **propagate their states:** increase their prosperity

81. **personate:** represent; **frame:** build; temper

82. **ivory:** i.e., ivory-white; **wafts:** beckons

83–84. **Whose present . . . rivals:** i.e., Fortune's instant favor to Timon immediately transforms his former competitors into his **slaves and servants**

85. **to scope:** to the purpose

86. **methinks:** i.e., it seems to me

88. **Bowing his head:** i.e., straining; **steepy:** steep

89–90. **be well . . . our condition:** i.e., find a striking parallel in our status (i.e., as artists); or, perhaps, **be well** presented in painting

91. **on:** further

92. **which:** i.e., who; **fellows:** equals; **but of late:** only lately

93. **better . . . value:** i.e., more worthy than he; or, worth more, in material terms, than he; **on the moment:** straightaway

94. **his lobbies:** i.e., corridors or anterooms of his dwelling; **tendance:** attendants

96. **through him:** i.e., only **through** his intercession

98. **marry:** i.e., indeed (originally an oath on the name of the Virgin Mary)

100. **Spurns down:** tramples, kicks

103. **declining:** descending, falling

(continued)

12

Feigned Fortune to be throned. The base o' th' mount
Is ranked with all deserts, all kind of natures
That labor on the bosom of this sphere
To propagate their states. Amongst them all
Whose eyes are on this sovereign lady fixed,   80
One do I personate of Lord Timon's frame,
Whom Fortune with her ivory hand wafts to her,
Whose present grace to present slaves and servants
Translates his rivals.
PAINTER   'Tis conceived to scope.   85
This throne, this Fortune, and this hill, methinks,
With one man beckoned from the rest below,
Bowing his head against the steepy mount
To climb his happiness, would be well expressed
In our condition.   90
POET   Nay, sir, but hear me on.
All those which were his fellows but of late,
Some better than his value, on the moment
Follow his strides, his lobbies fill with tendance,
Rain sacrificial whisperings in his ear,   95
Make sacred even his stirrup, and through him
Drink the free air.
PAINTER   Ay, marry, what of these?
POET
When Fortune in her shift and change of mood
Spurns down her late beloved, all his dependants,   100
Which labored after him to the mountain's top
Even on their knees and ⌜hands,⌝ let him ⌜slip⌝ down,
Not one accompanying his declining foot.
PAINTER   'Tis common.
A thousand moral paintings I can show   105
That shall demonstrate these quick blows of
    Fortune's
More pregnantly than words. Yet you do well
To show Lord Timon that mean eyes have seen
The foot above the head.   110

105. **moral paintings:** i.e., **paintings** that provide **moral** lessons

106. **demonstrate:** accent on second syllable

109. **mean eyes:** i.e., the **eyes** of the poor or socially inferior

110 SD. **Timon:** See "Timon" in "Historical Background," page 206.

112. **Five talents:** i.e., a great sum (See "Talents," especially parts a and b, pages 208–10.)

113. **strait:** strict, exacting

114. **Your honorable letter:** i.e., a **letter** from **your** Honor (i.e., you)

115. **those:** i.e., those who; **which failing:** i.e., the lack of which

116. **Periods:** brings to an end

118. **feather:** i.e., kind

119. **know him:** i.e., **know him** to be

122. **binds him:** i.e., obliges **him** to you

129. **father:** respectful term of address to an old man

*Trumpets sound. Enter Lord Timon, addressing himself
courteously to every suitor.* ⌜*He is accompanied by a
Messenger and followed by Lucilius and other
Servants.*⌝

TIMON   Imprisoned is he, say you?
MESSENGER
 Ay, my good lord. Five talents is his debt,
 His means most short, his creditors most strait.
 Your honorable letter he desires
 To those have shut him up, which failing   115
 Periods his comfort.
TIMON   Noble Ventidius. Well,
 I am not of that feather to shake off
 My friend when he must need me. I do know him
 A gentleman that well deserves a help,   120
 Which he shall have. I'll pay the debt and free him.
MESSENGER   Your Lordship ever binds him.
TIMON
 Commend me to him. I will send his ransom;
 And, being enfranchised, bid him come to me.
 'Tis not enough to help the feeble up,   125
 But to support him after. Fare you well.
MESSENGER   All happiness to your Honor.   *He exits.*

          Enter an old Athenian.

OLD MAN
 Lord Timon, hear me speak.
TIMON   Freely, good father.
OLD MAN
 Thou hast a servant named Lucilius.   130
TIMON   I have so. What of him?
OLD MAN
 Most noble Timon, call the man before thee.
TIMON
 Attends he here or no?—Lucilius!

135. **creature:** dependent (a contemptuous term)

137. **from my first:** i.e., **from** the beginning of **my** life

138. **more raised:** i.e., of higher social status

139. **one ... trencher:** i.e., a servant who waits on his master's table   **trencher:** wooden dish

142. **got:** acquired, amassed

143. **maid:** young woman; **o' th' ... bride:** i.e., only just the age to be marriageable

146. **Attempts:** endeavors to obtain or attract

147. **her resort:** access to her

150. **he will be:** i.e., **he will be** honorable (a primary meaning of **honest** [line 149])

151. **His honesty ... itself:** Proverbial: "Virtue is its own reward."

152. **bear my daughter:** i.e., carry off **my daughter** as well

154. **apt:** susceptible to impressions

155. **precedent:** former

158. **accepts of it:** receives it favorably

162. **all:** i.e., of everything

163. **How ... endowed:** i.e., what will her dowry be

164. **equal husband:** i.e., **husband** of her own status

LUCILIUS   Here, at your Lordship's service.

OLD MAN
  This fellow here, Lord Timon, this thy creature,   135
  By night frequents my house. I am a man
  That from my first have been inclined to thrift,
  And my estate deserves an heir more raised
  Than one which holds a trencher.

TIMON   Well. What further?   140

OLD MAN
  One only daughter have I, no kin else
  On whom I may confer what I have got.
  The maid is fair, o' th' youngest for a bride,
  And I have bred her at my dearest cost
  In qualities of the best. This man of thine   145
  Attempts her love. I prithee, noble lord,
  Join with me to forbid him her resort.
  Myself have spoke in vain.

TIMON   The man is honest.

OLD MAN   Therefore he will be, Timon.   150
  His honesty rewards him in itself;
  It must not bear my daughter.

TIMON   Does she love him?

OLD MAN   She is young and apt.
  Our own precedent passions do instruct us   155
  What levity 's in youth.

TIMON, ⌈*to Lucilius*⌉   Love you the maid?

LUCILIUS
  Ay, my good lord, and she accepts of it.

OLD MAN
  If in her marriage my consent be missing—
  I call the gods to witness—I will choose   160
  Mine heir from forth the beggars of the world
  And dispossess her all.

TIMON   How shall she be endowed
  If she be mated with an equal husband?

165. **Three talents:** See "Talents," especially parts a and b, pages 208–10. **on the present:** now

168. **in:** i.e., among

170. **weigh with her:** i.e., equal her (dowry's) weight in the scales (The image is of a balance with scales, on which the daughter's dowry is counterpoised by Timon's gift. See picture, page 20.)

172. **Pawn . . . honor:** i.e., if you guarantee **this** on **your honor**

175. **state:** prosperous condition

177. **Vouchsafe:** please accept

178. **anon:** soon

180. **piece of painting:** i.e., **painting** (literally, example of **painting**)

183. **natural man: man** free of affectation or artificiality

184. **traffics:** deals; intrigues, conspires

185. **but outside:** i.e., mere external appearance; **penciled:** painted

186. **give out:** i.e., profess (to be)

187. **Wait attendance:** i.e., **wait** (a phrase addressed to an inferior)

OLD MAN
  Three talents on the present; in future, all.   165
TIMON
  This gentleman of mine hath served me long.
  To build his fortune, I will strain a little,
  For 'tis a bond in men. Give him thy daughter.
  What you bestow, in him I'll counterpoise,
  And make him weigh with her.   170
OLD MAN   Most noble lord,
  Pawn me to this your honor, she is his.
TIMON
  My hand to thee; mine honor on my promise.
LUCILIUS
  Humbly I thank your Lordship. Never may
  That state or fortune fall into my keeping   175
  Which is not owed to you.
                    He exits ⌜*with the old Athenian.*⌝
POET, ⌜*presenting his poem to Timon*⌝
  Vouchsafe my labor, and long live your Lordship.
TIMON
  I thank you. You shall hear from me anon.
  Go not away.—What have you there, my friend?
PAINTER
  A piece of painting which I do beseech   180
  Your Lordship to accept.
TIMON   Painting is welcome.
  The painting is almost the natural man,
  For, since dishonor traffics with man's nature,
  He is but outside; these penciled figures are   185
  Even such as they give out. I like your work,
  And you shall find I like it. Wait attendance
  Till you hear further from me.
PAINTER   The gods preserve you.
TIMON
  Well fare you, gentleman. Give me your hand.   190

191. **must needs:** i.e., **must**

192. **suffered under praise:** i.e., been praised excessively (In line 193, the Jeweler replies as if **under praise** meant "adverse criticism.")

194. **A mere:** an absolute

196. **unclew:** ruin (literally, unwind)

199. **like:** the same

200. **prizèd . . . masters:** i.e., valued in relation to their owners' status

201. **mend the jewel:** render **the jewel** more excellent

202. **Well mocked:** perhaps Timon's compliment on the speciousness of the Jeweler's argument

205. **chid:** chided, scolded

206. **bear:** i.e., endure

208. **morrow:** morning

209. **stay . . . morrow:** i.e., you can wait for me to say "good morning"

210. **When . . . honest:** i.e., **when** the impossible happens (See longer note to 1.1.209–10, page 191.)

A balance. (1.1.169–70)
From Silvestro Pietrasanta, *Symbola heroica* (1682).

We must needs dine together.—Sir, your jewel
Hath suffered under praise.

JEWELER   What, my lord? Dispraise?

TIMON

A mere satiety of commendations.
If I should pay you for 't as 'tis extolled,   195
It would unclew me quite.

JEWELER   My lord, 'tis rated
As those which sell would give. But you well know
Things of like value, differing in the owners,
Are prizèd by their masters. Believe 't, dear lord,   200
You mend the jewel by the wearing it.

TIMON   Well mocked.

MERCHANT

No, my good lord. He speaks the common tongue,
Which all men speak with him.

Enter Apemantus.

TIMON   Look who comes here. Will you be chid?   205

JEWELER   We'll bear, with your Lordship.

MERCHANT   He'll spare none.

TIMON

Good morrow to thee, gentle Apemantus.

APEMANTUS

Till I be gentle, stay thou for thy good morrow—
When thou art Timon's dog, and these knaves honest.   210

TIMON

Why dost thou call them knaves? Thou know'st
    them not.

APEMANTUS   Are they not Athenians?

TIMON   Yes.

APEMANTUS   Then I repent not.   215

JEWELER   You know me, Apemantus?

APEMANTUS   Thou know'st I do. I called thee by thy
    name.

TIMON   Thou art proud, Apemantus.

222. **art:** i.e., are you

227. **innocence:** artlessness

228. **Wrought:** worked

231. **dog:** i.e., cynic (The word "**dog**" was a nickname for "Cynic," which derives from the Greek word meaning doglike or currish.) See longer note, page 191.

232. **generation:** breed, kind, race

236. **An:** i.e., if

243. **Not so . . . plain-dealing:** Proverbial: "**Plain-dealing** is a **jewel** but they that use it die beggars."

244. **a doit:** a bit (literally, a small Dutch coin of little monetary value)

254. **Then thou liest:** Proverbial: "Travelers and poets have leave to lie." (See also *As You Like It* 3.3.18–19, "the truest poetry is the most feigning," where "feigning" means [1] imaginative, inventive; and [2] deceitful, untrue.)

255. **him:** i.e., Timon

APEMANTUS   Of nothing so much as that I am not like   220
   Timon.

TIMON   Whither art going?

APEMANTUS   To knock out an honest Athenian's brains.

TIMON   That's a deed thou'lt die for.

APEMANTUS   Right, if doing nothing be death by th' law.   225

TIMON   How lik'st thou this picture, Apemantus?

APEMANTUS   The best, for the innocence.

TIMON   Wrought he not well that painted it?

APEMANTUS   He wrought better that made the painter,
   and yet he's but a filthy piece of work.   230

PAINTER   You're a dog.

APEMANTUS   Thy mother's of my generation. What's
   she, if I be a dog?

TIMON   Wilt dine with me, Apemantus?

APEMANTUS   No. I eat not lords.   235

TIMON   An thou shouldst, thou'dst anger ladies.

APEMANTUS   O, they eat lords. So they come by great
   bellies.

TIMON   That's a lascivious apprehension.

APEMANTUS   So thou apprehend'st it. Take it for thy   240
   labor.

TIMON   How dost thou like this jewel, Apemantus?

APEMANTUS   Not so well as plain-dealing, which will
   not ⌜cost⌝ a man a doit.

TIMON   What dost thou think 'tis worth?   245

APEMANTUS   Not worth my thinking.—How now, poet?

POET   How now, philosopher?

APEMANTUS   Thou liest.

POET   Art not one?

APEMANTUS   Yes.   250

POET   Then I lie not.

APEMANTUS   Art not a poet?

POET   Yes.

APEMANTUS   Then thou liest. Look in thy last work,
   where thou hast feigned him a worthy fellow.   255

265. **Wherefore:** why

266. **That I . . . lord:** A puzzling line that means, perhaps, "that in being **a lord,** I could no longer exhibit the anger that I can in being a philosopher"; or, perhaps, "that I was so witless in my anger that I chose to be **a lord**" (Apemantus's speeches are often riddles.)

269. **Traffic:** trade, commerce, business; **confound:** destroy, ruin

275. **of companionship:** i.e., in a single company

276. **entertain them:** receive **them;** allow **them** to enter; **Give them guide:** conduct **them**

279. **of your sights:** i.e., at the sight of you; to see you

279 SD. **Alcibiades:** See "Alcibiades" in "Historical Background," page 205, and picture, page 94.

282. **starve:** atrophy, wither, destroy

POET   That's not feigned. He is so.

APEMANTUS   Yes, he is worthy of thee, and to pay thee
   for thy labor. He that loves to be flattered is worthy
   o' th' flatterer. Heavens, that I were a lord!

TIMON   What wouldst do then, Apemantus?   260

APEMANTUS   E'en as Apemantus does now—hate a lord
   with my heart.

TIMON   What? Thyself?

APEMANTUS   Ay.

TIMON   Wherefore?   265

APEMANTUS   That I had no angry wit to be a lord.—Art
   not thou a merchant?

MERCHANT   Ay, Apemantus.

APEMANTUS   Traffic confound thee, if the gods will not.

MERCHANT   If traffic do it, the gods do it.   270

APEMANTUS   Traffic's thy god, and thy god confound
   thee!

Trumpet sounds. Enter a Messenger.

TIMON   What trumpet's that?

MESSENGER
   'Tis Alcibiades and some twenty horse,
   All of companionship.   275

TIMON
   Pray, entertain them. Give them guide to us.
                      ⌜*Some Servants exit with Messenger.*⌝
   You must needs dine with me. Go not you hence
   Till I have thanked you.—When dinner's done
   Show me this piece.—I am joyful of your sights.

Enter Alcibiades with the rest.

   Most welcome, sir.   ⌜*They bow to each other.*⌝   280

APEMANTUS, ⌜*apart*⌝   So, so, there!
   Aches contract and starve your supple joints!
   That there should be small love amongst these sweet
      knaves,

285. **bred out:** degenerated
287. **saved:** anticipated and so prevented
288. **hungerly:** hungrily
290. **depart:** separate
294. **That ... still: Time** always provides **that** opportunity. **still:** always
297. **meat:** food
301. **Shouldst:** i.e., you should
306. **unpeaceable:** contentious; **spurn:** kick
308. **opposite:** hostile, antagonistic

A baboon. (1.1.286).
From Edward Topsell, *The historie of foure-footed beastes . . .* (1607).

26

And all this courtesy! The strain of man's bred out   285
Into baboon and monkey.

ALCIBIADES, ⌐*to Timon*¬
  Sir, you have saved my longing, and I feed
  Most hungerly on your sight.

TIMON   Right welcome, sir.
  Ere we depart, we'll share a bounteous time   290
  In different pleasures. Pray you, let us in.
                              ⌐*All but Apemantus*¬ *exit.*

                    Enter two Lords.

FIRST LORD What time o' day is 't, Apemantus?
APEMANTUS Time to be honest.
FIRST LORD That time serves still.
APEMANTUS
  The most accursèd thou, that still omit'st it.   295
SECOND LORD Thou art going to Lord Timon's feast?
APEMANTUS
  Ay, to see meat fill knaves, and wine heat fools.
SECOND LORD Fare thee well, fare thee well.
APEMANTUS
  Thou art a fool to bid me farewell twice.
SECOND LORD Why, Apemantus?   300
APEMANTUS
  Shouldst have kept one to thyself, for I mean to give
    thee none.
FIRST LORD Hang thyself.
APEMANTUS
  No, I will do nothing at thy bidding.
  Make thy requests to thy friend.   305
SECOND LORD
  Away, unpeaceable dog, or I'll spurn thee hence.
APEMANTUS I will fly, like a dog, the heels o' th' ass.
                              ⌐*He exits.*¬
FIRST LORD
  He's opposite to humanity. ⌐Come,¬ shall we in

312. **meed:** gift

315. **All use of quittance:** i.e., repayment of the value of the **gift** with normal interest **use:** interest **quittance:** repayment

316. **carries:** bears within him

1.2 Timon lavishly entertains friends and suitors with food and drink and a masque of Cupid and Amazons, and displays his bounty by refusing repayment of his loan to Ventidius and by giving his guests elaborate gifts. As counterpoint to Timon's displays of generosity, Apemantus rails against the other guests' flattery of Timon while Timon's steward Flavius makes clear that Timon is spending money that he no longer possesses.

---

0 SD. **Hautboys:** powerful double-reed woodwind instruments, forerunners to the present-day oboe (See picture, page 90.) **States:** rulers; **which:** i.e., whom; **dropping:** perhaps an error for "drooping"; **like himself:** perhaps, in his typical manner; or, perhaps, in his usual attire, rather than in fine clothes

6. **free:** generous, noble

7. **service:** respect, devotion

And taste Lord Timon's bounty? He outgoes
The very heart of kindness.   310
SECOND LORD
  He pours it out. Plutus, the god of gold,
  Is but his steward. No meed but he repays
  Sevenfold above itself. No gift to him
  But breeds the giver a return exceeding
  All use of quittance.   315
FIRST LORD   The noblest mind he carries
  That ever governed man.
SECOND LORD
  Long may he live in fortunes. Shall we in?
  I'll keep you company.
                                               They exit.

                      ⌜Scene 2⌝

*Hautboys playing loud music. A great banquet served
in, and then enter Lord Timon, the States, the Athenian
Lords ⌜(including Lucius), Alcibiades, and⌝ Ventidius
(which Timon redeemed from prison). ⌜Flavius and others are in attendance.⌝ Then comes dropping after all
Apemantus discontentedly like himself.*

VENTIDIUS   Most honored Timon,
  It hath pleased the gods to remember my father's age
  And call him to long peace.
  He is gone happy and has left me rich.
  Then, as in grateful virtue I am bound   5
  To your free heart, I do return those talents,
  Doubled with thanks and service, from whose help
  I derived liberty.   ⌜*He offers a purse.*⌝
TIMON   O, by no means,
  Honest Ventidius. You mistake my love.   10
  I gave it freely ever, and there's none
  Can truly say he gives if he receives.

13. **that game:** i.e., receiving back again what they have given

14. **Faults . . . fair:** Proverbial: "Rich men have no **faults**."

16. **ceremony:** ceremoniousness, formality (This moment in the play is sometimes staged with Timon's guests making elaborately formal gestures of deference to him.)

18. **goodness:** generosity

19. **none:** i.e., no ceremoniousness

22. **confessed it:** i.e., acknowledged the truth of what you say

23. **"confessed it"? Hanged it:** Proverbial: "Confess and be hanged." (In the proverb, *confess* refers to shriving or to admitting to a crime.)

27. **humor:** temperament, disposition (See longer note, page 192.)

28. **Does:** i.e., that **does; much to blame:** i.e., very blameworthy

29. **Ira . . . est:** Wrath is a brief madness (Horace, *Epistles* 1.2.62)

31. **affect:** like; seek out

33. **thine apperil:** i.e., your peril or risk

34. **on 't:** i.e., of it

36. **would have no power:** i.e., do not wish for **power** (to **make thee silent**)

37. **meat:** food

40. **eats:** i.e., eat

42. **all the madness:** i.e., the maddest thing about it

45. **Methinks . . . knives:** a reference to the custom, in Shakespeare's day, of guests providing their own **knives** for meals (See longer note, page 192.)

If our betters play at that game, we must not dare
To imitate them. Faults that are rich are fair.

VENTIDIUS   A noble spirit!   15

TIMON
Nay, my lords, ceremony was but devised at first
To set a gloss on faint deeds, hollow welcomes,
Recanting goodness, sorry ere 'tis shown;
But where there is true friendship, there needs none.
Pray, sit. More welcome are you to my fortunes   20
Than my fortunes to me.   ⌜*They sit.*⌝

FIRST LORD   My lord, we always have confessed it.

APEMANTUS
Ho, ho, "confessed it"? Hanged it, have you not?

TIMON   O Apemantus, you are welcome.

APEMANTUS   No, you shall not make me welcome.   25
I come to have thee thrust me out of doors.

TIMON
Fie, thou 'rt a churl. You've got a humor there
Does not become a man. 'Tis much to blame.—
They say, my lords, *Ira furor brevis est*, but yond
man is ⌜ever⌝ angry. Go, let him have a table by   30
himself, for he does neither affect company, nor is
he fit for 't indeed.

APEMANTUS   Let me stay at thine apperil, Timon. I
come to observe; I give thee warning on 't.

TIMON   I take no heed of thee. Thou 'rt an Athenian,   35
therefore welcome. I myself would have no power;
prithee, let my meat make thee silent.

APEMANTUS   I scorn thy meat. 'Twould choke me, for I
should ne'er flatter thee. (⌜*Apart.*⌝) O you gods,
what a number of men eats Timon, and he sees 'em   40
not! It grieves me to see so many dip their meat in
one man's blood; and all the madness is, he cheers
them up too.
I wonder men dare trust themselves with men.
Methinks they should invite them without knives.   45

46. **their meat:** i.e., the host's food
48. **parts:** shares
48–49. **pledges . . . of him:** i.e., toasts his health
49. **divided draft:** i.e., a drink that they take from the same cup
50–51. **huge man: man** of great rank, power, and/or possessions
53. **notes:** i.e., signs (indicating **dangerous** vulnerability), with wordplay on musical **notes** in association with the word **pipe's** (line 52)
54. **harness:** armor (See picture below.)
58. **brave:** splendid
59. **tides:** times, occasions, opportunities (with wordplay on the **flow** of the sea)
60. **state:** condition (including his financial **state,** or his wealth)
63. **odds:** difference, inequality
64. **Feasts:** i.e., those at **feasts**
67. **fond:** foolish
71. **keeper:** jailer
75. **dich:** i.e., may it do
76. **field:** battlefield

A gorget, or "harness" for the throat. (1.2.54–55)
From Louis de Gaya, *Traité des armes, des machines de guerre . . .* (1678).

Good for their meat, and safer for their lives.
  There's much example for 't. The fellow that sits
  next him, now parts bread with him, pledges the
  breath of him in a divided draft, is the readiest
  man to kill him. 'T 'as been proved. If I were a huge   50
  man, I should fear to drink at meals,
Lest they should spy my wind-pipe's dangerous
  notes.
Great men should drink with harness on their
  throats.   55
TIMON, ⌜*responding to a toast*⌝
  My lord, in heart! And let the health go round.
SECOND LORD   Let it flow this way, my good lord.
APEMANTUS, ⌜*apart*⌝ "Flow this way"? A brave fellow.
  He keeps his tides well. Those healths will make
  thee and thy state look ill, Timon.   60
Here's that which is too weak to be a sinner,
Honest water, which ne'er left man i' th' mire.
This and my food are equals. There's no odds.
Feasts are too proud to give thanks to the gods.

Apemantus' grace.

  Immortal gods, I crave no pelf.   65
  I pray for no man but myself.
  Grant I may never prove so fond
  To trust man on his oath or bond,
  Or a harlot for her weeping,
  Or a dog that seems a-sleeping,   70
  Or a keeper with my freedom,
  Or my friends if I should need 'em.
  Amen. So fall to 't.
  Rich men sin, and I eat root.
                 ⌜*He eats and drinks.*⌝
Much good dich thy good heart, Apemantus!   75
TIMON   Captain Alcibiades, your heart's in the field now.
ALCIBIADES   My heart is ever at your service, my lord.

78. **of enemies:** made up **of enemies**
79. **of friends:** i.e., with **friends**
80. **So:** i.e., provided that
85. **bid me to 'em:** i.e., invite me to eat them
89. **perfect:** contented, satisfied
93. **charitable title:** loving name (i.e., **friends**); **from:** i.e., **from** among
94. **told:** (1) narrated, related; (2) counted
95. **of you:** i.e., regarding your merits
101. **instruments:** musical **instruments; keeps:** i.e., keep
105. **properer:** more appropriately
108. **made away:** destroyed (i.e., by tears)
110. **To forget their faults:** i.e., deliberately to neglect my eyes' weakness

The arrival of guests for a feast. (1.2.0 SD)
From Matteo Maria Boiardo, *Timone, comedia* . . . [1517].

TIMON   You had rather be at a breakfast of enemies
than a dinner of friends.

ALCIBIADES   So they were bleeding new, my lord,   80
there's no meat like 'em. I could wish my best
friend at such a feast.

APEMANTUS, ⌈*apart*⌉   Would all those flatterers were
thine enemies, then, that then thou mightst kill
'em and bid me to 'em.   85

FIRST LORD   Might we but have that happiness, my
lord, that you would once use our hearts, whereby
we might express some part of our zeals, we
should think ourselves forever perfect.

TIMON   O, no doubt, my good friends, but the gods   90
themselves have provided that I shall have much
help from you. How had you been my friends else?
Why have you that charitable title from thousands,
did not you chiefly belong to my heart? I have told
more of you to myself than you can with modesty   95
speak in your own behalf. And thus far I confirm
you. O you gods, think I, what need we have any
friends if we should ne'er have need of 'em? They
were the most needless creatures living, should we
ne'er have use for 'em, and would most resemble   100
sweet instruments hung up in cases, that keeps
their sounds to themselves. Why, I have often
wished myself poorer that I might come nearer to
you. We are born to do benefits. And what better or
properer can we call our own than the riches of   105
our friends? O, what a precious comfort 'tis to
have so many, like brothers, commanding one
another's fortunes. O, joy's e'en made away ere 't
can be born! Mine eyes cannot hold out water,
methinks. To forget their faults, I drink to you.   110

APEMANTUS, ⌈*apart*⌉   Thou weep'st to make them drink,
Timon.

114. **sprung up:** (1) leaped in the womb; (2) streamed out (i.e., in tears)

117 SD. **tucket:** trumpet signal

118. **trump:** trumpet

122. **What are their wills:** i.e., **what** do they want

123. **forerunner:** herald, introducer

124. **which:** i.e., who; **pleasures:** wishes

125 SD. **Cupid:** i.e., a boy dressed as the Roman god of love

129. **gratulate:** hail, compliment, show gratitude for; **plenteous bosom:** i.e., bountiful heart

129–30. **There . . . rise:** i.e., of the **five senses,** several have been gratified at Timon's **table** (Some editors print "Th'ear, taste, touch, smell, all pleased. . . .")

131. **They:** i.e., those about to enter; **only . . . but:** i.e., **now come only**

134. **ample:** i.e., amply

134 SD. **masque:** a popular court entertainment at the time this play was written (See longer note, page 192.) **Amazons:** members of a mythological tribe of female warriors, reputed to have lived in Scythia, near the Black Sea

135. **Hoy-day:** an exclamation calling attention to something

SECOND LORD
  Joy had the like conception in our eyes
  And, at that instant, like a babe sprung up.
APEMANTUS, ⌈*apart*⌉
  Ho, ho! I laugh to think that babe a bastard.   115
THIRD LORD
  I promise you, my lord, you moved me much.
APEMANTUS, ⌈*apart*⌉ Much!   *Sound tucket.*
TIMON What means that trump?

                    Enter Servant.

                              How now?
SERVANT Please you, my lord, there are certain ladies   120
  most desirous of admittance.
TIMON Ladies? What are their wills?
SERVANT There comes with them a forerunner, my lord,
  which bears that office to signify their pleasures.
TIMON I pray, let them be admitted.   ⌈*Servant exits.*⌉ 125

                    Enter "Cupid."

CUPID
  Hail to thee, worthy Timon, and to all
  That of his bounties taste! The five best senses
  Acknowledge thee their patron, and come freely
  To gratulate thy plenteous bosom. There
  Taste, touch, all, pleased from thy table rise;   130
  They only now come but to feast thine eyes.
TIMON
  They're welcome all. Let 'em have kind admittance.
  Music, make their welcome!
LUCIUS
  You see, my lord, how ample you're beloved.

  ⌈*Music.*⌉ *Enter the masque of Ladies* ⌈*as*⌉ *Amazons,*
    with lutes in their hands, dancing and playing.

APEMANTUS, ⌈*apart*⌉ Hoy-day!   135

136. **vanity:** This could mean, for example, "worthlessness," "futility," "triviality," and "folly," as well as "conceit and desire for admiration." All of these may be intended here.

138–39. **Like madness ... root:** i.e., a similar **madness** is the splendor **of this life,** as is shown in the contrast between the **pomp** of this celebration and life's bare necessities

141. **drink:** (1) **drink** to, toast; (2) consume

142. **Upon whose age:** i.e., **upon** whom, when they grow old; **void:** vomit

144. **depravèd:** disparaged, vilified

146. **gift:** i.e., giving

149. **Men ... setting sun:** Proverbial: "The rising, not the **setting, sun** is worshipped by most **men.**"

151. **Set ... on:** i.e., beautifully enhanced

152. **was not:** i.e., **was not** before you came

154. **mine own device:** i.e., (as if it were) a masque of my **own** invention or creation (See longer note, page 192.)

156. **take ... best:** i.e., give us the most favorable reception

157. **worst:** i.e., **worst** part

158. **would not hold taking:** i.e., could not endure being considered or handled (Apemantus's wordplay on **taking** as sexually possessing implies that the lady has venereal disease.) **doubt me:** i.e., fear

159. **an idle:** a trifling, frivolous; **banquet:** perhaps, dessert, including fruit and wine; **attends:** awaits

What a sweep of vanity comes this way.
They dance? They are madwomen.
Like madness is the glory of this life
As this pomp shows to a little oil and root.
We make ourselves fools to disport ourselves   140
And spend our flatteries to drink those men
Upon whose age we void it up again
With poisonous spite and envy.
Who lives that's not depravèd or depraves?
Who dies that bears not one spurn to their graves   145
Of their friends' gift?
I should fear those that dance before me now
Would one day stamp upon me. 'T 'as been done.
Men shut their doors against a setting sun.

*The Lords rise from table, with much adoring of Timon,
and to show their loves each single out an Amazon, and
all dance, men with women, a lofty strain or two to the
hautboys, and cease.*

TIMON
You have done our pleasures much grace, fair ladies,   150
Set a fair fashion on our entertainment,
Which was not half so beautiful and kind.
You have added worth unto 't and luster,
And entertained me with mine own device.
I am to thank you for 't.   155
FIRST ⌜LADY⌝
My lord, you take us even at the best.
APEMANTUS, ⌜*apart*⌝ Faith, for the worst is filthy and
    would not hold taking, I doubt me.
TIMON
Ladies, there is an idle banquet attends you.
Please you to dispose yourselves.   160
ALL LADIES   Most thankfully, my lord.
                              ⌜*Cupid and Ladies*⌝ *exit.*
TIMON   Flavius.

166. **crossing:** opposing; **humor:** inclination; habitual tendency (See longer note to 1.2.27, page 192.)

168. **be crossed:** perhaps, have his debts **crossed,** or canceled; or, perhaps, have coins that are stamped with crosses; **an:** i.e., if

169. **had ... behind:** i.e., was not prudent or cautious (literally, did not have **eyes** at the back of the head)

170. **for his mind:** i.e., because of his (generous) purposes or intentions

177. **advance:** prefer, or make appear more worthy

179. **am so far already in:** i.e., **already** have so many of

183. **fairly:** entirely

185. **near:** closely

186. **Near ... thee:** Compare *Julius Caesar* 3.1.6–8: "O Caesar, read mine first, for mine's a suit / That touches Caesar nearer. . . . CAESAR What touches us ourself shall be last served."

FLAVIUS
  My lord?
TIMON   The little casket bring me hither.
FLAVIUS   Yes, my lord. (⌈*Aside.*⌉) More jewels yet?   165
  There is no crossing him in 's humor;
  Else I should tell him well, i' faith I should.
  When all's spent, he'd be crossed then, an he could.
  'Tis pity bounty had not eyes behind,
  That man might ne'er be wretched for his mind.   170
                                        He exits.

FIRST LORD   Where be our men?
SERVANT   Here, my lord, in readiness.
SECOND LORD
  Our horses.

              Enter Flavius, ⌈with the casket.⌉

TIMON   O my friends, I have one word
  To say to you. Look you, my good lord,   175
  I must entreat you, honor me so much
  As to advance this jewel. Accept it and wear it,
  Kind my lord.
FIRST LORD
  I am so far already in your gifts—
ALL   So are we all.   180

              Enter a Servant.

SERVANT
  My lord, there are certain nobles of the Senate
  Newly alighted and come to visit you.
TIMON
  They are fairly welcome.   ⌈*Servant exits.*⌉
FLAVIUS   I beseech your Honor,
  Vouchsafe me a word. It does concern you near.   185
TIMON
  Near? Why, then, another time I'll hear thee.

192. **trapped in silver:** adorned with trappings decorated with **silver** (A *trapping* is cloth or covering spread over the harness or saddle of a horse.)

193. **fairly:** courteously

194. **worthily entertained:** nobly or fittingly accepted

199. **brace:** pairs

205. **yield me this:** i.e., provide me with the opportunity

208. **state:** wealth, possessions

211. **put to their books:** i.e., mortgaged to those on whom he lavishes gifts

"A great banquet served in." (1.2.0 SD)
From Bartolomeo Scappi, *Opera* . . . (1605).

I prithee, let's be provided to show them
    entertainment.
FLAVIUS, ⌜*aside*⌝   I scarce know how.

                    Enter another Servant.

⌜SECOND⌝ SERVANT
    May it please your Honor, Lord Lucius,   190
    Out of his free love, hath presented to you
    Four milk-white horses trapped in silver.
TIMON
    I shall accept them fairly. Let the presents
    Be worthily entertained.   ⌜*Servant exits.*⌝

                    Enter a third Servant.

                    How now? What news?   195
THIRD SERVANT   Please you, my lord, that honorable
    gentleman Lord Lucullus entreats your company
    tomorrow to hunt with him and has sent your
    Honor two brace of greyhounds.
TIMON
    I'll hunt with him; and let them be received,   200
    Not without fair reward.   ⌜*Servant exits.*⌝
FLAVIUS, ⌜*aside*⌝   What will this come to?
    He commands us to provide, and give great gifts,
    And all out of an empty coffer.
    Nor will he know his purse or yield me this—   205
    To show him what a beggar his heart is,
    Being of no power to make his wishes good.
    His promises fly so beyond his state
    That what he speaks is all in debt; he owes
    For ev'ry word. He is so kind that he   210
    Now pays interest for 't. His land 's put to their books.
    Well, would I were gently put out of office
    Before I were forced out.
    Happier is he that has no friend to feed

215. **Than ... exceed:** i.e., **than such** friends that ruin him faster than would **enemies**

222–23. **gave good words:** i.e., spoke complimentarily

223. **courser:** stallion, or swift horse

225. **O ... that:** a polite refusal of the gift

227. **affect:** like

228. **weigh ... own:** give the same importance to **my friends'** desires as to my **own**

229. **call to:** visit

231. **all and your several:** i.e., **your** collective and individual

232. **kind:** i.e., kindly; **'tis ... give:** i.e., that there is not **enough** in my possession to meet my desire **to give**

236. **It ... thee:** i.e., my gifts to you are true **charity; living:** (1) life, existence; (2) means of making a **living;** (3) lands

238. **pitched field:** a **field** in which troops are arrayed for battle

239. **defiled land:** wordplay on the proverb "He that toucheth pitch shall be defiled with it" (Ecclesiasticus 13.1)

A greyhound. (1.2.199)
From Edward Topsell, *The historie of foure-footed beastes* . . . (1607).

Than such that do e'en enemies exceed.   215
I bleed inwardly for my lord.   *He exits.*
TIMON, ⌐*to Lords*⌐   You do yourselves much wrong.
   You bate too much of your own merits.
   (⌐*Offering a gift.*⌐) Here, my lord, a trifle of our love.
SECOND LORD
   With more than common thanks I will receive it.   220
THIRD LORD   O, he's the very soul of bounty!
TIMON   And now I remember, my lord, you gave good
      words the other day of a bay courser I rode on. 'Tis
      yours because you liked it.
FIRST LORD
   O, I beseech you, pardon me, my lord, in that.   225
TIMON
   You may take my word, my lord. I know no man
   Can justly praise but what he does affect.
   I weigh my friends' affection with mine own.
   I'll tell you true, I'll call to you.
ALL LORDS   O, none so welcome.   230
TIMON
   I take all and your several visitations
   So kind to heart, 'tis not enough to give.
   Methinks I could deal kingdoms to my friends
   And ne'er be weary.—Alcibiades,
   Thou art a soldier, therefore seldom rich.   235
   It comes in charity to thee, for all thy living
   Is 'mongst the dead, and all the lands thou hast
   Lie in a pitched field.
ALCIBIADES   Ay, defiled land, my lord.
FIRST LORD   We are so virtuously bound—   240
TIMON   And so am I to you.
SECOND LORD   So infinitely endeared—
TIMON   All to you.—Lights, more lights.
FIRST LORD
   The best of happiness, honor, and fortunes
   Keep with you, Lord Timon.   245

247. **coil:** noisy disturbance

248. **becks:** bows

249. **legs:** (1) lower limbs; (2) bows

252. **lay out:** spend; **court'sies:** (1) curtsies, or bows; (2) courtesies

255. **I'll nothing:** i.e., **I'll** accept **nothing**

258. **fear me:** i.e., **fear**

263. **with better music:** i.e., when you can sing another song (proverbial)

264. **Thou:** i.e., if you

265. **lock thy heaven from thee:** perhaps, continue to come between you and your pleasures; or, perhaps, refuse to give you the counsel that would save you (Proverbial: "He that refuses to buy counsel cheap shall buy repentance dear.")

Crows, symbolizing flattery, feed on a dead body. (1.2.267)
From Guillaume de La Perrière,
Le théâtre des bons engins . . . [1539?].

TIMON   Ready for his friends.
                    ⌜*All but Timon and Apemantus*⌝ *exit.*
APEMANTUS   What a coil 's here,
   Serving of becks and jutting-out of bums!
   I doubt whether their legs be worth the sums
   That are given for 'em. Friendship's full of dregs.   250
   Methinks false hearts should never have sound legs.
   Thus honest fools lay out their wealth on court'sies.
TIMON
   Now, Apemantus, if thou wert not sullen,
   I would be good to thee.
APEMANTUS   No, I'll nothing, for if I should be bribed   255
   too, there would be none left to rail upon thee, and
   then thou wouldst sin the faster. Thou giv'st so
   long, Timon, I fear me thou wilt give away thyself
   in paper shortly. What needs these feasts, pomps,
   and vainglories?   260
TIMON   Nay, an you begin to rail on society once, I am
   sworn not to give regard to you. Farewell, and
   come with better music.   *He exits.*
APEMANTUS   So. Thou wilt not hear me now, thou shalt
   not then. I'll lock thy heaven from thee.   265
   O, that men's ears should be
   To counsel deaf, but not to flattery!
                                              He exits.

TIMON
OF
ATHENS

ACT 2

2.1 A senator, predicting the end of Timon's days of glory, sends a servant to Timon to collect overdue loans.

---

1. **late:** recently
4. **hold:** continue, endure
5. **steal:** i.e., all I need do is **steal**
9. **foals me straight:** i.e., immediately provides **me** with horses
10. **And able horses:** i.e., **and** provides mature **horses** (as gifts from Timon), not mere foals; **porter:** gatekeeper responsible for keeping out unwanted visitors
11. **still:** always
13. **sound:** (1) speak aloud; (2) measure or test as with a fathom line; **state:** i.e., financial condition
17. **ceased:** quieted, silenced
18–20. **when . . . thus:** i.e., when you are greeted with polite subservience (To remove one's **cap**—so that it **plays in the right hand thus**—was a mark of respect to a social superior and thus an act of subservience to a social equal, as Caphis would be to one of Timon's servants.)
21. **uses:** needs, necessities

⌜ACT 2⌝

⌜Scene 1⌝

Enter a Senator, ⌜with papers.⌝

SENATOR
And late five thousand. To Varro and to Isidore
He owes nine thousand, besides my former sum,
Which makes it five-and-twenty. Still in motion
Of raging waste! It cannot hold; it will not.
If I want gold, steal but a beggar's dog   5
And give it Timon, why, the dog coins gold.
If I would sell my horse and buy twenty more
Better than he, why, give my horse to Timon—
Ask nothing; give it him—it foals me straight,
And able horses. No porter at his gate   10
But rather one that smiles and still invites
All that pass by. It cannot hold. No reason
Can sound his state in safety.—Caphis, ho!
Caphis, I say!

Enter Caphis.

CAPHIS   Here, sir. What is your pleasure?   15
SENATOR
Get on your cloak and haste you to Lord Timon.
Importune him for my moneys. Be not ceased
With slight denial, nor then silenced when
"Commend me to your master" and the cap
Plays in the right hand thus; but tell him   20
My uses cry to me. I must serve my turn

51

22. **days and times:** i.e., the **days and times** specified for his repayments

23. **fracted:** broken (by the failure to repay on time)

24. **smit:** tainted, tarnished

29. **aspect:** accent on second syllable

31–32. **When . . . gull:** Proverbial: "If every bird should take his own feathers, you would be **naked.**" (See picture, page 86.) **Gull** means both (1) an unfledged bird and (2) a dupe or fool.

33. **Which:** i.e., who; **phoenix:** mythical bird, only one of which was alive at a single time—a rare and precious creature (See picture, page 54.)

36. **have the dates in:** i.e., mark the due dates, rather than just the periods (e.g., six months), on **the bonds** so that it is obvious that they are overdue (Many editors emend "in. Come" to "in compt," which means "reckoned.")

2.2 Servants of Timon's creditors gather and confront Timon, demanding immediate repayment of loans. Learning that he is bankrupt, Timon dispatches his own servants to seek large sums of money from his friends.

---

1. **senseless:** unmindful

2. **know:** learn

3. **riot:** wasteful living, reveling; **Takes:** i.e., he **takes**

4–5. **resumes . . . continue:** i.e., assumes any responsibility to provide what he needs **to continue** (his extravagance)

(continued)

Out of mine own. His days and times are past,
And my reliances on his fracted dates
Have smit my credit. I love and honor him
But must not break my back to heal his finger.   25
Immediate are my needs, and my relief
Must not be tossed and turned to me in words
But find supply immediate. Get you gone.
Put on a most importunate aspect,
A visage of demand, for I do fear   30
When every feather sticks in his own wing
Lord Timon will be left a naked gull,
Which flashes now a phoenix. Get you gone.

CAPHIS   I go, sir.

SENATOR
"I go, sir"? Take the bonds along with you   35
And have the dates in. Come.

                              ⌜*He hands Caphis papers.*⌝

CAPHIS   I will, sir.

SENATOR   Go.

                                        They exit.

                    ⌜Scene 2⌝

Enter Steward ⌜*Flavius,*⌝ *with many bills in his hand.*

FLAVIUS
No care, no stop, so senseless of expense
That he will neither know how to maintain it
Nor cease his flow of riot. Takes no account
How things go from him nor ⌜resumes⌝ no care
Of what is to continue. Never mind   5
Was to be so unwise to be so kind.
What shall be done? He will not hear till feel.
I must be round with him, now he comes from
    hunting.
Fie, fie, fie, fie!   10

5–6. **Never . . . kind:** i.e., there was **never** a **mind so unwise** in being **so kind**

7. **till feel:** i.e., until he is hurt

8. **round:** blunt

11. **Good even:** i.e., **good** afternoon (**Even** refers to any time after noon.) **Varro:** i.e., Varro's servant (See longer note, page 193.) **What:** an interjection introducing a question

15. **discharged:** paid

16. **fear it:** i.e., doubt (that we will be paid)

17 SD. **train:** followers, retinue

18. **dinner's:** Dinner was the noontime meal. **forth:** i.e., go out

21. **dues:** debts

26. **To the . . . days:** i.e., from one day to another

29. **with . . . suit:** i.e., **you'll** act in accord **with your other noble** qualities

32. **repair:** return

A phoenix. (2.1.33)
From Geoffrey Whitney, *A choice of emblemes . . .* (1586).

Enter Caphis, ⌜and the Men of⌝ Isidore and Varro.

CAPHIS
　Good even, Varro. What, you come for money?
⌜VARRO'S MAN⌝ Is 't not your business too?
CAPHIS It is. And yours too, Isidore?
⌜ISIDORE'S MAN⌝ It is so.
CAPHIS Would we were all discharged!　　　　　　　　　15
⌜VARRO'S MAN⌝ I fear it.
CAPHIS Here comes the lord.

Enter Timon, and his train, ⌜with Alcibiades.⌝

TIMON
　So soon as dinner's done we'll forth again,
　My Alcibiades. (⌜*To Caphis.*⌝) With me? What is your
　　will?　　　　　　　　　　　　　　　　　　　20
CAPHIS, ⌜*offering Timon a paper*⌝
　My lord, here is a note of certain dues.
TIMON Dues? Whence are you?
CAPHIS Of Athens here, my lord.
TIMON Go to my steward.
CAPHIS
　Please it your Lordship, he hath put me off　　　　25
　To the succession of new days this month.
　My master is awaked by great occasion
　To call upon his own and humbly prays you
　That with your other noble parts you'll suit
　In giving him his right.　　　　　　　　　　　30
TIMON　　　　　　　　　Mine honest friend,
　I prithee but repair to me next morning.
CAPHIS
　Nay, good my lord—
TIMON　　　　　　　Contain thyself, good friend.
⌜VARRO'S MAN, *offering a paper*⌝　　One Varro's servant,　35
　my good lord—

39. **wants:** needs

40. **on forfeiture:** on pain of forfeiting the collateral securing the loan

43. **breath:** i.e., room to breathe

44. **keep on:** i.e., continue on (without me)

45. **wait . . . instantly:** i.e., be back in your company immediately

49. **detention:** withholding

50. **Against my honor:** contrary to my good reputation

53. **importunacy:** i.e., persistence in making demands

54. **That:** i.e., so **that**

55. **Wherefore:** why

58. **Pray, draw near:** This line may be directed to Timon or to the creditors' men.

58 SD. **Fool:** In the drama of Shakespeare's time, the Fool is usually a servant who makes his living by amusing his aristocratic patron. In this play, the Fool seems to serve a brothel-keeper.

62. **dog:** See longer note to 1.1.231, page 191.

⌜ISIDORE'S MAN, *offering a paper*⌝
  From Isidore. He humbly prays your speedy
    payment.
CAPHIS
  If you did know, my lord, my master's wants—
⌜VARRO'S MAN⌝
  'Twas due on forfeiture, my lord, six weeks and past.   40
⌜ISIDORE'S MAN⌝
  Your steward puts me off, my lord, and I
  Am sent expressly to your Lordship.
TIMON   Give me breath.—
  I do beseech you, good my lords, keep on.
  I'll wait upon you instantly.   45
                    ⌜*Alcibiades and Timon's train exit.*⌝
  ⌜*To Flavius.*⌝   Come hither. Pray you,
  How goes the world that I am thus encountered
  With clamorous demands of debt, broken bonds,
  And the detention of long-since-due debts
  Against my honor?   50
FLAVIUS, ⌜*to the creditors' Men*⌝   Please you, gentlemen,
  The time is unagreeable to this business.
  Your importunacy cease till after dinner,
  That I may make his Lordship understand
  Wherefore you are not paid.   55
TIMON   Do so, my friends.—
  See them well entertained.
FLAVIUS   Pray, draw near.
                    ⌜*Timon and Flavius*⌝ *exit.*

            Enter Apemantus and Fool.

CAPHIS   Stay, stay, here comes the Fool with Apeman-
    tus. Let's ha' some sport with 'em.   60
⌜VARRO'S MAN⌝   Hang him! He'll abuse us.
⌜ISIDORE'S MAN⌝   A plague upon him, dog!
⌜VARRO'S MAN⌝   How dost, Fool?
APEMANTUS   Dost dialogue with thy shadow?
⌜VARRO'S MAN⌝   I speak not to thee.   65

66. **'tis to thyself:** i.e., you are the one properly to be called "Fool" (line 63)

68–69. **There's . . . already:** i.e., you have **already** had the name **fool** affixed to **your back**

70–71. **thou . . . yet:** i.e., you, the Fool, are still standing alone and have **not yet** been put **on** his **back**

72. **Where's the fool now:** i.e., who is really the Fool

73. **He:** i.e., **he** who (i.e., Caphis)

74. **usurers' men:** servants of those who collect interest when lending money, contrary to Christian teaching in Shakespeare's day; **bawds:** panders, go-betweens

81. **Gramercies:** thanks

83–84. **She's . . . are:** The Fool draws an analogy between the practice of immersing chickens in boiling water to remove their feathers and the practice of treating victims of venereal disease by putting them in sweating-tubs. (See picture, page 126.)

84. **Corinth:** The Greek city famous for its luxurious brothels, **Corinth** seems here to be used for the brothel district of Athens, where the Fool apparently resides. Proverbial: "It is not given to every man to go to **Corinth**." (See map, page xii.)

89. **rod:** stick (to beat you with)

90. **profitably:** i.e., for your benefit (by teaching you a lesson)

91–92. **superscription of:** i.e., addresses on

APEMANTUS   No, 'tis to thyself. (⌈*To the Fool.*⌉) Come
away.

⌈ISIDORE'S MAN, *to Varro's Man*⌉   There's the fool hangs
on your back already.

APEMANTUS   No, thou stand'st single; thou 'rt not on   70
him yet.

CAPHIS, ⌈*to Isidore's Man*⌉   Where's the fool now?

APEMANTUS   He last asked the question. Poor rogues
and usurers' men, bawds between gold and want.

ALL ⌈THE MEN⌉   What are we, Apemantus?   75

APEMANTUS   Asses.

ALL ⌈THE MEN⌉   Why?

APEMANTUS   That you ask me what you are, and do not
know yourselves.—Speak to 'em, Fool.

FOOL   How do you, gentlemen?   80

ALL ⌈THE MEN⌉   Gramercies, good Fool. How does your
mistress?

FOOL   She's e'en setting on water to scald such chickens as you are. Would we could see you at Corinth!

APEMANTUS   Good. Gramercy.   85

Enter Page.

FOOL   Look you, here comes my master's page.

PAGE, ⌈*to Fool*⌉   Why, how now, captain? What do you in
this wise company?—How dost thou, Apemantus?

APEMANTUS   Would I had a rod in my mouth that I
might answer thee profitably.   90

PAGE   Prithee, Apemantus, read me the superscription
of these letters. I know not which is which.

⌈*He shows some papers.*⌉

APEMANTUS   Canst not read?

PAGE   No.

APEMANTUS   There will little learning die, then, that   95
day thou art hanged. This is to Lord Timon, this to
Alcibiades. Go. Thou wast born a bastard, and
thou'lt die a bawd.

99. **whelped:** born (literally, brought forth as a whelp or puppy)

99–100. **famish ... death:** starve to **death** like **a dog**

104. **If ... home:** Apemantus suggests either that Timon is a fool himself (and thus Apemantus will leave a fool at Timon's house if Timon is there) or that Timon will be good company for the Fool.

106. **Would:** i.e., we wish

112. **one:** not a usurer, apparently, but a brothel-keeper, like the Fool's master, whose effect on his customers the Fool then compares to a usurer's (lines 112–15) In *Measure for Measure* 3.2.6, fornication and moneylending are called "two usuries." And line 74, above, compares "usurers' men" to "bawds."

123. **a spirit:** i.e., a being capable of shifting its shape

125. **stones:** testicles; **than 's:** i.e., **than** his; **artificial one:** philosopher's (i.e., alchemist's) stone, which transmutes base metals into gold (wordplay on **artificial** as "created through art," with "art" referring to that of the alchemist) See picture, page 170.

PAGE   Thou wast whelped a dog, and thou shalt famish
    a dog's death. Answer not. I am gone.   *He exits.*   100

APEMANTUS   E'en so thou outrunn'st grace.—Fool, I
    will go with you to Lord Timon's.

FOOL   Will you leave me there?

APEMANTUS   If Timon stay at home.—You three serve
    three usurers?   105

ALL ⌜THE MEN⌝   Ay. Would they served us!

APEMANTUS   So would I—as good a trick as ever hang-
    man served thief.

FOOL   Are you three usurers' men?

ALL ⌜THE MEN⌝   Ay, fool.   110

FOOL   I think no usurer but has a fool to his servant.
    My mistress is one, and I am her Fool. When men
    come to borrow of your masters, they approach
    sadly and go away merry, but they enter my mas-
    ter's house merrily and go away sadly. The reason   115
    of this?

⌜VARRO'S MAN⌝   I could render one.

APEMANTUS   Do it then, that we may account thee a
    whoremaster and a knave, which notwithstanding,
    thou shalt be no less esteemed.   120

⌜VARRO'S MAN⌝   What is a whoremaster, fool?

FOOL   A fool in good clothes, and something like thee.
    'Tis a spirit; sometime 't appears like a lord, some-
    time like a lawyer, sometime like a philosopher,
    with two stones more than 's artificial one. He is   125
    very often like a knight, and generally in all shapes
    that man goes up and down in from fourscore to
    thirteen, this spirit walks in.

⌜VARRO'S MAN⌝   Thou art not altogether a Fool.

FOOL   Nor thou altogether a wise man. As much fool-   130
    ery as I have, so much wit thou lack'st.

APEMANTUS   That answer might have become Apemantus.

ALL ⌜THE MEN⌝   Aside, aside! Here comes Lord Timon.

135–36. **lover . . . woman:** types of people proverbially represented as fools (Proverbial: "It is impossible to love and be wise"; "The younger brother has the more wit"; and "Women have no souls.")

137. **walk near:** i.e., stay close by; **anon:** soon

138. **wherefore:** why

139. **state:** financial affairs

140. **rated my expense:** calculated or estimated my expenditures

141. **As . . . means:** i.e., according to what my **means** allowed

143. **At many leisures:** i.e., many a time when you were unoccupied

144. **Go to:** an expression of derisive incredulity

145. **single vantages:** particular opportunities

147–48. **that unaptness . . . yourself:** i.e., you made my unwillingness to hear you on those occasions into your excuse for never raising the matter again **minister:** i.e., means

154. **so much:** i.e., **so much** more than the **present** was worth

155. **'gainst . . . manners:** i.e., in violation of good **manners**

156. **hold . . . close:** i.e., spend less

157. **checks:** rebukes

158. **in:** i.e., during

161. **The greatest of your having:** i.e., your wealth when it was at its **greatest; lacks a half:** i.e., is not enough by **a half**

197. **conscience:** sense, heart

198. **Secure thy heart:** i.e., free your **heart** from apprehension

199. **broach the vessels of my love:** Here, those who love Timon are imaged as casks ready to be tapped.

200. **try . . . hearts:** i.e., put to the test my friends' protestations of love

201. **frankly:** unconditionally, lavishly

203. **Assurance . . . thoughts:** i.e., may **your thoughts** be confirmed

204. **sort:** way

205. **That:** i.e., so **that**

206. **try:** test

210. **severally:** individually, separately

215. **occasions:** needs; **time:** i.e., a chance; **toward:** i.e., for

216. **fifty talents:** See "Talents," especially parts a and b, pages 208–10.

220. **even . . . health:** perhaps a reference to Timon's great service to the city-state of Athens, mentioned by Alcibiades at 4.3.105–6 (But see longer note, page 194.)

224. **For that:** because; **general:** usual; or, perhaps, expeditious.

225. **To them to use:** i.e., in going **to them** and in using; **signet:** a small seal, usually on a finger ring (possession of which would identify the steward as Timon's authorized agent)

Enter Timon and Steward ⌜Flavius.⌝

APEMANTUS   Come with me, fool, come.

FOOL   I do not always follow lover, elder brother, and   135
woman; sometime the philosopher.

           ⌜*Apemantus and the Fool exit.*⌝

FLAVIUS, ⌜*to the creditors' Men*⌝
Pray you, walk near. I'll speak with you anon.

           ⌜*The Men*⌝ *exit.*

TIMON
You make me marvel wherefore ere this time
Had you not fully laid my state before me,
That I might so have rated my expense   140
As I had leave of means.

FLAVIUS   You would not hear me.
At many leisures I ⌜proposed⌝—

TIMON   Go to.
Perchance some single vantages you took   145
When my indisposition put you back,
And that unaptness made your minister
Thus to excuse yourself.

FLAVIUS   O, my good lord,
At many times I brought in my accounts,   150
Laid them before you. You would throw them off
And say you ⌜found⌝ them in mine honesty.
When for some trifling present you have bid me
Return so much, I have shook my head and wept—
Yea, 'gainst th' authority of manners prayed you   155
To hold your hand more close. I did endure
Not seldom nor no slight checks when I have
Prompted you in the ebb of your estate
And your great flow of debts. My lovèd lord,
Though you hear now too late, yet now's a time.   160
The greatest of your having lacks a half
To pay your present debts.

TIMON   Let all my land be sold.

164. **engaged:** mortgaged

166. **dues:** debts

169. **Lacedaemon:** i.e., Sparta (See map, page xii.)

174. **husbandry:** household management

176. **set . . . proof:** subject me to the test

177. **offices:** rooms, especially the kitchen and rooms connected to it

178. **riotous:** reveling; **feeders:** those who eat at the expense of others; dependents (a contemptuous term); **vaults:** wine cellars (but **vaults** also could mean "drains")

180. **minstrelsy:** playing and singing

181. **retired me to a wasteful cock:** perhaps, **retired to** a winebarrel with a leaking tap (This puzzling line is often changed by editors in an attempt to clarify it. Some editors print *like* a wasteful cock" or "*from* a wasteful cock"; others recommend changing "wasteful cock" to "wakeful cot" or "wakeful couch.")

186. **Who is not Timon's:** i.e., **who** does not profess himself entirely devoted to Timon?

192. **Feast-won, fast-lost:** i.e., anything achieved by giving feasts is quickly lost (with wordplay on **fast** as a period of abstaining from food—the opposite of **feast**)

193. **are couched:** hide under cover

194. **sermon me:** i.e., preach to **me**

FLAVIUS
'Tis all engaged, some forfeited and gone,
And what remains will hardly stop the mouth   165
Of present dues. The future comes apace.
What shall defend the interim? And at length
How goes our reck'ning?

TIMON
To Lacedaemon did my land extend.

FLAVIUS
O my good lord, the world is but a word.   170
Were it all yours to give it in a breath,
How quickly were it gone!

TIMON   You tell me true.

FLAVIUS
If you suspect my husbandry ⌜of⌝ falsehood,
Call me before th' exactest auditors,   175
And set me on the proof. So the gods bless me,
When all our offices have been oppressed
With riotous feeders, when our vaults have wept
With drunken spilth of wine, when every room
Hath blazed with lights and brayed with minstrelsy,   180
I have retired me to a wasteful cock
And set mine eyes at flow.

TIMON   Prithee, no more.

FLAVIUS
Heavens, have I said, the bounty of this lord!
How many prodigal bits have slaves and peasants   185
This night englutted. Who is not Timon's?
What heart, head, sword, force, means, but is Lord
    Timon's?
Great Timon, noble, worthy, royal Timon!
Ah, when the means are gone that buy this praise,   190
The breath is gone whereof this praise is made.
Feast-won, fast-lost. One cloud of winter showers,
These flies are couched.

TIMON   Come, sermon me no further.

No villainous bounty yet hath passed my heart;   195
Unwisely, not ignobly, have I given.
Why dost thou weep? Canst thou the conscience lack
To think I shall lack friends? Secure thy heart.
If I would broach the vessels of my love
And try the argument of hearts by borrowing,   200
Men and men's fortunes could I frankly use
As I can bid thee speak.
FLAVIUS   Assurance bless your thoughts!
TIMON
And in some sort these wants of mine are crowned,
That I account them blessings. For by these   205
Shall I try friends. You shall perceive how you
Mistake my fortunes. I am wealthy in my friends.—
Within there! ⌜Flaminius!⌝—Servilius!

Enter three Servants, ⌜Flaminius, Servilius, and another.⌝

SERVANTS   My lord, my lord.
TIMON   I will dispatch you severally. (⌜*To Servilius*⌝)   210
    You to Lord Lucius, (⌜*to Flaminius*⌝) to Lord
    Lucullus you—I hunted with his Honor today; (⌜*to
    the third Servant*⌝) you to Sempronius. Commend
    me to their loves, and I am proud, say, that my
    occasions have found time to use 'em toward a   215
    supply of money. Let the request be fifty talents.
FLAMINIUS   As you have said, my lord.   ⌜*Servants exit.*⌝
FLAVIUS, ⌜*aside*⌝   Lord Lucius and Lucullus? Humh!
TIMON   Go you, sir, to the Senators,
Of whom, even to the state's best health, I have   220
Deserved this hearing. Bid 'em send o' th' instant
A thousand talents to me.
FLAVIUS   I have been bold—
For that I knew it the most general way—
To them to use your signet and your name,   225
But they do shake their heads, and I am here
No richer in return.

229. **corporate:** united

230. **at fall:** i.e., at a low ebb; **want:** lack

234. **catch:** incur

235. **intending:** bending their attention to

236. **hard:** unyielding, harsh; **fractions:** i.e., scraps (of sentences)

237. **half-caps:** salutations that are only half-courteous; **cold-moving:** (1) chilly; (2) chilling

240. **cheerly:** cheerful

242. **caked:** coagulated, congealed

243. **kindly:** (1) natural; (2) friendly

244. **earth:** i.e., the grave

247. **ingeniously:** ingenuously, candidly

251. **in scarcity of:** i.e., without

252. **cleared him:** i.e., paid his debts and thereby released **him** from (debtors') prison

253. **good:** genuine

255. **That had, give 't:** i.e., when you have the **five talents, give** them to

256. **instant:** now

260. **free:** noble, generous

TIMON   Is 't true? Can 't be?
FLAVIUS
  They answer in a joint and corporate voice
  That now they are at fall, want treasure, cannot   230
  Do what they would, are sorry. You are honorable,
  But yet they could have wished—they know not—
  Something hath been amiss—a noble nature
  May catch a wrench—would all were well—'tis pity.
  And so, intending other serious matters,   235
  After distasteful looks and these hard fractions,
  With certain half-caps and cold-moving nods
  They froze me into silence.
TIMON   You gods, reward them!
  Prithee, man, look cheerly. These old fellows   240
  Have their ingratitude in them hereditary.
  Their blood is caked, 'tis cold, it seldom flows;
  'Tis lack of kindly warmth they are not kind;
  And nature, as it grows again toward earth,
  Is fashioned for the journey, dull and heavy.   245
  Go to Ventidius. Prithee, be not sad.
  Thou art true and honest—ingeniously I speak—
  No blame belongs to thee. Ventidius lately
  Buried his father, by whose death he's stepped
  Into a great estate. When he was poor,   250
  Imprisoned, and in scarcity of friends,
  I cleared him with five talents. Greet him from me.
  Bid him suppose some good necessity
  Touches his friend, which craves to be remembered
  With those five talents. That had, give 't these fellows   255
  To whom 'tis instant due. Ne'er speak or think
  That Timon's fortunes 'mong his friends can sink.
                                        ⌜*He exits.*⌝
FLAVIUS I would I could not think it.
  That thought is bounty's foe;
  Being free itself, it thinks all others so.   260
                                        ⌜*He*⌝ *exits.*

TIMON

OF

ATHENS

ACT 3

3.1 Timon's servant Flaminius approaches Timon's friend Lucullus for money and is denied.

---

6. **hits right:** i.e., is just as it should be
8. **respectively:** respectfully
9. **Fill me:** i.e., pour
10. **complete:** consummate
19. **supply:** fill; **who:** i.e., Timon; **instant occasion:** pressing need

"Basin and ewer." (3.1.7)
From Bartolomeo Scappi, *Opera* . . . (1605).

⌜ACT 3⌝

⌜Scene 1⌝

⌜*Enter*⌝ *Flaminius waiting to speak with* ⌜*Lucullus,*⌝
from his master.

⌜*Enter*⌝ *a Servant to him.*

SERVANT I have told my lord of you. He is coming
down to you.

FLAMINIUS I thank you, sir.

Enter Lucullus.

SERVANT Here's my lord.

LUCULLUS, ⌜*aside*⌝ One of Lord Timon's men? A gift, I   5
warrant. Why, this hits right. I dreamt of a silver
basin and ewer tonight.—Flaminius, honest
Flaminius, you are very respectively welcome, sir.
(⌜*To Servant.*⌝) Fill me some wine. (⌜*Servant exits.*⌝)
And how does that honorable, complete, free-   10
hearted gentleman of Athens, thy very bountiful
good lord and master?

FLAMINIUS His health is well, sir.

LUCULLUS I am right glad that his health is well, sir.
And what hast thou there under thy cloak, pretty   15
Flaminius?

FLAMINIUS Faith, nothing but an empty box, sir, which
in my lord's behalf I come to entreat your Honor
to supply; who, having great and instant occasion

73

21. **present:** immediate

25. **keep ... house:** i.e., indulge in such lavish hospitality

26. **on 't:** i.e., of it

27. **of purpose:** i.e., with the **purpose; have him:** i.e., persuade **him** to

29. **by my:** i.e., from my

30. **honesty:** generosity, hospitality

35. **speaks your pleasure:** i.e., is pleased to say so

36. **towardly:** friendly, well-disposed, tractable

37. **prompt:** willing and ready

39. **parts:** qualities

40. **sirrah:** term of address to a socially inferior male

45–46. **solidares:** coins (This word, invented by Shakespeare and used only here, was perhaps intended to suggest the plural of *solidus*, or shilling.)

47. **wink at me:** i.e., shut your eyes; disregard or overlook **me**

49. **differ:** change

to use fifty talents, hath sent to your Lordship to 20
furnish him, nothing doubting your present assis-
tance therein.

LUCULLUS La, la, la, la. "Nothing doubting" says he?
Alas, good lord! A noble gentleman 'tis, if he would
not keep so good a house. Many a time and often I 25
ha' dined with him and told him on 't, and come
again to supper to him of purpose to have him
spend less, and yet he would embrace no counsel,
take no warning by my coming. Every man has his
fault, and honesty is his. I ha' told him on 't, but I 30
could ne'er get him from 't.

Enter Servant with wine.

SERVANT Please your Lordship, here is the wine.

LUCULLUS Flaminius, I have noted thee always wise.
Here's to thee.   ⌜*He drinks.*⌝

FLAMINIUS Your Lordship speaks your pleasure.   35

LUCULLUS I have observed thee always for a towardly
prompt spirit—give thee thy due—and one that
knows what belongs to reason and canst use the
time well, if the time use thee well. Good parts in
thee.—Get you gone, sirrah.   ⌜*Servant exits.*⌝ 40
Draw nearer, honest Flaminius. Thy lord's a bountiful gentleman, but thou art wise and thou
know'st well enough, although thou com'st to me,
that this is no time to lend money, especially upon
bare friendship, without security. Here's three soli- 45
dares for thee. (⌜*Gives him money.*⌝) Good boy,
wink at me, and say thou saw'st me not. Fare thee
well.

FLAMINIUS
Is 't possible the world should so much differ,
And we alive that lived? Fly, damnèd baseness,   50
To him that worships thee!
            ⌜*He throws the money back at Lucullus.*⌝

54–55. **May . . . damnation:** a seeming reference to the idea that the eternal punishment of the avaricious, in keeping with his sin, is to have **molten coin** poured down his throat

58. **turns:** (1) changes; (2) becomes sour

59–60. **This . . . honor:** i.e., this man who is so slavish in preserving his sense of **honor** (perhaps ironic)

60. **meat:** food

67. **his hour:** i.e., the **hour** of his death, the delay of which will add to his suffering

3.2 Timon's servant Servilius approaches Timon's friend Lucius for money and is refused. Three strangers condemn the ingratitude of Timon's "friends" and praise Timon's goodness.

———————

5. **which:** i.e., one **which**

6. **happy:** fortunate

8. **want for:** lack

12. **fifty talents:** See "Talents," especially part c, pages 210–11.

54–55. **May . . . damnation:** a seeming reference to the idea that the eternal punishment of the avaricious, in keeping with his sin, is to have **molten coin** poured down his throat

58. **turns:** (1) changes; (2) becomes sour

59–60. **This . . . honor:** i.e., this man who is so slavish in preserving his sense of **honor** (perhaps ironic)

60. **meat:** food

67. **his hour:** i.e., the **hour** of his death, the delay of which will add to his suffering

3.2 Timon's servant Servilius approaches Timon's friend Lucius for money and is refused. Three strangers condemn the ingratitude of Timon's "friends" and praise Timon's goodness.

---

5. **which:** i.e., one **which**

6. **happy:** fortunate

8. **want for:** lack

12. **fifty talents:** See "Talents," especially part c, pages 210–11.

to use fifty talents, hath sent to your Lordship to   20
furnish him, nothing doubting your present assis-
tance therein.

LUCULLUS   La, la, la, la. "Nothing doubting" says he?
Alas, good lord! A noble gentleman 'tis, if he would
not keep so good a house. Many a time and often I   25
ha' dined with him and told him on 't, and come
again to supper to him of purpose to have him
spend less, and yet he would embrace no counsel,
take no warning by my coming. Every man has his
fault, and honesty is his. I ha' told him on 't, but I   30
could ne'er get him from 't.

Enter Servant with wine.

SERVANT   Please your Lordship, here is the wine.

LUCULLUS   Flaminius, I have noted thee always wise.
Here's to thee.   ⌈*He drinks.*⌉

FLAMINIUS   Your Lordship speaks your pleasure.   35

LUCULLUS   I have observed thee always for a towardly
prompt spirit—give thee thy due—and one that
knows what belongs to reason and canst use the
time well, if the time use thee well. Good parts in
thee.——Get you gone, sirrah.   ⌈*Servant exits.*⌉   40
Draw nearer, honest Flaminius. Thy lord's a bountiful gentleman, but thou art wise and thou
know'st well enough, although thou com'st to me,
that this is no time to lend money, especially upon
bare friendship, without security. Here's three soli-   45
dares for thee. (⌈*Gives him money.*⌉) Good boy,
wink at me, and say thou saw'st me not. Fare thee
well.

FLAMINIUS
Is 't possible the world should so much differ,
And we alive that lived? Fly, damnèd baseness,   50
To him that worships thee!
          ⌈*He throws the money back at Lucullus.*⌉

21. **present:** immediate

25. **keep . . . house:** i.e., indulge in such lavish hospitality

26. **on 't:** i.e., of it

27. **of purpose:** i.e., with the **purpose; have him:** i.e., persuade **him** to

29. **by my:** i.e., from my

30. **honesty:** generosity, hospitality

35. **speaks your pleasure:** i.e., is pleased to say so

36. **towardly:** friendly, well-disposed, tractable

37. **prompt:** willing and ready

39. **parts:** qualities

40. **sirrah:** term of address to a socially inferior male

45–46. **solidares:** coins (This word, invented by Shakespeare and used only here, was perhaps intended to suggest the plural of *solidus*, or shilling.)

47. **wink at me:** i.e., shut your eyes; disregard or overlook **me**

49. **differ:** change

⌜ACT 3⌝

⌜Scene 1⌝

⌜*Enter*⌝ *Flaminius waiting to speak with* ⌜*Lucullus,*⌝
from his master.

⌜*Enter*⌝ *a Servant to him.*

SERVANT I have told my lord of you. He is coming
down to you.

FLAMINIUS I thank you, sir.

Enter Lucullus.

SERVANT Here's my lord.

LUCULLUS, ⌜*aside*⌝ One of Lord Timon's men? A gift, I   5
warrant. Why, this hits right. I dreamt of a silver
basin and ewer tonight.—Flaminius, honest
Flaminius, you are very respectively welcome, sir.
(⌜*To Servant.*⌝) Fill me some wine. (⌜*Servant exits.*⌝)
And how does that honorable, complete, free-   10
hearted gentleman of Athens, thy very bountiful
good lord and master?

FLAMINIUS His health is well, sir.

LUCULLUS I am right glad that his health is well, sir.
And what hast thou there under thy cloak, pretty   15
Flaminius?

FLAMINIUS Faith, nothing but an empty box, sir, which
in my lord's behalf I come to entreat your Honor
to supply; who, having great and instant occasion

3.1   Timon's servant Flaminius approaches Timon's friend Lucullus for money and is denied.

———————

   6. **hits right:** i.e., is just as it should be
   8. **respectively:** respectfully
   9. **Fill me:** i.e., pour
   10. **complete:** consummate
   19. **supply:** fill; **who:** i.e., Timon; **instant occasion:** pressing need

"Basin and ewer." (3.1.7)
From Bartolomeo Scappi, *Opera . . .* (1605).

TIMON

OF

ATHENS

ACT 3

TIMON   Is 't true? Can 't be?

FLAVIUS
They answer in a joint and corporate voice
That now they are at fall, want treasure, cannot   230
Do what they would, are sorry. You are honorable,
But yet they could have wished—they know not—
Something hath been amiss—a noble nature
May catch a wrench—would all were well—'tis pity.
And so, intending other serious matters,   235
After distasteful looks and these hard fractions,
With certain half-caps and cold-moving nods
They froze me into silence.

TIMON   You gods, reward them!
Prithee, man, look cheerly. These old fellows   240
Have their ingratitude in them hereditary.
Their blood is caked, 'tis cold, it seldom flows;
'Tis lack of kindly warmth they are not kind;
And nature, as it grows again toward earth,
Is fashioned for the journey, dull and heavy.   245
Go to Ventidius. Prithee, be not sad.
Thou art true and honest—ingeniously I speak—
No blame belongs to thee. Ventidius lately
Buried his father, by whose death he's stepped
Into a great estate. When he was poor,   250
Imprisoned, and in scarcity of friends,
I cleared him with five talents. Greet him from me.
Bid him suppose some good necessity
Touches his friend, which craves to be remembered
With those five talents. That had, give 't these fellows   255
To whom 'tis instant due. Ne'er speak or think
That Timon's fortunes 'mong his friends can sink.
⌜*He exits.*⌝

FLAVIUS   I would I could not think it.
That thought is bounty's foe;
Being free itself, it thinks all others so.   260
⌜*He*⌝ *exits.*

229. **corporate:** united

230. **at fall:** i.e., at a low ebb; **want:** lack

234. **catch:** incur

235. **intending:** bending their attention to

236. **hard:** unyielding, harsh; **fractions:** i.e., scraps (of sentences)

237. **half-caps:** salutations that are only half-courteous; **cold-moving:** (1) chilly; (2) chilling

240. **cheerly:** cheerful

242. **caked:** coagulated, congealed

243. **kindly:** (1) natural; (2) friendly

244. **earth:** i.e., the grave

247. **ingeniously:** ingenuously, candidly

251. **in scarcity of:** i.e., without

252. **cleared him:** i.e., paid his debts and thereby released **him** from (debtors') prison

253. **good:** genuine

255. **That had, give 't:** i.e., when you have the **five talents, give** them to

256. **instant:** now

260. **free:** noble, generous

No villainous bounty yet hath passed my heart;   195
Unwisely, not ignobly, have I given.
Why dost thou weep? Canst thou the conscience lack
To think I shall lack friends? Secure thy heart.
If I would broach the vessels of my love
And try the argument of hearts by borrowing,   200
Men and men's fortunes could I frankly use
As I can bid thee speak.

FLAVIUS   Assurance bless your thoughts!

TIMON
And in some sort these wants of mine are crowned,
That I account them blessings. For by these   205
Shall I try friends. You shall perceive how you
Mistake my fortunes. I am wealthy in my friends.—
Within there! ⌈Flaminius!⌉—Servilius!

Enter three Servants, ⌈Flaminius, Servilius, and another.⌉

SERVANTS   My lord, my lord.
TIMON   I will dispatch you severally. (⌈*To Servilius*⌉)   210
You to Lord Lucius, (⌈*to Flaminius*⌉) to Lord
Lucullus you—I hunted with his Honor today; (⌈*to
the third Servant*⌉) you to Sempronius. Commend
me to their loves, and I am proud, say, that my
occasions have found time to use 'em toward a   215
supply of money. Let the request be fifty talents.
FLAMINIUS   As you have said, my lord.   ⌈*Servants exit.*⌉
FLAVIUS, ⌈*aside*⌉   Lord Lucius and Lucullus? Humh!
TIMON   Go you, sir, to the Senators,
Of whom, even to the state's best health, I have   220
Deserved this hearing. Bid 'em send o' th' instant
A thousand talents to me.

FLAVIUS   I have been bold—
For that I knew it the most general way—
To them to use your signet and your name,   225
But they do shake their heads, and I am here
No richer in return.

Enter Timon and Steward ⌐Flavius.⌐

APEMANTUS   Come with me, fool, come.
FOOL   I do not always follow lover, elder brother, and   135
    woman; sometime the philosopher.
                       ⌐Apemantus and the Fool exit.⌐
FLAVIUS, *⌐to the creditors' Men⌐*
    Pray you, walk near. I'll speak with you anon.
                             ⌐The Men⌐ exit.

TIMON
    You make me marvel wherefore ere this time
    Had you not fully laid my state before me,
    That I might so have rated my expense   140
    As I had leave of means.
FLAVIUS   You would not hear me.
    At many leisures I ⌐proposed⌐—
TIMON   Go to.
    Perchance some single vantages you took   145
    When my indisposition put you back,
    And that unaptness made your minister
    Thus to excuse yourself.
FLAVIUS   O, my good lord,
    At many times I brought in my accounts,   150
    Laid them before you. You would throw them off
    And say you ⌐found⌐ them in mine honesty.
    When for some trifling present you have bid me
    Return so much, I have shook my head and wept—
    Yea, 'gainst th' authority of manners prayed you   155
    To hold your hand more close. I did endure
    Not seldom nor no slight checks when I have
    Prompted you in the ebb of your estate
    And your great flow of debts. My lovèd lord,
    Though you hear now too late, yet now's a time.   160
    The greatest of your having lacks a half
    To pay your present debts.
TIMON   Let all my land be sold.

164. **engaged:** mortgaged

166. **dues:** debts

169. **Lacedaemon:** i.e., Sparta (See map, page xii.)

174. **husbandry:** household management

176. **set . . . proof:** subject me to the test

177. **offices:** rooms, especially the kitchen and rooms connected to it

178. **riotous:** reveling; **feeders:** those who eat at the expense of others; dependents (a contemptuous term); **vaults:** wine cellars (but **vaults** also could mean "drains")

180. **minstrelsy:** playing and singing

181. **retired me to a wasteful cock:** perhaps, **retired to** a winebarrel with a leaking tap (This puzzling line is often changed by editors in an attempt to clarify it. Some editors print "*like* a wasteful cock" or "*from* a wasteful cock"; others recommend changing "wasteful cock" to "wakeful cot" or "wakeful couch.")

186. **Who is not Timon's:** i.e., **who** does not profess himself entirely devoted to Timon?

192. **Feast-won, fast-lost:** i.e., anything achieved by giving feasts is quickly lost (with wordplay on **fast** as a period of abstaining from food—the opposite of **feast**)

193. **are couched:** hide under cover

194. **sermon me:** i.e., preach to **me**

FLAVIUS
　'Tis all engaged, some forfeited and gone,
　And what remains will hardly stop the mouth   165
　Of present dues. The future comes apace.
　What shall defend the interim? And at length
　How goes our reck'ning?
TIMON
　To Lacedaemon did my land extend.
FLAVIUS
　O my good lord, the world is but a word.   170
　Were it all yours to give it in a breath,
　How quickly were it gone!
TIMON   You tell me true.
FLAVIUS
　If you suspect my husbandry ⌐of⌐ falsehood,
　Call me before th' exactest auditors,   175
　And set me on the proof. So the gods bless me,
　When all our offices have been oppressed
　With riotous feeders, when our vaults have wept
　With drunken spilth of wine, when every room
　Hath blazed with lights and brayed with minstrelsy,   180
　I have retired me to a wasteful cock
　And set mine eyes at flow.
TIMON   Prithee, no more.
FLAVIUS
　Heavens, have I said, the bounty of this lord!
　How many prodigal bits have slaves and peasants   185
　This night englutted. Who is not Timon's?
　What heart, head, sword, force, means, but is Lord
　　Timon's?
　Great Timon, noble, worthy, royal Timon!
　Ah, when the means are gone that buy this praise,   190
　The breath is gone whereof this praise is made.
　Feast-won, fast-lost. One cloud of winter showers,
　These flies are couched.
TIMON   Come, sermon me no further.

197. **conscience:** sense, heart

198. **Secure thy heart:** i.e., free your **heart** from apprehension

199. **broach the vessels of my love:** Here, those who love Timon are imaged as casks ready to be tapped.

200. **try ... hearts:** i.e., put to the test my friends' protestations of love

201. **frankly:** unconditionally, lavishly

203. **Assurance ... thoughts:** i.e., may **your thoughts** be confirmed

204. **sort:** way

205. **That:** i.e., so that

206. **try:** test

210. **severally:** individually, separately

215. **occasions:** needs; **time:** i.e., a chance; **toward:** i.e., for

216. **fifty talents:** See "Talents," especially parts a and b, pages 208–10.

220. **even ... health:** perhaps a reference to Timon's great service to the city-state of Athens, mentioned by Alcibiades at 4.3.105–6 (But see longer note, page 194.)

224. **For that:** because; **general:** usual; or, perhaps, expeditious.

225. **To them to use:** i.e., in going **to them** and in using; **signet:** a small seal, usually on a finger ring (possession of which would identify the steward as Timon's authorized agent)

LUCULLUS   Ha! Now I see thou art a fool and fit for thy
    master.   *Lucullus exits.*

FLAMINIUS
    May these add to the number that may scald thee!
    Let molten coin be thy damnation,   55
    Thou disease of a friend and not himself!
    Has friendship such a faint and milky heart
    It turns in less than two nights? O you gods,
    I feel my master's passion. This slave
    Unto his honor has my lord's meat in him.   60
    Why should it thrive and turn to nutriment
    When he is turned to poison?
    O, may diseases only work upon 't,
    And when he's sick to death, let not that part of
        nature   65
    Which my lord paid for be of any power
    To expel sickness, but prolong his hour.
                                              He exits.

⌜Scene 2⌝

Enter Lucius, with three Strangers.

LUCIUS   Who, the Lord Timon? He is my very good
    friend and an honorable gentleman.
FIRST STRANGER   We know him for no less, though we
    are but strangers to him. But I can tell you one
    thing, my lord, and which I hear from common   5
    rumors: now Lord Timon's happy hours are done
    and past, and his estate shrinks from him.
LUCIUS   Fie, no, do not believe it. He cannot want for
    money.
SECOND STRANGER   But believe you this, my lord, that 10
    not long ago one of his men was with the Lord
    Lucullus to borrow ⌜fifty⌝ talents, nay, urged
    extremely for 't, and showed what necessity
    belonged to 't, and yet was denied.

15. **How:** i.e., what did you say

21. **plate:** silver or gold utensils or ornaments

23. **his:** i.e., what Timon has given Lucullus; **had he mistook him:** i.e., if Timon had made a mistake

24. **denied . . . talents:** i.e., **denied** him **fifty talents** in his need

25. **hap:** fortune, chance; **my lord:** i.e., Lucius

26. **sweat:** i.e., sweated, exerted myself strongly

30. **exquisite:** excellent

33. **endeared:** obliged

36. **occasion:** need

37–38. **supply . . . use:** i.e., provide him immediately

40. **want fifty-five hundred talents:** i.e., lack an enormous fortune (See "Talents," especially part b, pages 208–10.)

41. **wants:** wordplay on **want** as "desire, wish"

42. **were not virtuous:** i.e., did not arise from the practice of virtue, i.e., generosity

LUCIUS How?   15
SECOND STRANGER I tell you, denied, my lord.
LUCIUS What a strange case was that! Now, before the
  gods, I am ashamed on 't. Denied that honorable
  man? There was very little honor showed in 't. For
  my own part, I must needs confess I have received   20
  some small kindnesses from him, as money, plate,
  jewels, and suchlike trifles, nothing comparing to
  his; yet had he mistook him and sent to me, I
  should ne'er have denied his occasion ⌜fifty⌝ talents.

Enter Servilius.

SERVILIUS, ⌜*aside*⌝ See, by good hap, yonder's my lord.   25
  I have sweat to see his Honor. ⌜*To Lucius.*⌝ My
  honored lord.
LUCIUS Servilius. You are kindly met, sir. Fare thee
  well. Commend me to thy honorable virtuous lord,
  my very exquisite friend.   ⌜*He turns to exit.*⌝   30
SERVILIUS May it please your Honor, my lord hath
  sent—
LUCIUS Ha! What has he sent? I am so much endeared
  to that lord; he's ever sending. How shall I thank
  him, think'st thou? And what has he sent now?   35
SERVILIUS Has only sent his present occasion now, my
  lord, requesting your Lordship to supply his
  instant use with ⌜fifty⌝ talents.
LUCIUS
  I know his Lordship is but merry with me.
  He cannot want fifty-five hundred talents.   40
SERVILIUS
  But in the meantime he wants less, my lord.
  If his occasion were not virtuous,
  I should not urge it half so faithfully.
LUCIUS
  Dost thou speak seriously, Servilius?
SERVILIUS Upon my soul, 'tis true, sir.   45

46–47. disfurnish . . . time: i.e., deprive **myself** (of what is needed) just before such a **good** opportunity

49. purchase: strive

50. little part: perhaps, **little part** of honor (which would parallel or balance **great deal of honor** at the end of this sentence); **undo:** destroy

52. use: make use of (probably, borrow from)

53–54. I would not . . . I had done 't: i.e., I wish . . . that I **had not done** it

64. I'll look you out a good turn: i.e., **I'll** be on the lookout for something I can do for **you**

66. speed: prosper

69. world's soul: principle that animates the world

69–70. just . . . piece: i.e., exactly the **same**

72. dips . . . dish: Compare Matthew 26.23: "He that dippeth his hand with me in **the dish,** he shall betray me."

74. kept his: i.e., sustained Lucius's; **with his:** i.e., **with** Timon's own

LUCIUS What a wicked beast was I to disfurnish
myself against such a good time, when I might ha'
shown myself honorable! How unluckily it happened that I should purchase the day before for a
little part, and undo a great deal of honor! Servil-   50
ius, now before the gods, I am not able to do—the
more beast, I say!—I was sending to use Lord
Timon myself, these gentlemen can witness; but I
would not for the wealth of Athens I had done 't
now. Commend me bountifully to his good Lord-   55
ship, and I hope his Honor will conceive the fairest
of me, because I have no power to be kind. And tell
him this from me: I count it one of my greatest
afflictions, say, that I cannot pleasure such an honorable gentleman. Good Servilius, will you   60
befriend me so far as to use mine own words to
him?
SERVILIUS Yes, sir, I shall.
LUCIUS I'll look you out a good turn, Servilius.
                                    Servilius exits.
True, as you said, Timon is shrunk indeed,   65
And he that's once denied will hardly speed.
                                    He exits.
FIRST STRANGER Do you observe this, Hostilius?
SECOND STRANGER Ay, too well.
FIRST STRANGER
Why, this is the world's soul, and just of the same
    piece   70
Is every flatterer's sport. Who can call him his friend
That dips in the same dish? For, in my knowing,
Timon has been this lord's father
And kept his credit with his purse,
Supported his estate, nay, Timon's money   75
Has paid his men their wages. He ne'er drinks
But Timon's silver treads upon his lip.
And yet—O, see the monstrousness of man

79. **looks out:** appears

80. **He:** i.e., Lucius; **in respect of his:** i.e., in comparison to Lucius's total wealth

87. **For:** because of

88. **carriage:** conduct, behavior

90. **put . . . donation:** i.e., made a gift of **my wealth**

91. **best half:** greater part; **returned:** i.e., gone back as if to its previous owner

94. **policy:** cunning dissimulation

3.3 Timon's servant approaches Timon's friend Sempronius for money and is refused.

---

1. **in 't:** i.e., with it

7. **touched . . . metal:** i.e., tested and **found** of no value (an image from testing **metal** by rubbing it against a touchstone) See picture below.

10. **Has:** i.e., have

Metal being tested on a touchstone. (3.3.7; 4.3.435)
From George Wither, *A collection of emblemes . . .* (1635).

When he looks out in an ungrateful shape!—
He does deny him, in respect of his,   80
What charitable men afford to beggars.
THIRD STRANGER
  Religion groans at it.
FIRST STRANGER   For mine own part,
  I never tasted Timon in my life,
  Nor came any of his bounties over me   85
  To mark me for his friend. Yet I protest,
  For his right noble mind, illustrious virtue,
  And honorable carriage,
  Had his necessity made use of me,
  I would have put my wealth into donation,   90
  And the best half should have returned to him,
  So much I love his heart. But I perceive
  Men must learn now with pity to dispense,
  For policy sits above conscience.
                                              They exit.

⌜Scene 3⌝

Enter a Third Servant ⌜of Timon's⌝ with Sempronius,
another of Timon's friends.

SEMPRONIUS
  Must he needs trouble me in 't? Hum! 'Bove all others?
  He might have tried Lord Lucius or Lucullus;
  And now Ventidius is wealthy too,
  Whom he redeemed from prison. All these
  Owes their estates unto him.   5
SERVANT My lord,
  They have all been touched and found base metal,
  For they have all denied him.
SEMPRONIUS How? Have they denied him?
  Has Ventidius and Lucullus denied him,   10
  And does he send to me? Three? Humh!

13–14. **His friends . . . over:** Proverbial: "**Physicians** enriched **give over** their patients." **give over:** declare incurable

15. **Has:** i.e., he **has**

16. **That . . . place:** i.e., who should have granted me precedence among his friends; **sense:** reason

17. **his occasions:** i.e., he, in his need

18. **in my conscience:** truly

22. **argument:** subject, theme for

25. **Had:** i.e., he **had; but . . . sake:** i.e., if only because of my feelings toward him

26. **a courage:** an intention, inclination

29. **goodly:** splendid, excellent

31. **politic:** cunning; **crossed:** thwarted

32–33. **set him clear:** perhaps, prove **him** or make **him** appear innocent

33. **fairly:** beautifully; completely, fully

34. **Takes virtuous copies to be wicked:** perhaps, he patterns himself on the virtuous in order to do harm

35. **under:** i.e., **under** the guise of; or, **under** the influence of

40. **wards:** locks (literally, the ridges projecting from the inside plate of a lock)

44. **keep his house:** i.e., stay in **his house** so as not to be arrested for debt

It shows but little love or judgment in him.
Must I be his last refuge? His friends, like physicians,
Thrive, give him over. Must I take th' cure upon me?
Has much disgraced me in 't. I'm angry at him   15
That might have known my place. I see no sense for 't
But his occasions might have wooed me first;
For, in my conscience, I was the first man
That e'er received gift from him.
And does he think so backwardly of me now   20
That I'll requite it last? No.
So it may prove an argument of laughter
To th' rest, and ⌈I⌉ 'mongst lords be thought a fool.
I'd rather than the worth of thrice the sum
Had sent to me first, but for my mind's sake;   25
I'd such a courage to do him good. But now return,
And with their faint reply this answer join:
Who bates mine honor shall not know my coin.
                                                 He exits.
SERVANT Excellent! Your Lordship's a goodly villain.
    The devil knew not what he did when he made   30
    man politic. He crossed himself by 't, and I cannot
    think but, in the end, the villainies of man will set
    him clear. How fairly this lord strives to appear
    foul! Takes virtuous copies to be wicked, like those
    that under hot ardent zeal would set whole realms   35
    on fire.
Of such a nature is his politic love.
This was my lord's best hope. Now all are fled,
Save only the gods. Now his friends are dead,
Doors that were ne'er acquainted with their wards   40
Many a bounteous year must be employed
Now to guard sure their master.
And this is all a liberal course allows:
Who cannot keep his wealth must keep his house.
                                                 He exits.

3.4 The servants of Timon's creditors gather at his gates. He confronts them in a rage and, after they are gone, orders Flavius once again to invite all his friends to dinner.

———————

0 SD. **Men of:** i.e., servants of (See longer note to 2.2.11, page 193.)

1. **morrow:** morning

2. **like:** same

4. **What:** an interjection introducing a question

10. **at once:** i.e., to all of you (literally, at one sweep, once for all)

21. **recoverable:** (1) capable of being retraced; (2) capable of being recovered or regained

Jackdaws with borrowed feathers. (2.1.31)
From Aesop, . . . *Fabulae* . . . (1587).

⌜Scene 4⌝

Enter Varro's ⌜two Men,⌝ meeting ⌜Titus and⌝ others, all
⌜being Men of⌝ Timon's creditors to wait for his coming
out. Then enter ⌜Lucius' Man⌝ and Hortensius.

VARRO'S ⌜FIRST⌝ MAN
  Well met. Good morrow, Titus and Hortensius.
TITUS
  The like to you, kind Varro.
HORTENSIUS   Lucius!
  What, do we meet together?
⌜LUCIUS' MAN⌝   Ay, and I think   5
  One business does command us all,
  For mine is money.
TITUS   So is theirs and ours.

Enter Philotus.

⌜LUCIUS' MAN⌝
  And, sir, Philotus' too.
PHILOTUS   Good day at once.   10
⌜LUCIUS' MAN⌝   Welcome, good brother.
  What do you think the hour?
PHILOTUS   Laboring for nine.
⌜LUCIUS' MAN⌝
  So much?
PHILOTUS   Is not my lord seen yet?   15
⌜LUCIUS' MAN⌝   Not yet.
PHILOTUS
  I wonder on 't. He was wont to shine at seven.
⌜LUCIUS' MAN⌝
  Ay, but the days are waxed shorter with him.
  You must consider that a prodigal course
  Is like the sun's,   20
  But not, like his, recoverable. I fear
  'Tis deepest winter in Lord Timon's purse:

32. **Mark:** notice, consider
36. **charge:** task
38. **stealth:** stealing
39. **crowns:** See "Talents," especially pages 212–13.
41. **much:** very
42. **mine:** i.e., my master's
43. **his:** i.e., **his sum**
48. **attend:** wait for
50. **diligent:** attentive

Fortune on her throne. (1.1.76)
From Charles de Bouelles, *Que hoc volumine continentur* . . . [1510].

That is, one may reach deep enough and yet
Find little.

PHILOTUS　　　I am of your fear for that.　　　　　　25

TITUS
I'll show you how t' observe a strange event.
Your lord sends now for money?

HORTENSIUS　　　　　　　　　Most true, he does.

TITUS
And he wears jewels now of Timon's gift,
For which I wait for money.　　　　　　　　　　30

HORTENSIUS　It is against my heart.

⌜LUCIUS' MAN⌝　Mark how strange it shows:
Timon in this should pay more than he owes,
And e'en as if your lord should wear rich jewels
And send for money for 'em.　　　　　　　　　35

HORTENSIUS
I'm weary of this charge, the gods can witness.
I know my lord hath spent of Timon's wealth,
And now ingratitude makes it worse than stealth.

⌜VARRO'S FIRST MAN⌝
Yes, mine's three thousand crowns. What's yours?

⌜LUCIUS' MAN⌝　Five thousand mine.　　　　　　40

⌜VARRO'S FIRST MAN⌝
'Tis much deep, and it should seem by th' sum
Your master's confidence was above mine,
Else surely his had equaled.

Enter Flaminius.

TITUS　One of Lord Timon's men.

⌜LUCIUS' MAN⌝　Flaminius? Sir, a word. Pray, is my lord　45
ready to come forth?

FLAMINIUS　No, indeed he is not.

TITUS　We attend his Lordship. Pray, signify so much.

FLAMINIUS　I need not tell him that. He knows you are
too diligent.　　　　　　　　　　　⌜*He exits.*⌝　50

Enter ⌜Flavius, the⌝ Steward in a cloak, muffled.

56. **certain:** i.e., some particular sums of
58. **certain:** sure to come, dependable
60. **preferred:** offered, presented
61. **eat:** ate (pronounced "et"); **meat:** food
64. **do yourselves but:** i.e., only **do yourselves**
66. **have made an end:** are finished
68. **will not serve:** does not satisfy
70. **you serve:** i.e., **you** act as servants to
74. **broader:** i.e., with less reserve or restraint
79. **repair:** return
80. **derive:** gain

"Hautboys playing loud music." (1.2.0 SD)
From Balthasar Küchler, *Repraesentatio der fürstlichen Auffzug . . .* [1611].

⌜LUCIUS' MAN⌝
　Ha! Is not that his steward muffled so?
　He goes away in a cloud. Call him, call him.
TITUS　Do you hear, sir?
VARRO'S SECOND MAN　By your leave, sir.
FLAVIUS　What do you ask of me, my friend? 55
TITUS
　We wait for certain money here, sir.
FLAVIUS　　　　　　　　　　　　Ay,
　If money were as certain as your waiting,
　'Twere sure enough.
　Why then preferred you not your sums and bills 60
　When your false masters eat of my lord's meat?
　Then they could smile and fawn upon his debts
　And take down th' int'rest into their glutt'nous maws.
　You do yourselves but wrong to stir me up.
　Let me pass quietly. 65
　Believe 't, my lord and I have made an end.
　I have no more to reckon, he to spend.
⌜LUCIUS' MAN⌝　Ay, but this answer will not serve.
FLAVIUS
　If 'twill not serve, 'tis not so base as you,
　For you serve knaves.　　　　　　⌜*He exits.*⌝ 70
VARRO'S FIRST MAN　How? What does his cashiered
　Worship mutter?
VARRO'S SECOND MAN　No matter what. He's poor, and
　that's revenge enough. Who can speak broader
　than he that has no house to put his head in? Such 75
　may rail against great buildings.

　　　　　　Enter Servilius.

TITUS　O, here's Servilius. Now we shall know some
　answer.
SERVILIUS　If I might beseech you, gentlemen, to repair
　some other hour, I should derive much from 't. For 80
　take 't of my soul, my lord leans wondrously to dis-

82. **comfortable:** cheerful

84. **chambers are:** i.e., **chambers** who **are**

87. **clear:** unobstructed (with wordplay on the meaning "debt-free")

90 SD. **within:** i.e., from offstage

92. **free:** with wordplay on the meaning "generous"

93. **retentive:** confining (with possible wordplay on the meaning "stingy")

96. **Put in:** i.e., present (your claim)

102. **Knock . . . girdle:** Timon plays on the meaning of **bill** as a long-handled bladed weapon. (See picture below.) **girdle:** belt

106. **Tell out my blood:** i.e., use **my blood** as payment (**Tell** means "count.")

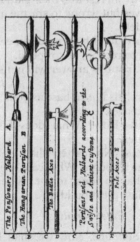

Bills (halberds) and other bladed weapons. (3.4.101)
From Louis de Gaya, *A treatise of the arms . . .* (1678).

content. His comfortable temper has forsook him.
He's much out of health and keeps his chamber.

⌜LUCIUS' MAN⌝
  Many do keep their chambers are not sick;
  And if it be so far beyond his health,   85
  Methinks he should the sooner pay his debts
  And make a clear way to the gods.

SERVILIUS   Good gods!

TITUS   We cannot take this for answer, sir.

FLAMINIUS, *within*   Servilius, help! My lord, my lord!   90

                Enter Timon in a rage.

TIMON
  What, are my doors opposed against my passage?
  Have I been ever free, and must my house
  Be my retentive enemy, my jail?
  The place which I have feasted, does it now,
  Like all mankind, show me an iron heart?   95

⌜LUCIUS' MAN⌝   Put in now, Titus.

TITUS   My lord, here is my bill.

⌜LUCIUS' MAN⌝   Here's mine.

⌜HORTENSIUS⌝   And mine, my lord.

VARRO'S SECOND MAN   And ours, my lord.   100

PHILOTUS   All our bills.

TIMON
  Knock me down with 'em! Cleave me to the girdle.

⌜LUCIUS' MAN⌝   Alas, my lord—

TIMON   Cut my heart in sums!

TITUS   Mine, fifty talents.   105

TIMON   Tell out my blood.

⌜LUCIUS' MAN⌝   Five thousand crowns, my lord.

TIMON
  Five thousand drops pays that.—What yours?—And
    yours?

VARRO'S FIRST MAN   My lord—   110

VARRO'S SECOND MAN   My lord—

112. **fall upon:** i.e., rush to attack

113–14. **throw their caps at:** give up for lost

115. **desperate:** beyond recovery (with wordplay on the meaning "infuriated from despair," with reference to Timon)

123. **fitly:** readily

128. **furnish out:** provide enough for

Alcibiades.
From Guillaume Rouillé, . . . *Promptuarii iconum* . . . (1553).

TIMON
  Tear me, take me, and the gods fall upon you!
                              Timon exits.
HORTENSIUS Faith, I perceive our masters may throw
    their caps at their money. These debts may well be
    called desperate ones, for a madman owes 'em.   115
                              They exit.

                Enter Timon ⌐and Flavius.⌐

TIMON
  They have e'en put my breath from me, the slaves!
  Creditors? Devils!
FLAVIUS   My dear lord—
TIMON   What if it should be so?
FLAVIUS   My lord—   120
TIMON
  I'll have it so.—My steward!
FLAVIUS   Here, my lord.
TIMON
  So fitly? Go, bid all my friends again,
  Lucius, Lucullus, and Sempronius, all.
  I'll once more feast the rascals.   125
FLAVIUS   O my lord,
  You only speak from your distracted soul.
  There's not so much left to furnish out
  A moderate table.
TIMON   Be it not in thy care. Go,   130
  I charge thee, invite them all. Let in the tide
  Of knaves once more. My cook and I'll provide.
                              They exit.

3.5 Alcibiades pleads in vain before three Athenian senators for the life of one of his soldiers. Frustrated at being denied, he provokes the senators, who banish him from Athens.

_____

1. **to 't:** i.e., in support of it; **fault's:** offense is
2. **he should die:** See longer note, page 194.
3. **Nothing . . . mercy:** Proverbial: "Pardon makes offenders."
4. **bruise:** crush, smash
8. **the virtue:** the excellence
9. **it:** i.e., **the law**
16. **fact:** crime
17. **buys out:** redeems; **fault:** culpability
19. **touched to death:** i.e., injured or tainted intolerably
21. **unnoted:** unobserved (because concealed or controlled)
22. **behave:** manage
24. **undergo:** undertake
26. **took:** i.e., taken
27. **form:** good order
27–28. **set . . . valor:** i.e., associate violent altercation with the highest form of **valor**
28. **which:** i.e., **quarreling**

⌈Scene 5⌉

Enter three Senators at one door, Alcibiades meeting
them, with Attendants.

FIRST SENATOR, ⌈*to the Second Senator*⌉
  My lord, you have my voice to 't. The fault's
  Bloody. 'Tis necessary he should die.
  Nothing emboldens sin so much as mercy.
SECOND SENATOR   Most true. The law shall bruise 'em.
ALCIBIADES
  Honor, health, and compassion to the Senate!   5
FIRST SENATOR   Now, captain?
ALCIBIADES
  I am an humble suitor to your virtues,
  For pity is the virtue of the law,
  And none but tyrants use it cruelly.
  It pleases time and fortune to lie heavy   10
  Upon a friend of mine, who in hot blood
  Hath stepped into the law, which is past depth
  To those that without heed do plunge into 't.
  He is a man—setting his fate aside—
  Of comely virtues.   15
  Nor did he soil the fact with cowardice—
  ⌈An⌉ honor in him which buys out his fault—
  But with a noble fury and fair spirit,
  Seeing his reputation touched to death,
  He did oppose his foe;   20
  And with such sober and unnoted passion
  He did ⌈behave⌉ his anger, ere 'twas spent,
  As if he had but proved an argument.
FIRST SENATOR
  You undergo too strict a paradox,
  Striving to make an ugly deed look fair.   25
  Your words have took such pains as if they labored
  To bring manslaughter into form and set quarreling
  Upon the head of valor—which indeed

29. **misbegot:** misbegotten, illegitimately fathered

32. **breathe:** speak

33. **his wrongs:** i.e., the **wrongs** he endures

35. **prefer:** present

37. **us kill:** i.e., **us** to **kill**

38. **ill:** evil

40. **clear:** innocent

41. **bear:** endure

42. **under favor:** with all submission (a polite phrase, here introducing a rebuttal)

44. **fond:** foolish

47. **repugnancy:** opposition, fighting back

48–49. **what . . . / Abroad:** i.e., why do we go on foreign military expeditions in defense of our state?

50. **carry it:** gains the advantage; wins the day

52. **Loaden with irons:** laden with iron shackles

54. **pitifully:** compassionately

56. **gust:** (1) blast (as of wind); (2) act of satisfying the appetite; flavor; liking

57. **by mercy:** i.e., if interpreted mercifully

59. **not:** i.e., never

61. **breathe:** speak

Is valor misbegot, and came into the world
When sects and factions were newly born.   30
He's truly valiant that can wisely suffer
The worst that man can breathe
And make his wrongs his outsides,
To wear them like his raiment, carelessly,
And ne'er prefer his injuries to his heart   35
To bring it into danger.
If wrongs be evils and enforce us kill,
What folly 'tis to hazard life for ill!

ALCIBIADES
My lord—

FIRST SENATOR   You cannot make gross sins look clear.   40
To revenge is no valor, but to bear.

ALCIBIADES
My lords, then, under favor, pardon me
If I speak like a captain.
Why do fond men expose themselves to battle
And not endure all threats? Sleep upon 't,   45
And let the foes quietly cut their throats
Without repugnancy? If there be
Such valor in the bearing, what make we
Abroad? Why, then, women are more valiant
That stay at home, if bearing carry it,   50
And the ass more captain than the lion, the ⌈felon⌉
Loaden with irons wiser than the judge,
If wisdom be in suffering. O my lords,
As you are great, be pitifully good.
Who cannot condemn rashness in cold blood?   55
To kill, I grant, is sin's extremest gust,
But in defense, by mercy, 'tis most just.
To be in anger is impiety,
But who is man that is not angry?
Weigh but the crime with this.   60

SECOND SENATOR   You breathe in vain.

ALCIBIADES   In vain? His service done

63. **Lacedaemon and Byzantium:** See "Alcibiades" in "Historical Background," page 205, and map, page xii.

66. **has done:** i.e., he **has done; fair:** fine

71. **sworn:** inveterate; **rioter:** reveler

72. **drowns him:** In *Twelfth Night*, Shakespeare had earlier used the metaphor of drowning to describe drunkenness: "What's a drunken man like . . . ?" "Like a drowned man, a fool, and a madman. One draught above heat makes him a fool, the second mads him, and a third **drowns him**" (1.5.128–31).

73. **that were enough:** i.e., his drinking would be **enough**

76. **inferred:** mentioned, reported

80. **parts:** qualities

83. **to his:** i.e., in addition **to his**

84. **for:** because

85. **Security:** (1) safety; (2) collateral to secure a loan (Wordplay on financial terms continues with **pawn, good returns,** and **owes.**)

91. **On height of our:** i.e., at the risk of incurring our highest

92. **another:** i.e., another's

At Lacedaemon and Byzantium
Were a sufficient briber for his life.
FIRST SENATOR   What's that?   65
ALCIBIADES
Why, ⌜I⌝ say, my lords, has done fair service
And slain in fight many of your enemies.
How full of valor did he bear himself
In the last conflict, and made plenteous wounds!
SECOND SENATOR
He has made too much plenty with ⌜'em.⌝   70
He's a sworn rioter. He has a sin
That often drowns him and takes his valor prisoner.
If there were no foes, that were enough
To overcome him. In that beastly fury,
He has been known to commit outrages   75
And cherish factions. 'Tis inferred to us
His days are foul and his drink dangerous.
FIRST SENATOR
He dies.
ALCIBIADES   Hard fate! He might have died in war.
My lords, if not for any parts in him—   80
Though his right arm might purchase his own time
And be in debt to none—yet, more to move you,
Take my deserts to his and join 'em both.
And, for I know your reverend ages love
Security, I'll pawn my victories, all   85
My honor, to you, upon his good returns.
If by this crime he owes the law his life,
Why, let the war receive 't in valiant gore,
For law is strict, and war is nothing more.
FIRST SENATOR
We are for law. He dies. Urge it no more,   90
On height of our displeasure. Friend or brother,
He forfeits his own blood that spills another.
ALCIBIADES   Must it be so? It must not be.
My lords, I do beseech you, know me.

95. **How:** i.e., what do you mean
100. **sue:** petition
108. **two days' shine:** i.e., two days
109. **Attend:** expect, look out for
110. **spirit:** angry or hostile feeling
115. **told:** counted; **let out:** loaned
121. **spleen:** indignation
123. **lay for hearts:** i.e., win men to my cause
lay for: ambush, waylay
125. **should . . . gods:** i.e., **should** not tolerate **wrongs** any more than the **gods** do

A usurer. (2.2.74, 109, 111; 3.5.106; 4.3.126)
From John Blaxton, *The English vsurer . . .* (1634).

SECOND SENATOR How?   95
ALCIBIADES Call me to your remembrances.
THIRD SENATOR What?
ALCIBIADES
  I cannot think but your age has forgot me.
  It could not else be I should prove so base
  To sue and be denied such common grace.   100
  My wounds ache at you.
FIRST SENATOR   Do you dare our anger?
  'Tis in few words, but spacious in effect:
  We banish thee forever.
ALCIBIADES   Banish me?   105
  Banish your dotage, banish usury,
  That makes the Senate ugly!
FIRST SENATOR
  If after two days' shine Athens contain thee,
  Attend our weightier judgment.
  And, not to swell our spirit,   110
  He shall be executed presently.   ⌜*Senators*⌝ *exit.*
ALCIBIADES
  Now the gods keep you old enough that you may live
  Only in bone, that none may look on you!—
  I'm worse than mad. I have kept back their foes
  While they have told their money and let out   115
  Their coin upon large interest, I myself
  Rich only in large hurts. All those for this?
  Is this the balsam that the usuring Senate
  Pours into captains' wounds? Banishment.
  It comes not ill. I hate not to be banished.   120
  It is a cause worthy my spleen and fury,
  That I may strike at Athens. I'll cheer up
  My discontented troops and lay for hearts.
  'Tis honor with most lands to be at odds.
  Soldiers should brook as little wrongs as gods.   125
                                        He exits.

3.6 Timon's friends come to dinner again, but this time he serves them only water and stones and drives them away.

O SD. **Friends:** See "Timon's 'Friends,' " especially page 214.

3. **try:** test

4. **tiring:** tearing, pulling (as a bird of prey, in feeding, does to its victim)

7. **by the persuasion:** i.e., on the evidence

10. **inviting:** invitation; **many my near occasions:** i.e., the **many** needs closely affecting me

11. **conjured:** entreated, implored (with wordplay on the sense "summoned up as if I were a spirit"—wordplay that continues in the next line with **appear**)

12. **needs:** of necessity

21. **pieces:** i.e., coins (See "Talents," especially part d, pages 211–13.)

26. **my heart:** sincerity and the utmost of goodwill

31. **willing:** i.e., willingly

⌜Scene 6⌝

⌜*Music.*⌝ *Enter divers Friends at several doors.*

FIRST FRIEND   The good time of day to you, sir.

SECOND FRIEND   I also wish it to you. I think this honorable lord did but try us this other day.

FIRST FRIEND   Upon that were my thoughts tiring when we encountered. I hope it is not so low with him as 5
he made it seem in the trial of his several friends.

SECOND FRIEND   It should not be, by the persuasion of his new feasting.

FIRST FRIEND   I should think so. He hath sent me an earnest inviting, which many my near occasions 10
did urge me to put off; but he hath conjured me beyond them, and I must needs appear.

SECOND FRIEND   In like manner was I in debt to my importunate business, but he would not hear my excuse. I am sorry, when he sent to borrow of me, 15
that my provision was out.

FIRST FRIEND   I am sick of that grief too, as I understand how all things go.

SECOND FRIEND   Every man here's so. What would he have borrowed of you? 20

FIRST FRIEND   A thousand pieces.

SECOND FRIEND   A thousand pieces!

FIRST FRIEND   What of you?

SECOND FRIEND   He sent to me, sir—

Enter Timon and Attendants.

Here he comes. 25

TIMON   With all my heart, gentlemen both! And how fare you?

FIRST FRIEND   Ever at the best, hearing well of your Lordship.

SECOND FRIEND   The swallow follows not summer 30
more willing than we your Lordship.

32–33. **Nor . . . men:** Proverbial: "Swallows, like false friends, fly away upon the approach of **winter.**" (See picture below.)

34. **stay:** delay, waiting

35–36. **fare so harshly o' th':** i.e., be entertained with food as rough or unpleasant as the

36. **shall to 't:** i.e., sit down to feast

38. **empty:** i.e., empty-handed

41. **what cheer:** how are you?

47. **cumber:** trouble; **better remembrance:** i.e., memory, which is **better** employed with other things

58. **upon what:** i.e., for **what** reason?

61. **toward:** approaching, imminent

62. **old:** long-familiar

63. **hold:** continue, endure

64. **time will:** perhaps, "**time will** tell"

DE HIRVNDINE DOMESTICA, ET
in genere.

A swallow. (3.6.30–33)
From Konrad Gesner, . . . *Historiae animalium* . . . (1585–1604).

TIMON, ⌜*aside*⌝ Nor more willingly leaves winter, such
   summer birds are men.—Gentlemen, our dinner
   will not recompense this long stay. Feast your ears
   with the music awhile, if they will fare so harshly   35
   o' th' trumpets' sound. We shall to 't presently.
FIRST FRIEND I hope it remains not unkindly with your
   Lordship that I returned you an empty messenger.
TIMON O, sir, let it not trouble you.
SECOND FRIEND My noble lord—   40
TIMON Ah, my good friend, what cheer?
SECOND FRIEND My most honorable lord, I am e'en
   sick of shame that when your Lordship this other
   day sent to me, I was so unfortunate a beggar.
TIMON Think not on 't, sir.   45
SECOND FRIEND If you had sent but two hours before—
TIMON Let it not cumber your better remembrance.

                  The banquet brought in.

   Come, bring in all together.
SECOND FRIEND All covered dishes!
FIRST FRIEND Royal cheer, I warrant you.   50
THIRD FRIEND Doubt not that, if money and the season
   can yield it.
FIRST FRIEND How do you? What's the news?
THIRD FRIEND Alcibiades is banished. Hear you of it?
FIRST AND SECOND FRIENDS Alcibiades banished?   55
THIRD FRIEND 'Tis so. Be sure of it.
FIRST FRIEND How? How?
SECOND FRIEND I pray you, upon what?
TIMON My worthy friends, will you draw near?
THIRD FRIEND I'll tell you more anon. Here's a noble   60
   feast toward.
SECOND FRIEND This is the old man still.
THIRD FRIEND Will 't hold? Will 't hold?
SECOND FRIEND It does, but time will—and so—
THIRD FRIEND I do conceive.   65

67–68. **Your diet ... alike:** i.e., you will all be served the same food

68. **city feast:** i.e., formal banquet of **city** dignitaries seated in order of precedence, with the greatest accorded **first place** (line 69)

69. **meat:** food

71. **society:** company

73. **reserve still to give:** i.e., always keep something back when you **give**

80. **fees:** offerings, tribute

82. **tag:** rabble

91. **mouth-friends:** (1) those who only mouth their friendship; (2) those who are friends only so long as one feasts them

93. **your perfection:** i.e., the perfect thing for you

94. **stuck:** adorned

TIMON Each man to his stool, with that spur as he
would to the lip of his mistress. Your diet shall
be in all places alike. Make not a city feast of it, to let
the meat cool ere we can agree upon the first place.
Sit, sit. (⌜*They sit.*⌝) The gods require our thanks: 70

You great benefactors, sprinkle our society with
thankfulness. For your own gifts make yourselves
praised, but reserve still to give, lest your deities be
despised. Lend to each man enough, that one need
not lend to another; for, were your godheads to 75
borrow of men, men would forsake the gods. Make
the meat be beloved more than the man that gives
it. Let no assembly of twenty be without a score of
villains. If there sit twelve women at the table, let a
dozen of them be as they are. The rest of your fees, 80
O gods, the Senators of Athens, together with the
common ⌜tag⌝ of people, what is amiss in them,
you gods, make suitable for destruction. For these
my present friends, as they are to me nothing, so
in nothing bless them, and to nothing are they wel- 85
come.

Uncover, dogs, and lap.
⌜*The dishes are uncovered. They contain
only water and stones.*⌝
SOME SPEAK   What does his Lordship mean?
SOME OTHER   I know not.
TIMON
May you a better feast never behold, 90
You knot of mouth-friends! Smoke and lukewarm
water
Is your perfection. This is Timon's last,
Who, stuck and spangled ⌜with your⌝ flatteries,
Washes it off and sprinkles in your faces 95
Your reeking villainy. (⌜*He throws water in their
faces.*⌝) Live loathed and long,

101. **Cap-and-knee slaves:** i.e., servile creatures who are always doffing their caps and bowing; **minute-jacks:** people who change their minds every moment (Literally, **a jack** is a mechanical figure that strikes the hours on a clock. See picture, page 140.)

102. **Of . . . malady:** i.e., may every dreadful disease **of man and beast**

105. **Soft:** wait; **physic:** medicine

117. **humors:** whims (See longer note to **humor,** 1.2.27, page 192.)

123. **stay:** delay

ΕΛΛΑΔΟΣ ΕΛΛΑΣ ΑΘΗΝΑΙ

The walled city of Athens. (4.1.1–3)
From Thucydides, *Eight bookes of the Peloponnesian warre . . .* (1629).

Most smiling, smooth, detested parasites,
Courteous destroyers, affable wolves, meek bears,
You fools of fortune, trencher-friends, time's flies,   100
Cap-and-knee slaves, vapors, and minute-jacks.
Of man and beast the infinite malady
Crust you quite o'er! (⌜*They stand.*⌝) What, dost thou
          go?
Soft! Take thy physic first—thou too—and thou.—   105
Stay. I will lend thee money, borrow none.
                    ⌜*He attacks them and forces them out.*⌝
What? All in motion? Henceforth be no feast
Whereat a villain's not a welcome guest.
Burn, house! Sink, Athens! Henceforth hated be
Of Timon man and all humanity!   ⌜*He exits.*⌝ 110

Enter ⌜*Timon's Friends,*⌝ *the Senators, with other Lords.*

FIRST FRIEND   How now, my lords?
SECOND FRIEND   Know you the quality of Lord Timon's
          fury?
THIRD FRIEND   Push! Did you see my cap?
FOURTH FRIEND   I have lost my gown.   115
FIRST FRIEND   He's but a mad lord, and naught but
          humors sways him. He gave me a jewel th' other
          day, and now he has beat it out of my hat. Did you
          see my jewel?
SECOND FRIEND   Did you see my cap?   120
THIRD FRIEND   Here 'tis.
FOURTH FRIEND   Here lies my gown.
FIRST FRIEND   Let's make no stay.
SECOND FRIEND
     Lord Timon's mad.
THIRD FRIEND   I feel 't upon my bones.   125
FOURTH FRIEND
     One day he gives us diamonds, next day stones.
                    The Senators ⌜*and the others*⌝ *exit.*

TIMON

OF

ATHENS

ACT 4

4.1 Timon abandons Athens and retires to the woods.

---

1. **wall:** See picture, page 110.
3. **turn incontinent:** become unchaste
6. **minister:** administer, i.e., govern; **filths:** prostitutes
7. **green virginity:** i.e., young, inexperienced virgins
10. **your trusters' throats:** i.e., the **throats** of those who trusted you; **Bound:** indentured
11. **Large-handed:** grasping, rapacious
12. **pill:** pillage
14. **lined:** padded
16. **Religion to:** devotion to, reverence for
17. **Domestic awe:** i.e., respect for authority within households; **neighborhood:** neighborliness
18. **manners:** morals; **mysteries:** occupations, professions, skills
19. **Degrees:** ranks
20. **Decline to:** sink or descend into; **your confounding contraries:** i.e., the opposites (of the virtues in lines 15–19), which confound or destroy
21. **And yet confusion live:** i.e., but let destruction escape obliteration
23. **ripe for stroke:** i.e., ready to be struck

⌜ACT 4⌝

⌜Scene 1⌝

Enter Timon.

TIMON
Let me look back upon thee. O thou wall
That girdles in those wolves, dive in the earth
And fence not Athens! Matrons, turn incontinent!
Obedience fail in children! Slaves and fools,
Pluck the grave wrinkled Senate from the bench   5
And minister in their steads! To general filths
Convert o' th' instant, green virginity!
Do 't in your parents' eyes! Bankrupts, hold fast!
Rather than render back, out with your knives
And cut your trusters' throats! Bound servants, steal!   10
Large-handed robbers your grave masters are,
And pill by law. Maid, to thy master's bed!
Thy mistress is o' th' brothel. ⌜Son⌝ of sixteen,
Pluck the lined crutch from thy old limping sire;
With it beat out his brains! Piety and fear,   15
Religion to the gods, peace, justice, truth,
Domestic awe, night rest, and neighborhood,
Instruction, manners, mysteries, and trades,
Degrees, observances, customs, and laws,
Decline to your confounding contraries,   20
And yet confusion live! Plagues incident to men,
Your potent and infectious fevers heap
On Athens, ripe for stroke! Thou cold sciatica,

24. **halt:** limp

25. **liberty:** license, disregard for what is right and proper

28. **riot:** revelry

31. **society:** association (with each other)

32. **merely poison:** entirely poisonous

33. **detestable:** with accents on the first and third syllables

34. **Take thou that too:** perhaps stripping off some of his garments; **bans:** curses

35. **will:** i.e., **will** go

36. **more kinder:** (1) **more** natural; (2) **more** friendly or benevolent

37. **confound:** destroy, utterly defeat

39. **grows:** ages

4.2 Flavius shares his remaining money with his fellow servants as they disperse.

―――――――――

2. **undone:** ruined; **cast off:** abandoned

3. **Alack:** an expression of sorrow; **fellows:** comrades, companions, co-workers (with the added meaning of "equals, peers")

6. **broke:** ruined, destroyed

Cripple our senators, that their limbs may halt
As lamely as their manners! Lust and liberty,   25
Creep in the minds and marrows of our youth,
That 'gainst the stream of virtue they may strive
And drown themselves in riot! Itches, blains,
Sow all th' Athenian bosoms, and their crop
Be general leprosy! Breath infect breath,   30
That their society, as their friendship, may
Be merely poison! Nothing I'll bear from thee
But nakedness, thou detestable town!
Take thou that too, with multiplying bans!
Timon will to the woods, where he shall find   35
Th' unkindest beast more kinder than mankind.
The gods confound—hear me, you good gods all!—
Th' Athenians both within and out that wall,
And grant, as Timon grows, his hate may grow
To the whole race of mankind, high and low!   40
Amen.

He exits.

⌜Scene 2⌝

Enter Steward ⌜Flavius⌝ with two or three Servants.

FIRST SERVANT
  Hear you, Master Steward, where's our master?
  Are we undone, cast off, nothing remaining?
FLAVIUS
  Alack, my fellows, what should I say to you?
  Let me be recorded by the righteous gods,
  I am as poor as you.   5
FIRST SERVANT   Such a house broke?
  So noble a master fall'n, all gone, and not
  One friend to take his fortune by the arm
  And go along with him?
SECOND SERVANT   As we do turn our backs   10

15. **dedicated beggar to the air:** i.e., **beggar** who has committed himself to living in the open **air**

23. **mates:** comrades (with wordplay on **mates** as ship's officers)

24. **threat:** threaten

27. **latest:** last

35. **fierce:** merciless, violent

40. **state:** pomp, high status, wealth; **compounds:** constitutes

41. **varnished:** simulated, pretended

From our companion thrown into his grave,
So his familiars to his buried fortunes
Slink all away, leave their false vows with him,
Like empty purses picked; and his poor self,
A dedicated beggar to the air,   15
With his disease of all-shunned poverty,
Walks, like contempt, alone.

                    Enter other Servants.

                              More of our fellows.
FLAVIUS
    All broken implements of a ruined house.
THIRD SERVANT
    Yet do our hearts wear Timon's livery.   20
    That see I by our faces. We are fellows still,
    Serving alike in sorrow. Leaked is our bark,
    And we, poor mates, stand on the dying deck,
    Hearing the surges threat. We must all part
    Into this sea of air.   25
FLAVIUS   Good fellows all,
    The latest of my wealth I'll share amongst you.
    Wherever we shall meet, for Timon's sake
    Let's yet be fellows. Let's shake our heads and say,
    As 'twere a knell unto our master's fortunes,   30
    "We have seen better days." (⌜*He offers them
        money.*⌝) Let each take some.
    Nay, put out all your hands. Not one word more.
    Thus part we rich in sorrow, parting poor.
            ⌜*The Servants*⌝ *embrace and part several ways.*
    O, the fierce wretchedness that glory brings us!   35
    Who would not wish to be from wealth exempt,
    Since riches point to misery and contempt?
    Who would be so mocked with glory, or to live
    But in a dream of friendship,
    To have his pomp and all what state compounds   40
    But only painted, like his varnished friends?

43. **blood:** i.e., disposition, temper
46. **do:** i.e., does
52. **has he:** i.e., **has he** anything; **supply:** maintain, support
53. **command:** secure

4.3 Timon, digging for roots to eat, finds gold. He is visited by Alcibiades and his concubines, to whom he gives gold for the purpose of advancing the destruction of Athens. He is then visited by Apemantus, with whom he violently argues; then by thieves, to whom he gives gold; and, finally, by Flavius.

———————

2. **thy sister's orb:** the moon (In classical mythology, Diana, goddess of the moon, and Apollo, god of the **sun,** are sister and brother.)
5. **Scarce:** i.e., scarcely; **dividant:** divided, separate; **touch:** i.e., if you test; **with several:** i.e., by giving them different
6. **The greater:** i.e., then the more fortunate; **Not nature:** i.e., **not** even **nature**
7. **To whom . . . siege:** i.e., which is subject to all kinds of suffering
8. **contempt of nature:** i.e., being contemptuous **of nature**
9. **Raise me:** i.e., **raise** (The word **me** is an ethical dative that does not affect sense but enlivens the expression.) **deny 't:** i.e., **deny** wealth and social elevation to

(continued)

Poor honest lord, brought low by his own heart,
Undone by goodness! Strange unusual blood
When man's worst sin is he does too much good!
Who then dares to be half so kind again?   45
For bounty, that makes gods, do still mar men.
My dearest lord, blest to be most accursed,
Rich only to be wretched, thy great fortunes
Are made thy chief afflictions. Alas, kind lord!
He's flung in rage from this ingrateful seat   50
Of monstrous friends,
Nor has he with him to supply his life,
Or that which can command it.
I'll follow and inquire him out.
I'll ever serve his mind with my best will.   55
Whilst I have gold, I'll be his steward still.

                                        He exits.

                    ⌜Scene 3⌝

        Enter Timon in the woods, ⌜with a spade.⌝

TIMON
O blessèd breeding sun, draw from the earth
Rotten humidity! Below thy sister's orb
Infect the air! ⌜Twinned⌝ brothers of one womb,
Whose procreation, residence, and birth
Scarce is dividant, touch them with several fortunes,   5
The greater scorns the lesser. Not nature,
To whom all sores lay siege, can bear great fortune
But by contempt of nature.
Raise me this beggar, and deny 't that lord;
The Senators shall bear contempt hereditary,   10
The beggar native honor.
It is the pasture lards the brother's sides,
The want that makes him ⌜lean.⌝ Who dares, who
    dares

10. **contempt hereditary:** i.e., the **contempt** endured by those born into low rank

11. **native honor:** i.e., the **honor** enjoyed by those born into high rank

12–13. **It is . . . lean:** perhaps, it is the land (**pasture**) that the one brother (lines 3–6 above) possesses that makes him rich, proud, and flattered, and the **want** of it that makes the other brother poor and an object of contempt. See longer note, page 195.

17. **grise:** i.e., step in a staircase (or, in this context, the person occupying the step)

18. **smoothed:** flattered

19. **Ducks:** i.e., bows awkwardly and obsequiously; **obliquy:** obliquity, or deviation from proper conduct

20. **level:** direct (with possible wordplay on the sense "not oblique")

21. **direct:** downright (again with possible wordplay on the sense "not oblique")

22. **societies:** companies

23. **semblable:** fellow

24. **fang:** seize upon

25. **of thee:** i.e., from **thee**

26. **operant:** powerful

29. **votarist:** votary, i.e., one bound by a special vow

30. **clear:** bright, pure; **this:** i.e., gold

37. **Pluck . . . heads:** Compare Ben Jonson's *Volpone* (c. 1606): " 'Tis but to pluck the pillow from his head, / And he is throttled." **stout:** strong, hardy

40. **hoar:** white; **place:** put in office

41. **knee:** reverence

(continued)

In purity of manhood stand upright   15
And say "This man's a flatterer"? If one be,
So are they all, for every grise of fortune
Is smoothed by that below. The learnèd pate
Ducks to the golden fool. All's obliquy.
There's nothing level in our cursèd natures   20
But direct villainy. Therefore be abhorred
All feasts, societies, and throngs of men.
His semblable, yea, himself, Timon disdains.
Destruction fang mankind! Earth, yield me roots!
Who seeks for better of thee, sauce his palate   25
With thy most operant poison! (⌜*Digging, he finds*
    gold.⌝) What is here?
Gold? Yellow, glittering, precious gold?
No, gods, I am no idle votarist.
Roots, you clear heavens! Thus much of this will   30
    make
Black white, foul fair, wrong right,
Base noble, old young, coward valiant.
Ha, you gods! Why this? What this, you gods? Why,
    this   35
Will lug your priests and servants from your sides,
Pluck stout men's pillows from below their heads.
This yellow slave
Will knit and break religions, bless th' accursed,
Make the hoar leprosy adored, place thieves   40
And give them title, knee, and approbation
With senators on the bench. This is it
That makes the wappened widow wed again;
She whom the spital house and ulcerous sores
Would cast the gorge at, this embalms and spices   45
To th' April day again. Come, damnèd earth,
Thou common whore of mankind, that puts odds
Among the rout of nations, I will make thee
Do thy right nature. (*March afar off.*) Ha? A drum?
    Thou 'rt quick,   50

42. **With:** i.e., as if they were

43. **wappened:** a word not recorded anywhere else, but possibly a form of "wappered," or "fatigued"

44. **spital house and ulcerous sores:** i.e., inmates of hospitals and men suffering from purulent ulcers

45. **cast the gorge at:** i.e., vomit at the sight of (The image is from falconry: falcons have a **gorge** they fill with food.)

46. **To th' April day:** i.e., until she looks and smells like an **April day; earth:** a disparaging term for precious metal

47. **puts odds:** causes strife

49. **Do:** i.e., act according to

50. **quick:** rapid in action (with wordplay on the sense "alive")

51. **go:** walk, move

53. **for earnest:** as a pledge or installment

53 SD. **Drum and Fife:** i.e., soldiers playing the **drum and fife**

55. **The canker:** cancer (or, perhaps, the canker-worm, an insect larva that destroys buds and leaves of plants)

59. **Misanthropos:** hater of humankind (from the Greek) See longer note, page 195.

61. **something:** to some extent

63. **strange:** unacquainted

66. **gules:** red (a term from heraldry)

70. **cherubin:** angelic, innocently childlike

75. **wanting:** lacking

But yet I'll bury thee. Thou'lt go, strong thief,
When gouty keepers of thee cannot stand.
Nay, stay thou out for earnest.
⌐*He buries the gold, keeping some out.*⌐

Enter Alcibiades, with Drum and Fife, in warlike
manner, and Phrynia and Timandra.

ALCIBIADES   What art thou there? Speak.

TIMON
A beast, as thou art. The canker gnaw thy heart   55
For showing me again the eyes of man!

ALCIBIADES
What is thy name? Is man so hateful to thee
That art thyself a man?

TIMON
I am Misanthropos and hate mankind.
For thy part, I do wish thou wert a dog,   60
That I might love thee something.

ALCIBIADES   I know thee well.
But in thy fortunes am unlearned and strange.

TIMON
I know thee too, and more than that I know thee
I not desire to know. Follow thy drum.   65
With man's blood paint the ground gules, gules!
Religious canons, civil laws are cruel.
Then what should war be? This fell whore of thine
Hath in her more destruction than thy sword,
For all her cherubin look.   70

PHRYNIA   Thy lips rot off!

TIMON
I will not kiss thee. Then the rot returns
To thine own lips again.

ALCIBIADES
How came the noble Timon to this change?

TIMON
As the moon does, by wanting light to give.   75

83–84. **confound thee:** i.e., may you be destroyed

85. **in some sort:** to some extent

88. **with:** i.e., by

90. **Voiced:** spoke of

95. **salt:** lecherous, salacious (with wordplay on "condiment," since **salt** is followed by **Season,** itself a pun on "fit, prepare" and "add flavor")

96. **tubs and baths:** sweating treatments for venereal diseases (See picture below.)

97. **tub-fast:** abstinence during treatment in the sweating-tub; **the diet:** i.e., **the** curative **diet**

A sweating-tub for treating venereal disease. (4.3.96)
From Thomas Randolph, *Cornelianum dolium . . .* (1638).

But then renew I could not, like the moon;
There were no suns to borrow of.

ALCIBIADES
Noble Timon, what friendship may I do thee?

TIMON
None, but to maintain my opinion.

ALCIBIADES   What is it, Timon?   80

TIMON   Promise me friendship, but perform none. If
thou wilt not promise, the gods plague thee, for
thou art a man. If thou dost perform, confound
thee, for thou art a man.

ALCIBIADES
I have heard in some sort of thy miseries.   85

TIMON
Thou saw'st them when I had prosperity.

ALCIBIADES
I see them now. Then was a blessèd time.

TIMON
As thine is now, held with a brace of harlots.

TIMANDRA
Is this th' Athenian minion whom the world
Voiced so regardfully?   90

TIMON   Art thou Timandra?

TIMANDRA   Yes.

TIMON
Be a whore still. They love thee not that use thee.
.Give them diseases, leaving with thee their lust.
Make use of thy salt hours. Season the slaves   95
For tubs and baths. Bring down rose-cheeked youth
To the tub-fast and the diet.

TIMANDRA   Hang thee, monster!

ALCIBIADES
Pardon him, sweet Timandra, for his wits
Are drowned and lost in his calamities.—   100
I have but little gold of late, brave Timon,
The want whereof doth daily make revolt

103. **penurious:** needy, poverty-stricken

106. **trod:** would have **trod**

116. **confound:** destroy

121. **Put up:** put away

122. **planetary plague:** fatal infectious epidemic produced by the malignant influence of a planet (See longer note, page 195.) **Jove:** in Roman mythology, king of the gods

123. **high-viced:** i.e., extremely wicked

124. **sick:** i.e., corrupt

126. **Strike me:** i.e., **strike;** or, perhaps, **strike for me,** or **strike** on my behalf

127. **habit:** clothing, dress; **honest:** chaste

129. **trenchant:** sharp; **milk paps:** nipples

130. **window-bars:** perhaps, the open work in the bodice of a dress; or, perhaps, a set of bars fitted into a window (Proverbial: "A woman at a window [is] as grapes on a highway.")

Timandra. (4.3.53 SD; 4.3.91)
From Guillaume Rouillé, . . . *Promptuarii iconum* . . . (1553).

In my penurious band. I have heard and grieved
How cursèd Athens, mindless of thy worth,
Forgetting thy great deeds when neighbor states,   105
But for thy sword and fortune, trod upon them—

TIMON
I prithee, beat thy drum and get thee gone.

ALCIBIADES
I am thy friend and pity thee, dear Timon.

TIMON
How dost thou pity him whom thou dost trouble?
I had rather be alone.   110

ALCIBIADES
Why, fare thee well. Here is some gold for thee.

TIMON   Keep it. I cannot eat it.

ALCIBIADES
When I have laid proud Athens on a heap—

TIMON
Warr'st thou 'gainst Athens?

ALCIBIADES   Ay, Timon, and have cause.   115

TIMON
The gods confound them all in thy conquest,
And thee after, when thou hast conquered!

ALCIBIADES
Why me, Timon?

TIMON   That by killing of villains
Thou wast born to conquer my country.   120
Put up thy gold. Go on. Here's gold. Go on.
Be as a planetary plague when Jove
Will o'er some high-viced city hang his poison
In the sick air. Let not thy sword skip one.
Pity not honored age for his white beard;   125
He is an usurer. Strike me the counterfeit matron;
It is her habit only that is honest,
Herself's a bawd. Let not the virgin's cheek
Make soft thy trenchant sword, for those milk paps,
That through the ⌈window-bars⌉ bore at men's eyes,   130

132. **set them down:** i.e., record **them** as
134. **exhaust:** draw out
137. **doubtfully:** ambiguously; **the throat shall cut:** perhaps, **shall cut** thy **throat** (See longer note, page 196.)
138. **sans:** without; **remorse:** compassion; **Swear against objects:** perhaps, take an oath to listen to no objections (that would deter you from atrocities)
140. **proof:** impenetrability; **nor yells . . . babes:** i.e., neither **yells of mothers, maids,** or **babes**
144. **confusion:** ruin
148. **Dost . . . not:** i.e., whether you do or **not**
151. **to make whores a bawd:** perhaps, to turn **whores** into bawds
152. **mountant:** mounting, rising (suggesting a pseudo-heraldic meaning in which the apron raised for sexual activity becomes the sign of the **whore**)
153. **oathable:** fit or able to be sworn to an oath
155. **strong:** severe
157. **conditions:** moral natures; social positions
159. **strong in whore:** steadfast in remaining whores; **burn him up:** i.e., in the fires of lust; and, in the fever of venereal disease
160. **Let . . . smoke:** wordplay on the proverbs "**Fire** is quenched in its own **smoke**" and "No **smoke** without some **fire**" **close:** secret **predominate:** dominate, prevail over
161–62. **Yet . . . contrary:** This puzzling sentence places some kind of vague curse on the women.
162–63. **thatch . . . dead:** i.e., cover your scalp, made bald with venereal disease, with a wig made from the hair **of the dead**

Are not within the leaf of pity writ,
But set them down horrible traitors. Spare not the
    babe,
Whose dimpled smiles from fools exhaust their
    mercy;   135
Think it a bastard whom the oracle
Hath doubtfully pronounced the throat shall cut,
And mince it sans remorse. Swear against objects;
Put armor on thine ears and on thine eyes,
Whose proof nor yells of mothers, maids, nor babes, 140
Nor sight of priests in holy vestments bleeding,
Shall pierce a jot. (⌐*He offers gold.*¬) There's gold to
    pay thy soldiers.
Make large confusion and, thy fury spent,
Confounded be thyself! Speak not. Begone.   145

ALCIBIADES
Hast thou gold yet? I'll take the gold thou givest me,
Not all thy counsel.

TIMON
Dost thou or dost thou not, heaven's curse upon thee!

BOTH ⌐WOMEN¬
Give us some gold, good Timon. Hast thou more?

TIMON
Enough to make a whore forswear her trade,   150
And to make whores a bawd. Hold up, you sluts,
Your aprons mountant. (⌐*He begins throwing gold
    into their aprons.*¬) You are not oathable,
Although I know you'll swear—terribly swear
Into strong shudders and to heavenly agues   155
Th' immortal gods that hear you. Spare your oaths.
I'll trust to your conditions. Be whores still.
And he whose pious breath seeks to convert you,
Be strong in whore, allure him, burn him up.
Let your close fire predominate his smoke,   160
And be no turncoats. Yet may your pains six months
Be quite contrary. And thatch your poor thin roofs

166. **Paint . . . face:** i.e., apply such a thick coat of cosmetics that **a horse** may sink into **your face** as if into muddy ground

167. **pox of:** curse on

170. **Consumptions:** wasting diseases (presumably, venereal disease), which hollow out the **bones**

171. **sharp shins:** i.e., shinbones afflicted with painful nodes (another symptom of venereal disease)

172. **spurring:** i.e., horseback riding (with wordplay on the sex act)

174. **quillets:** subtle distinctions, quibbles; **Hoar:** whiten (perhaps, afflict with leprosy; or, perhaps, turn white the hair of); **flamen:** priest

175. **flesh:** sexual intercourse

176–77. **Down . . . away: The bridge** of **the nose** was often eaten **away** by venereal disease.

178. **his particular to foresee:** i.e., in order to provide for his personal interest or advantage

179. **Smells . . . weal:** i.e., fails to pay attention to the common good; **curled-pate:** curly-haired

184. **erection:** advancement, invigoration (with wordplay on the sexual sense)

186. **grave:** be the grave for

188. **whore:** i.e., whoring; **mischief:** disease; harm; wickedness

189. **earnest:** an installment

193. **If I hope well:** i.e., if my hopes are realized

With burdens of the dead—some that were hanged,
No matter; wear them, betray with them. Whore
   still.   165
Paint till a horse may mire upon your face.
A pox of wrinkles!
BOTH ⌜WOMEN⌝   Well, more gold. What then?
  Believe 't that we'll do anything for gold.
TIMON   Consumptions sow   170
  In hollow bones of man; strike their sharp shins,
  And mar men's spurring. Crack the lawyer's voice,
  That he may never more false title plead
  Nor sound his quillets shrilly. Hoar the flamen,
  That ⌜scolds⌝ against the quality of flesh   175
  And not believes himself. Down with the nose—
  Down with it flat, take the bridge quite away—
  Of him that, his particular to foresee,
  Smells from the general weal. Make curled-pate
    ruffians bald,   180
  And let the unscarred braggarts of the war
  Derive some pain from you. Plague all,
  That your activity may defeat and quell
  The source of all erection. There's more gold.
  Do you damn others, and let this damn you,   185
  And ditches grave you all!
BOTH ⌜WOMEN⌝
  More counsel with more money, bounteous Timon.
TIMON
  More whore, more mischief first! I have given you
    earnest.
ALCIBIADES
  Strike up the drum towards Athens.—Farewell,   190
    Timon.
  If I thrive well, I'll visit thee again.
TIMON
  If I hope well, I'll never see thee more.
ALCIBIADES   I never did thee harm.

197. **find it:** i.e., **find it** harmful (that others speak well of them)

198. **beagles:** a slang term for prostitutes (See the 17th-century play *The Telltale:* "You have brought your sweet beagle to follow the camp.")

200. **Strike:** i.e., sound the drum

201. **being sick of:** i.e., having surfeited on

202. **Common mother:** i.e., the earth (proverbial)

204–5. **Whose . . . feeds all:** i.e., **whose unmeasurable womb teems** (i.e., gives birth) and **whose infinite breast feeds all**

205. **mettle:** spirit (with wordplay on "metal," from which **mettle** had yet to be distinguished in spelling, meaning earthy matter or substance)

208. **worm:** perhaps, serpent; or, perhaps, blindworm

209. **crisp:** perhaps, clear, shining

210. **Hyperion's:** the sun-god's; **quick'ning:** lifegiving, animating

211. **do hate:** i.e., hates

213. **Ensear:** dry up; **conceptious:** prolific

215. **Go great:** be pregnant

216. **Teem:** be prolific, or fertile; **upward:** upturned

217. **marbled mansion:** i.e., the sky (called **marbled** perhaps because shining or streaked [with clouds] like marble)

219. **marrows:** the pith of plants and pulp of fruit; **leas:** meadows

220. **liquorish drafts:** delightful drinks (with wordplay on intoxicating liquors)

222. **That:** i.e., so that

225. **affect my manners:** i.e., assume or take on my ways of behaving

TIMON
　Yes, thou spok'st well of me.　　　　　　　　　195
ALCIBIADES　　　　　　　Call'st thou that harm?
TIMON
　Men daily find it. Get thee away, and take
　Thy beagles with thee.
ALCIBIADES, ⌜*to the Women*⌝　We but offend him.—
　Strike.　　　⌜*The drum sounds; all but Timon*⌝ *exit.*　200
TIMON
　That nature, being sick of man's unkindness,
　Should yet be hungry! (⌜*He digs.*⌝) Common mother,
　　thou
　Whose womb unmeasurable and infinite breast
　Teems and feeds all; whose selfsame mettle—　　205
　Whereof thy proud child, arrogant man, is puffed—
　Engenders the black toad and adder blue,
　The gilded newt and eyeless venomed worm,
　With all th' abhorrèd births below crisp heaven
　Whereon Hyperion's quick'ning fire doth shine:　210
　Yield him who all ⌜thy⌝ human sons do hate,
　From forth thy plenteous bosom, one poor root!
　Ensear thy fertile and conceptious womb;
　Let it no more bring out ingrateful man.
　Go great with tigers, dragons, wolves, and bears;　215
　Teem with new monsters, whom thy upward face
　Hath to the marbled mansion all above
　Never presented. O, a root! Dear thanks!
　Dry up thy marrows, vines, and plow-torn leas,
　Whereof ingrateful man with liquorish drafts　220
　And morsels unctuous greases his pure mind,
　That from it all consideration slips—

Enter Apemantus.

　More man? Plague, plague!
APEMANTUS
　I was directed hither. Men report
　Thou dost affect my manners and dost use them.　225

227. **Consumption:** wasting disease (of any sort)

231. **habit:** clothing, apparel

233. **perfumes:** perhaps, perfumed mistresses

235. **cunning:** art, craft; **carper:** faultfinder, censorious critic

237. **undone:** destroyed

238. **observe:** treat with ceremonious reverence

239. **Blow . . . cap:** Doffing one's **cap** was a mark of deference. **strain:** feature of character

240. **Thou wast told thus:** i.e., you were flattered in this way (with possible wordplay on "tolled" as "decoyed, enticed")

241. **tapsters:** tavern keepers

243. **just:** suitable, fitting

248. **so long:** i.e., for **so long**

249. **boisterous chamberlain:** i.e., incompetent or unskilled chamber attendant (personal servant), though with wordplay on **boisterous** as stormy (describing the **air**)

251. **eagle:** The **eagle** was proverbially long-lived. **page:** i.e., follow, like attentive pages, at

252. **point'st out:** i.e., indicate something you want or wish to have done for you

253. **Candied:** covered, encrusted; **caudle:** i.e., provide a **caudle** (warm gruel mixed with wine or ale) to

256. **wreakful:** vengeful

TIMON
      'Tis, then, because thou dost not keep a dog,
      Whom I would imitate. Consumption catch thee!
APEMANTUS
      This is in thee a nature but infected,
      A poor unmanly melancholy sprung
      From change of future. Why this spade? This place?   230
      This slavelike habit and these looks of care?
      Thy flatterers yet wear silk, drink wine, lie soft,
      Hug their diseased perfumes, and have forgot
      That ever Timon was. Shame not these woods
      By putting on the cunning of a carper.   235
      Be thou a flatterer now, and seek to thrive
      By that which has undone thee. Hinge thy knee,
      And let his very breath whom thou'lt observe
      Blow off thy cap; praise his most vicious strain,
      And call it excellent. Thou wast told thus.   240
      Thou gav'st thine ears, like tapsters that bade
         welcome,
      To knaves and all approachers. 'Tis most just
      That thou turn rascal. Had'st thou wealth again,
      Rascals should have 't. Do not assume my likeness.   245
TIMON
      Were I like thee, I'd throw away myself.
APEMANTUS
      Thou hast cast away thyself, being like thyself—
      A madman so long, now a fool. What, think'st
      That the bleak air, thy boisterous chamberlain,
      Will put thy shirt on warm? Will these moist trees,   250
      That have outlived the eagle, page thy heels
      And skip when thou point'st out? Will the cold brook,
      Candied with ice, caudle thy morning taste
      To cure thy o'ernight's surfeit? Call the creatures
      Whose naked natures live in all the spite   255
      Of wreakful heaven, whose bare unhousèd trunks,

258. **Answer:** stand up to; **mere nature:** unmitigated **nature,** or **nature** in all its severity and intensity

260. **fool of:** i.e., **fool** in

265. **caitiff:** wretch, villain

267. **vex:** seriously afflict or distress

268. **office:** function

272. **habit:** disposition, demeanor

274. **enforcedly:** under compulsion

275. **Willing misery:** i.e., poverty chosen or accepted without complaint

276. **incertain pomp:** i.e., uncertain splendor; **before:** sooner; or, perhaps, in advance, beforehand

277. **The one:** i.e., the life of **incertain pomp; filling still, never complete:** i.e., always less than contented

278. **The other at high wish:** i.e., the life of **willing misery** is perfectly contented

278–80. **Best state ... content:** i.e., the most fortunate are never contented and live unhappily in a disordered and bewildered state, which is **worse** than the state of the least fortunate who are contented

282. **by his breath that:** i.e., because of the words of one who

285. **swathe:** swaddling bands; **proceeded:** i.e., progressed or advanced through (*Proceed* is a technical term for the taking of advanced academic **degrees.**)

To the conflicting elements exposed,
Answer mere nature. Bid them flatter thee.
O, thou shalt find——

TIMON   A fool of thee. Depart.   260

APEMANTUS
I love thee better now than e'er I did.

TIMON
I hate thee worse.

APEMANTUS   Why?

TIMON   Thou flatter'st misery.

APEMANTUS
I flatter not but say thou art a caitiff.   265

TIMON   Why dost thou seek me out?

APEMANTUS   To vex thee.

TIMON
Always a villain's office or a fool's.
Dost please thyself in 't?

APEMANTUS   Ay.   270

TIMON   What, a knave too?

APEMANTUS
If thou didst put this sour cold habit on
To castigate thy pride, 'twere well, but thou
Dost it enforcedly. Thou'dst courtier be again
Wert thou not beggar. Willing misery   275
Outlives incertain pomp, is crowned before;
The one is filling still, never complete,
The other at high wish. Best state, contentless,
Hath a distracted and most wretched being,
Worse than the worst, content.   280
Thou shouldst desire to die, being miserable.

TIMON
Not by his breath that is more miserable.
Thou art a slave whom Fortune's tender arm
With favor never clasped but bred a dog.
Hadst thou, like us from our first swathe, proceeded   285
The sweet degrees that this brief world affords

290. **general riot:** wholesale dissipation
291. **different:** various
293. **game:** perhaps, amusement, diversion; or, perhaps, quarry
297. **At duty:** i.e., paying homage; **frame:** devise
300. **Fell:** i.e., fallen
303. **sufferance:** suffering
304. **made . . . in 't:** i.e., hardened or inured you to it
308. **in spite:** maliciously
308–9. **put stuff / To:** i.e., copulated with
309. **compounded:** composed
310. **hereditary:** by natural inheritance
313. **yet:** still
319. **That the:** i.e., I wish **that the**
321. **mend thy:** i.e., improve the quality of **thy**

"Jacks" striking the hour. (3.6.101)
From Angelo Rocca, *De campanis commentarius . . .* (1612).

To such as may the passive drugs of it
Freely ⌜command,⌝ thou wouldst have plunged
    thyself
In general riot, melted down thy youth   290
In different beds of lust, and never learned
The icy precepts of respect, but followed
The sugared game before thee. But myself—
Who had the world as my confectionary,
The mouths, the tongues, the eyes and hearts of   295
    men
At duty, more than I could frame employment,
That numberless upon me stuck as leaves
Do on the oak, have with one winter's brush
Fell from their boughs and left me open, bare,   300
For every storm that blows—I to bear this,
That never knew but better, is some burden.
Thy nature did commence in sufferance. Time
Hath made thee hard in 't. Why shouldst thou hate
    men?   305
They never flattered thee. What hast thou given?
If thou wilt curse, thy father, that poor rag,
Must be thy subject, who in spite put stuff
To some she-beggar and compounded thee
Poor rogue hereditary. Hence, begone.   310
If thou hadst not been born the worst of men,
Thou hadst been a knave and flatterer.
APEMANTUS
    Art thou proud yet?
TIMON   Ay, that I am not thee.
APEMANTUS   I, that I was no prodigal.   315
TIMON   I, that I am one now.
    Were all the wealth I have shut up in thee,
    I'd give thee leave to hang it. Get thee gone.
    That the whole life of Athens were in this!
    Thus would I eat it.   ⌜*He gnaws a root.*⌝ 320
APEMANTUS, ⌜*offering food*⌝   Here, I will mend thy feast.

324. **'Tis not:** i.e., your company is **not;** **mended:** repaired; **botched:** clumsily repaired

325. **would:** i.e., wish

332. **a-nights:** at night

333. **that's:** i.e., that which is

334. **a-days:** during the day

335. **meat:** food

337. **Would:** i.e., I wish

343. **gilt:** gold

344. **curiosity:** refinement, fastidiousness

346. **medlar:** small brown-skinned apple (See picture, below.)

350. **An:** if

352. **unthrift:** i.e., as a spendthrift or prodigal

353. **after his means:** (1) according to **his means;** (2) **after his means** were gone

A medlar. (4.3.346)
From *The grete herball* . . . [1529].

TIMON
First mend ⌜my⌝ company. Take away thyself.
APEMANTUS
So I shall mend mine own by th' lack of thine.
TIMON
'Tis not well mended so; it is but botched.
If not, I would it were.   325
APEMANTUS What wouldst thou have to Athens?
TIMON
Thee thither in a whirlwind. If thou wilt,
Tell them there I have gold. Look, so I have.
APEMANTUS
Here is no use for gold.
TIMON   The best and truest,   330
For here it sleeps and does no hired harm.
APEMANTUS Where liest a-nights, Timon?
TIMON Under that's above me. Where feed'st thou
    a-days, Apemantus?
APEMANTUS Where my stomach finds meat, or rather   335
    where I eat it.
TIMON Would poison were obedient and knew my
    mind!
APEMANTUS Where wouldst thou send it?
TIMON To sauce thy dishes.   340
APEMANTUS The middle of humanity thou never
    knewest, but the extremity of both ends. When
    thou wast in thy gilt and thy perfume, they
    mocked thee for too much curiosity. In thy rags
    thou know'st none, but art despised for the con-   345
    trary. There's a medlar for thee. Eat it.
TIMON On what I hate I feed not.
APEMANTUS Dost hate a medlar?
TIMON Ay, though it look like thee.
APEMANTUS An thou'dst hated meddlers sooner, thou   350
    shouldst have loved thyself better now. What man
    didst thou ever know unthrift that was beloved
    after his means?

365. **confusion:** destruction, perdition

372. **peradventure:** perchance

377–79. **Wert ... fury:** an allusion to the traditional story that **the unicorn** in its fury to attack the treed lion would impale its horn in the tree and thereby become the lion's helpless victim **confound:** destroy

382. **germane:** closely related

383. **spots of thy kindred:** moral blemishes of the lion (with wordplay on the **spots** on the leopard's skin)

383–84. **were jurors on:** i.e., would sit in judgment **on**

384. **All thy safety were remotion:** i.e., your only **safety** would lie in departing (or, perhaps, going from place to place)

OF THE VNICORNE.

A unicorn. (4.3.377–78)
From Edward Topsell, *The historie of foure-footed
beastes ...* (1607).

144

TIMON   Who, without those means thou talk'st of, didst
thou ever know beloved?   355
APEMANTUS   Myself.
TIMON   I understand thee. Thou hadst some means to
keep a dog.
APEMANTUS   What things in the world canst thou near-
est compare to thy flatterers?   360
TIMON   Women nearest, but men—men are the things
themselves. What wouldst thou do with the world,
Apemantus, if it lay in thy power?
APEMANTUS   Give it the beasts, to be rid of the men.
TIMON   Wouldst thou have thyself fall in the confusion   365
of men and remain a beast with the beasts?
APEMANTUS   Ay, Timon.
TIMON   A beastly ambition, which the gods grant thee
t' attain to! If thou wert the lion, the fox would
beguile thee. If thou wert the lamb, the fox would   370
eat thee. If thou wert the fox, the lion would suspect thee when peradventure thou wert accused by
the ass. If thou wert the ass, thy dullness would
torment thee, and still thou lived'st but as a breakfast to the wolf. If thou wert the wolf, thy greedi-   375
ness would afflict thee, and oft thou shouldst hazard thy life for thy dinner. Wert thou the unicorn,
pride and wrath would confound thee and
make thine own self the conquest of thy fury. Wert
thou a bear, thou wouldst be killed by the horse.   380
Wert thou a horse, thou wouldst be seized by the
leopard. Wert thou a leopard, thou wert germane
to the lion, and the spots of thy kindred were
jurors on thy life. All thy safety were remotion, and
thy defense absence. What beast couldst thou be   385
that were not subject to a beast? And what a beast
art thou already that seest not thy loss in transformation!
APEMANTUS   If thou couldst please me with speaking to

392. **How:** an interjection introducing a question

394. **Yonder ... painter:** These characters do not enter until Act 5.

396. **give way:** i.e., get out of the **way**

401. **cap:** i.e., foremost

404. **by:** in comparison with; **pure:** innocent

407. **I'll:** i.e., I would

❡ Of the ſtraunge and beaſtlie nature of Timon of Athenes, enemie to mankinds : with his death, buriall, and Epitaphe.

❡ The.xxviii.Nouell.

AL the beaſtes of the woꝛlde, doe ap-plie them ſelues to other beaſtes of their kinde, Timon of Athenes on-ly excepted, of whoſe ſtraunge na-ture, Plutarche is aſtonied, in the life of Marcus Antonius. Plato and Aristophanes, doe repoꝛte his mer-uaſlous nature, bicauſe he was a man but by ſhape one-lie, in qualities, he was the capital enemie of mākinde, whiche he confeſſed franckely, vtterlie to abhoꝛre and hate. He dwelte alone in a litle cabane in the fieldes, not farre

"Of the strange and beastly nature of Timon of Athens, enemy to mankind, with his death, burial, and epitaph."

"All the beasts of the world do apply themselves to [i.e., are drawn to] other beasts of their kind, Timon of Athens only excepted, of whose strange nature Plutarch is astonied [i.e., amazed] in the 'Life of Marcus Antonius.' Plato and Aristophanes do report his marvelous nature because he was a man but by shape only. In qualities, he was the capital enemy of mankind, which he confessed frankly utterly to abhor and hate. He dwelt alone in a little cabin in the fields. . . ."

From William Painter, *The pallace of pleasure* . . . (1569).

me, thou mightst have hit upon it here. The com-   390
monwealth of Athens is become a forest of beasts.

TIMON   How, has the ass broke the wall that thou art
out of the city?

APEMANTUS   Yonder comes a poet and a painter. The
plague of company light upon thee! I will fear to   395
catch it and give way. When I know not what else
to do, I'll see thee again.

TIMON   When there is nothing living but thee, thou
shalt be welcome. I had rather be a beggar's dog
than Apemantus.   400

APEMANTUS
Thou art the cap of all the fools alive.

TIMON
Would thou wert clean enough to spit upon!

APEMANTUS
A plague on thee! Thou art too bad to curse.

TIMON
All villains that do stand by thee are pure.

APEMANTUS
There is no leprosy but what thou speak'st.   405

TIMON   If I name thee.
I'll beat thee, but I should infect my hands.

APEMANTUS   I would my tongue could rot them off!

TIMON
Away, thou issue of a mangy dog!
Choler does kill me that thou art alive.   410
I swoon to see thee.

APEMANTUS
Would thou wouldst burst!

TIMON   Away, thou tedious rogue!
I am sorry I shall lose a stone by thee.
⌜*Timon throws a stone at Apemantus.*⌝

APEMANTUS   Beast!   415
TIMON   Slave!
APEMANTUS   Toad!

420. **But even:** except for

421. **presently:** immediately

428. **Hymen's:** In classical mythology, Hymen is the god of marriage. **Mars:** the Roman god of war (See picture, page 150.)

430. **blush:** shine

431. **Dian's:** Diana is the Roman goddess of chastity. (See picture, below.)

432. **sold'rest close:** i.e., solders together, unites

435. **touch:** touchstone (See picture, page 82.)

436. **virtue:** power

437. **Set ... odds:** i.e., set men in such conflict that all will be destroyed; **that:** i.e., so **that**

446. **quit:** free, clear (or, perhaps, rid [of Apemantus])

446 SD. **Banditti:** bandits, thieves

Diana. (4.3.431)
From Robert Whitcombe, *Janua divorum* ... (1678).

TIMON   Rogue, rogue, rogue!
  I am sick of this false world, and will love nought
  But even the mere necessities upon 't.   420
  Then, Timon, presently prepare thy grave.
  Lie where the light foam of the sea may beat
  Thy gravestone daily. Make thine epitaph,
  That death in me at others' lives may laugh.
  (⌈*To his gold.*⌉) O thou sweet king-killer and dear   425
      divorce
  'Twixt natural son and ⌈sire,⌉ thou bright defiler
  Of Hymen's purest bed, thou valiant Mars,
  Thou ever young, fresh, loved, and delicate wooer,
  Whose blush doth thaw the consecrated snow   430
  That lies on Dian's lap; thou visible god,
  That sold'rest close impossibilities
  And mak'st them kiss, that speak'st with every
      tongue
  To every purpose! O thou touch of hearts,   435
  Think thy slave, man, rebels, and by thy virtue
  Set them into confounding odds, that beasts
  May have the world in empire!
APEMANTUS   Would 'twere so!
  But not till I am dead. I'll say thou 'st gold;   440
  Thou wilt be thronged to shortly.
TIMON   Thronged to?
APEMANTUS   Ay.
TIMON
  Thy back, I prithee.
APEMANTUS   Live and love thy misery.   445
TIMON   Long live so, and so die. I am quit.

                  Enter the Banditti.

APEMANTUS
  More things like men.—Eat, Timon, and abhor
  ⌈them.⌉   *Apemantus exits.*
FIRST BANDIT   Where should he have this gold? It is

450. **ort:** scrap, bit

451. **mere:** very, sheer; **want:** lack

451–52. **falling-from:** i.e., desertion, defection

454. **assay:** attempt (with wordplay on **assay** as the determination of the quantity of a particular metal in ore)

455. **for 't:** i.e., **for** his gold

456. **shall 's:** i.e., **shall** we

463. **Save thee:** i.e., God **save thee** (a conventional greeting)

467. **want:** (1) lack; (2) need

468. **meat:** food

471. **mast:** fruit (usually food for swine); **hips:** fruit of **briars** (wild roses)

472. **huswife:** housewife (pronounced "hussif")

473. **mess:** course of dishes

477. **con:** offer

480. **limited:** i.e., exclusive

"Valiant Mars." (4.3.428)
From Vincenzo Cartari, *Le imagini de i dei de gli antichi* . . . (1587).

some poor fragment, some slender ort of his 450
remainder. The mere want of gold and the falling-
from of his friends drove him into this melancholy.

SECOND BANDIT   It is noised he hath a mass of treasure.

THIRD BANDIT   Let us make the assay upon him. If he
care not for 't, he will supply us easily. If he cov- 455
etously reserve it, how shall 's get it?

SECOND BANDIT   True, for he bears it not about him. 'Tis
hid.

FIRST BANDIT   Is not this he?

⌈OTHERS⌉   Where? 460

SECOND BANDIT   'Tis his description.

THIRD BANDIT   He. I know him.

ALL   Save thee, Timon.

TIMON   Now, thieves?

ALL
Soldiers, not thieves. 465

TIMON   Both, too, and women's sons.

ALL
We are not thieves, but men that much do want.

TIMON
Your greatest want is, you want much of meat.
Why should you want? Behold, the earth hath roots.
Within this mile break forth a hundred springs. 470
The oaks bear mast, the briars scarlet hips.
The bounteous huswife Nature on each bush
Lays her full mess before you. Want? Why want?

FIRST BANDIT
We cannot live on grass, on berries, water,
As beasts and birds and fishes. 475

TIMON
Nor on the beasts themselves, the birds and fishes;
You must eat men. Yet thanks I must you con
That you are thieves professed, that you work not
In holier shapes, for there is boundless theft
In limited professions. Rascal thieves, 480

482. **subtle:** (1) delicate; (2) insidiously treacherous

483. **seethe:** boil

487. **protest:** promise

488. **example you with:** i.e., provide **you** with examples or models of

489. **attraction:** drawing power

490. **arrant:** common, notorious

492–93. **The sea's ... tears:** The image of **the sea** dissolving **the moon into salt tears** draws on the moon's control of the tides. **resolves:** melts

494. **composture:** compost, manure

497. **Has unchecked theft:** i.e., have unrestrained power to steal

502. **for this:** i.e., because of **this**

503. **confound:** destroy; **howsoe'er:** in any case

504. **Has:** i.e., he **has**

506. **in the malice of:** i.e., because of his **malice** against

507–8. **mystery:** profession, trade (i.e., thievery)

509–10. **I'll ... trade:** perhaps an allusion to the proverb "It is lawful to learn even from **an enemy**"; or perhaps, "since he is **an enemy,** I will not **believe him,** and will not quit **my trade.**"

512. **true:** honest

Here's gold. (⌜*He gives them gold.*⌝) Go, suck the
  subtle blood o' th' grape
Till the high fever seethe your blood to froth,
And so 'scape hanging. Trust not the physician;
His antidotes are poison, and he slays   485
More than you rob. Take wealth and lives together.
Do, ⌜villainy,⌝ do, since you protest to do 't,
Like workmen. I'll example you with thievery.
The sun's a thief and with his great attraction
Robs the vast sea. The moon's an arrant thief,   490
And her pale fire she snatches from the sun.
The sea's a thief, whose liquid surge resolves
The moon into salt tears. The earth's a thief,
That feeds and breeds by a composture stol'n
From gen'ral excrement. Each thing 's a thief.   495
The laws, your curb and whip, in their rough power
Has unchecked theft. Love not yourselves. Away!
Rob one another. There's more gold. (⌜*He gives them*
  gold.⌝) Cut throats.
All that you meet are thieves. To Athens go.   500
Break open shops. Nothing can you steal
But thieves do lose it. Steal less for this I give you,
And gold confound you howsoe'er! Amen.
THIRD BANDIT Has almost charmed me from my pro-
  fession by persuading me to it.   505
FIRST BANDIT 'Tis in the malice of mankind that he
  thus advises us, not to have us thrive in our mys-
  tery.
SECOND BANDIT I'll believe him as an enemy and give
  over my trade.   510
FIRST BANDIT Let us first see peace in Athens. There is
  no time so miserable but a man may be true.
                            Thieves exit.

    Enter ⌜*Flavius,*⌝ *the Steward, to Timon.*

FLAVIUS O you gods!

514. **ruinous:** ruined
515. **failing:** weakness; failure
521. **rarely:** excellently; **it:** i.e., my observation that Timon has been destroyed by his **friends; guise:** fashion, style
522. **wished:** entreated, commanded
524. **mischief:** injure
539. **undone:** ruined
543. **give:** i.e., weep
544. **thorough:** through, i.e., as a consequence of

Capricious Fortune. (1.1.99)
From Giovanni Boccaccio, *A treatise . . . shewing . . . the falles of . . . princes . . .* (1554).

Is yond despised and ruinous man my lord?
Full of decay and failing? O, monument   515
And wonder of good deeds evilly bestowed!
What an alteration of honor has desp'rate want
    made!
What viler thing upon the earth than friends,
Who can bring noblest minds to basest ends!   520
How rarely does it meet with this time's guise,
When man was wished to love his enemies!
Grant I may ever love, and rather woo
Those that would mischief me than those that do!
Has caught me in his eye. I will present   525
My honest grief unto him and as my lord
Still serve him with my life.—My dearest master.

TIMON
Away! What art thou?

FLAVIUS   Have you forgot me, sir?

TIMON
Why dost ask that? I have forgot all men.   530
Then, if thou ⌜grant'st⌝ thou 'rt a man, I have forgot
    thee.

FLAVIUS   An honest poor servant of yours.

TIMON   Then I know thee not.
I never had honest man about me, I. All   535
I kept were knaves to serve in meat to villains.

FLAVIUS   The gods are witness,
Ne'er did poor steward wear a truer grief
For his undone lord than mine eyes for you.
                                         ⌜*He weeps.*⌝

TIMON
What, dost thou weep? Come nearer, then. I love   540
    thee
Because thou art a woman and disclaim'st
Flinty mankind, whose eyes do never give
But thorough lust and laughter. Pity's sleeping.

549. **entertain:** employ, retain
551. **comfortable:** comforting, consoling
555. **exceptless rashness:** lack of due consideration in allowing for exceptions
559. **fain:** gladly
562. **Methinks:** it seems to me
564. **service:** situation or position as a servant
566. **true:** i.e., truly
568. **subtle:** artfully contrived
569. **deal:** bestow
572. **suspect:** suspicion
575. **still:** always
576. **merely:** entirely

Strange times that weep with laughing, not with   545
   weeping!

FLAVIUS
  I beg of you to know me, good my lord,
  T' accept my grief, and, whilst this poor wealth lasts,
  To entertain me as your steward still.
                      ⌜*He offers money.*⌝

TIMON   Had I a steward   550
  So true, so just, and now so comfortable?
  It almost turns my dangerous nature ⌜mild.⌝
  Let me behold thy face. Surely this man
  Was born of woman.
  Forgive my general and exceptless rashness,   555
  You perpetual-sober gods. I do proclaim
  One honest man—mistake me not, but one;
  No more, I pray!—and he's a steward.
  How fain would I have hated all mankind,
  And thou redeem'st thyself. But all, save thee,   560
  I fell with curses.
  Methinks thou art more honest now than wise,
  For by oppressing and betraying me
  Thou mightst have sooner got another service;
  For many so arrive at second masters   565
  Upon their first lord's neck. But tell me true—
  For I must ever doubt, though ne'er so sure—
  Is not thy kindness subtle, covetous,
  A usuring kindness, and as rich men deal gifts,
  Expecting in return twenty for one?   570

FLAVIUS
  No, my most worthy master, in whose breast
  Doubt and suspect, alas, are placed too late.
  You should have feared false times when you did
     feast.
  Suspect still comes where an estate is least.   575
  That which I show, heaven knows, is merely love,
  Duty, and zeal to your unmatchèd mind,

578. **Care of:** concern for, attention to; **living:** livelihood, maintenance

580. **For:** i.e., as for; **points to:** i.e., is directed toward

581. **in hope:** i.e., in the future; **present:** the **present** time

583. **requite:** repay

584. **singly:** (1) uniquely; (2) truly

587. **Has:** i.e., have

588. **thus conditioned:** i.e., only under the following conditions; **from:** away from, at a distance from

593. **be men:** i.e., let **men** be

Care of your food and living. And believe it,
My most honored lord,
For any benefit that points to me,   580
Either in hope or present, I'd exchange
For this one wish, that you had power and wealth
To requite me by making rich yourself.

TIMON
Look thee, 'tis so. Thou singly honest man,
Here, take. (⌜*Timon offers gold.*⌝) The gods out of my   585
    misery
Has sent thee treasure. Go, live rich and happy,
But thus conditioned: thou shalt build from men;
Hate all, curse all, show charity to none,
But let the famished flesh slide from the bone   590
Ere thou relieve the beggar; give to dogs
What thou deniest to men; let prisons swallow 'em,
Debts wither 'em to nothing; be men like blasted
    woods,
And may diseases lick up their false bloods!   595
And so farewell and thrive.

FLAVIUS   O, let me stay
And comfort you, my master.

TIMON   If thou hat'st curses,
Stay not. Fly whilst thou art blest and free.   600
Ne'er see thou man, and let me ne'er see thee.
                                        ⌜*They*⌝ *exit.*

TIMON
OF
ATHENS

ACT 5

5.1 Timon is visited by the Poet and the Painter seeking the gold Timon is now rumored to possess. After he drives them away empty-handed, he receives a delegation of two Athenian senators, who plead in vain with him to return to Athens and rescue it from the approaching Alcibiades. Timon refuses and withdraws to die.

---

7. **soldiers:** The Banditti claimed to be **soldiers** at 4.3.465.

9. **breaking:** financial failure, bankruptcy; **try:** test

11. **palm:** perhaps an allusion to Psalm 92.12: "The righteous shall **flourish** like a **palm** tree."

13. **tender:** offer

14. **show honestly:** appear honorable

16. **travail:** (1) labor; (2) travel (The words *travail* and *travel* were not distinguished from each other.)

17. **having:** wealth

21. **intent:** project, design

⌜ACT 5⌝

⌜Scene 1⌝

Enter Poet and Painter.

PAINTER As I took note of the place, it cannot be far
where he abides.

POET What's to be thought of him? Does the rumor
hold for true that he's so full of gold?

PAINTER Certain. Alcibiades reports it. Phrynia and   5
Timandra had gold of him. He likewise enriched
poor straggling soldiers with great quantity. 'Tis
said he gave unto his steward a mighty sum.

POET Then this breaking of his has been but a try for
his friends?   10

PAINTER Nothing else. You shall see him a palm in
Athens again, and flourish with the highest. Therefore 'tis not amiss we tender our loves to him in
this supposed distress of his. It will show honestly
in us and is very likely to load our purposes with   15
what they travail for, if it be a just and true report
that goes of his having.

Enter Timon, ⌜behind them,⌝ from his cave.

POET What have you now to present unto him?

PAINTER Nothing at this time but my visitation. Only I
will promise him an excellent piece.   20

POET I must serve him so too—tell him of an intent
that's coming toward him.

163

23. **air:** manner, style

25. **his act:** i.e., its **act,** its fulfillment of the promise made; **but in:** i.e., except with

26–27. **deed of saying:** i.e., **performance** of what one has promised

27. **use:** practice, custom

33. **provided:** arranged

34. **personating of himself:** i.e., representation of Timon's own circumstances

35. **softness:** comfort; luxury; easy or voluptuous living

35–36. **discovery:** revelation, disclosure

38. **Must thou needs:** i.e., **must** you; **stand for:** represent, be in the place of

42. **estate:** material prosperity

45. **serves:** is available

51. **thou:** i.e., **gold; rigg'st . . . foam:** i.e., cause men to rig ships and sail the seas (by providing the motivation for exploration and colonization)

52. **Settlest . . . slave:** Perhaps, make **a slave** admire and reverence his master; or, perhaps, make even **a** former **slave** the object of admiration and reverence

53. **aye:** ever

55. **Fit:** perhaps, it is fitting that

PAINTER   Good as the best. Promising is the very air o'
th' time; it opens the eyes of expectation. Performance is ever the duller for his act, and but in the   25
plainer and simpler kind of people the deed of saying is quite out of use. To promise is most courtly
and fashionable. Performance is a kind of will or
testament which argues a great sickness in his
judgment that makes it.   30

TIMON, ⌜*aside*⌝ Excellent workman! Thou canst not
paint a man so bad as is thyself.

POET   I am thinking what I shall say I have provided
for him. It must be a personating of himself, a
satire against the softness of prosperity, with a dis-   35
covery of the infinite flatteries that follow youth
and opulency.

TIMON, ⌜*aside*⌝ Must thou needs stand for a villain in
thine own work? Wilt thou whip thine own faults
in other men? Do so. I have gold for thee.   40

POET   Nay, let's seek him.
   Then do we sin against our own estate
   When we may profit meet and come too late.

PAINTER   True.
   When the day serves, before black-cornered night,   45
   Find what thou want'st by free and offered light.
   Come.

TIMON, ⌜*aside*⌝
   I'll meet you at the turn. What a god's gold
   That he is worshiped in a baser temple
   Than where swine feed!   50
   'Tis thou that rigg'st the bark and plow'st the foam,
   Settlest admirèd reverence in a slave.
   To thee be ⌜worship,⌝ and thy saints for aye
   Be crowned with plagues, that thee alone obey!
   Fit I meet them.   ⌜*He comes forward.*⌝ 55

POET
   Hail, worthy Timon.

57. **late:** recently, not long since
58. **once:** i.e., indeed
60. **open:** liberal, generous
61. **retired:** withdrawn into seclusion; **fall'n off:** i.e., having deserted you
65. **starlike . . . influence:** In astrological thinking, **influence** streamed from the stars, shaping human character and destiny.
71. **them:** perhaps, ungrateful men; or, perhaps, their acts of ingratitude
77. **requite:** repay
82. **therefor:** for that reason
85. **counterfeit:** portrait, image, likeness

A painter at his easel. (1.1.0 SD; 5.1.0 SD)
From Randle Holme, *The academy of armory . . .* (1688).

PAINTER   Our late noble master.

TIMON
  Have I once lived to see two honest men?

POET Sir,
  Having often of your open bounty tasted,   60
  Hearing you were retired, your friends fall'n off,
  Whose thankless natures—O, abhorrèd spirits!
  Not all the whips of heaven are large enough—
  What, to you,
  Whose starlike nobleness gave life and influence   65
  To their whole being? I am rapt and cannot cover
  The monstrous bulk of this ingratitude
  With any size of words.

TIMON
  Let it go naked. Men may see 't the better.
  You that are honest, by being what you are   70
  Make them best seen and known.

PAINTER   He and myself
  Have travailed in the great shower of your gifts
  And sweetly felt it.

TIMON   Ay, you are honest ⌜men.⌝   75

PAINTER
  We are hither come to offer you our service.

TIMON
  Most honest men! Why, how shall I requite you?
  Can you eat roots and drink cold water? No?

BOTH
  What we can do we'll do to do you service.

TIMON
  You're honest men. You've heard that I have gold.   80
  I am sure you have. Speak truth. You're honest men.

PAINTER
  So it is said, my noble lord, but therefor
  Came not my friend nor I.

TIMON
  Good honest men. (⌜*To the Painter.*⌝) Thou draw'st a
     counterfeit   85

87. **counterfeit'st:** (1) draw images; (2) practice deceit; **lively:** vividly

89. **And for:** i.e., **and** as **for**

91. **stuff:** matter or substance; **smooth:** (1) pleasant; (2) speciously attractive, flattering

92. **thou art even natural:** i.e., (1) you rival nature; (2) you reveal your true self (with possible wordplay on a **natural** as an idiot)

96. **mend:** rectify, remove

97. **Beseech:** i.e., we **beseech**

99. **ill:** badly

106. **cog:** cheat, deceive

107. **patchery:** knavery, roguery

108. **Keep:** i.e., **keep** him

109. **made-up:** consummate, accomplished

113. **Rid me:** i.e., if you will **rid**

114. **draft:** privy

115. **Confound:** destroy

Best in all Athens. Thou 'rt indeed the best.
Thou counterfeit'st most lively.

PAINTER   So-so, my lord.

TIMON
E'en so, sir, as I say. (⌜*To the Poet.*⌝) And for thy
  fiction,   90
Why, thy verse swells with stuff so fine and smooth
That thou art even natural in thine art.
But for all this, my honest-natured friends,
I must needs say you have a little fault.
Marry, 'tis not monstrous in you, neither wish I   95
You take much pains to mend.

BOTH   Beseech your Honor
To make it known to us.

TIMON   You'll take it ill.

BOTH   Most thankfully, my lord.   100

TIMON   Will you indeed?

BOTH   Doubt it not, worthy lord.

TIMON
There's never a one of you but trusts a knave
That mightily deceives you.

BOTH   Do we, my lord?   105

TIMON
Ay, and you hear him cog, see him dissemble,
Know his gross patchery, love him, feed him,
Keep in your bosom. Yet remain assured
That he's a made-up villain.

PAINTER   I know none such, my lord.   110

POET   Nor I.

TIMON
Look you, I love you well. I'll give you gold.
Rid me these villains from your companies,
Hang them or stab them, drown them in a draft,
Confound them by some course, and come to me,   115
I'll give you gold enough.

BOTH
Name them, my lord, let 's know them.

125. **pack:** leave, depart
127. **work:** i.e., **a work** or poem
133. **he is set so only to:** i.e., **he is so** single-mindedly directed toward the consideration of
137. **part:** function, duty, business
140. **still:** always
141. **framed:** shaped; **with his:** i.e., **with its**

An alchemist at work. (2.2.124–25; 5.1.129)
From Konrad Gesner, *The newe iewell of health . . .* (1576).

TIMON
You that way and you this, but two in company.
Each man apart, all single and alone,
Yet an archvillain keeps him company. 120
(⌜*To one.*⌝) If where thou art, two villains shall not be,
Come not near him. (⌜*To the other.*⌝) If thou wouldst
    not reside
But where one villain is, then him abandon.—
Hence, pack. There's gold. You came for gold, you 125
    slaves.
(⌜*To one.*⌝) You have work for me. There's payment.
    Hence.
(⌜*To the other.*⌝) You are an alchemist; make gold of
    that. 130
Out, rascal dogs!
                    ⌜*Timon drives them out and then*⌝ *exits.*

        Enter Steward ⌜*Flavius,*⌝ *and two Senators.*

FLAVIUS
It is vain that you would speak with Timon,
For he is set so only to himself
That nothing but himself which looks like man
Is friendly with him. 135
FIRST SENATOR   Bring us to his cave.
It is our part and promise to th' Athenians
To speak with Timon.
SECOND SENATOR   At all times alike
Men are not still the same. 'Twas time and griefs 140
That framed him thus. Time, with his fairer hand
Offering the fortunes of his former days,
The former man may make him. Bring us to him,
And ⌜chance⌝ it as it may.
FLAVIUS   Here is his cave.— 145
Peace and content be here! Lord Timon! Timon!
Look out, and speak to friends. Th' Athenians
By two of their most reverend Senate greet thee.
Speak to them, noble Timon.

161. **What ... thee:** i.e., the offenses that **we ourselves are sorry for** having committed against you

162. **with one consent:** i.e., in a perfect accord or consensus

167. **general gross:** i.e., generally evident

168. **public body:** perhaps, Athens; or, perhaps, the senate of Athens

170. **withal:** because of that, or as a consequence of that

171. **it:** i.e., its; **fall:** descent from the moral high ground; **restraining:** withholding

172. **make ... render:** i.e., give their apology; offer an account of how sorry they are

173–74. **more fruitful ... dram:** i.e., that more than counterpoises **their offense** even according to the most exact measure **dram:** an exceptionally small unit of weight (in apothecaries' weight, 60 grains)

177. **write ... love:** Here Timon is imagined as an account book in which the **love** of **the Senators** is written down. (**Figures** could also mean images or letters of the alphabet.)

179. **witch:** enchant

Enter Timon out of his cave.

TIMON
  Thou sun that comforts, burn!—Speak and be   150
    hanged!
  For each true word a blister, and each false
  Be as a cauterizing to the root o' th' tongue,
  Consuming it with speaking.
FIRST SENATOR   Worthy Timon—   155
TIMON
  Of none but such as you, and you of Timon.
FIRST SENATOR
  The Senators of Athens greet thee, Timon.
TIMON
  I thank them and would send them back the plague,
  Could I but catch it for them.
FIRST SENATOR   O, forget   160
  What we are sorry for ourselves in thee.
  The Senators with one consent of love
  Entreat thee back to Athens, who have thought
  On special dignities which vacant lie
  For thy best use and wearing.   165
SECOND SENATOR   They confess
  Toward thee forgetfulness too general gross;
  Which now the public body, which doth seldom
  Play the recanter, feeling in itself
  A lack of Timon's aid, hath ⌜sense⌝ withal   170
  Of it own fall, restraining aid to Timon,
  And send forth us to make their sorrowed render,
  Together with a recompense more fruitful
  Than their offense can weigh down by the dram—
  Ay, even such heaps and sums of love and wealth   175
  As shall to thee blot out what wrongs were theirs
  And write in thee the figures of their love,
  Ever to read them thine.
TIMON   You witch me in it,

182. **beweep these comforts:** weep over these comforting reflections

183. **so please thee:** i.e., if it **please** you

186. **Allowed with:** granted, assigned, given

187. **Live:** i.e., continue to be associated

200. **contumelious:** insolent

204. **take 't at worst:** i.e., interpret what I say in the most unfavorable way (See longer note, page 196.)

205. **answer:** suffer the consequences; **For myself:** i.e., as **for myself**

206. **whittle:** large knife (carving knife, clasp knife); **th' unruly camp:** i.e., Alcibiades' military **camp,** called **unruly** because ungovernable by Athens

207. **at my love:** perhaps, in terms of **my love;** or, as worthy of **my love**

209. **prosperous:** auspicious, favorable

210. **keepers:** jailers

212. **writing of:** i.e., **writing**

Surprise me to the very brink of tears.   180
Lend me a fool's heart and a woman's eyes,
And I'll beweep these comforts, worthy senators.
FIRST SENATOR
Therefore, so please thee to return with us
And of our Athens, thine and ours, to take
The captainship, thou shalt be met with thanks;   185
Allowed with absolute power, and thy good name
Live with authority. So soon we shall drive back
Of Alcibiades th' approaches wild,
Who like a boar too savage doth root up
His country's peace.   190
SECOND SENATOR   And shakes his threat'ning sword
Against the walls of Athens.
FIRST SENATOR   Therefore, Timon—
TIMON
Well sir, I will. Therefore I will, sir, thus:
If Alcibiades kill my countrymen,   195
Let Alcibiades know this of Timon—
That Timon cares not. But if he sack fair Athens
And take our goodly agèd men by th' beards,
Giving our holy virgins to the stain
Of contumelious, beastly, mad-brained war,   200
Then let him know, and tell him Timon speaks it
In pity of our agèd and our youth,
I cannot choose but tell him that I care not,
And let him take 't at worst—for their knives care not,
While you have throats to answer. For myself,   205
There's not a whittle in th' unruly camp
But I do prize it at my love before
The reverend'st throat in Athens. So I leave you
To the protection of the prosperous gods
As thieves to keepers.   210
FLAVIUS, ⌜*to Senators*⌝ Stay not. All's in vain.
TIMON
Why, I was writing of my epitaph.

214. **mend:** improve
215. **nothing:** extinction
220. **common wrack:** destruction of the community
221. **common bruit:** popular report, rumor
226. **triumphers:** conquerors, victors
230. **aches:** pronounced "aitches"
231. **incident throes:** i.e., agonies that are likely to happen
235. **prevent:** (1) escape, frustrate; (2) anticipate
237. **close:** enclosure, yard
238. **use:** need; advantage
240. **the sequence of degree:** order of social precedence

A boar rooting up a vineyard. (5.1.189–90)
From Cornelis Zweerts, *K. Zweerts Zede-en Zinnebeelden* . . . (1707).

It will be seen tomorrow. My long sickness
Of health and living now begins to mend,
And nothing brings me all things. Go, live still.   215
Be Alcibiades your plague, you his,
And last so long enough!
FIRST SENATOR   We speak in vain.
TIMON
But yet I love my country and am not
One that rejoices in the common wrack,   220
As common bruit doth put it.
FIRST SENATOR   That's well spoke.
TIMON
Commend me to my loving countrymen.
FIRST SENATOR
These words become your lips as they pass through
    them.   225
SECOND SENATOR
And enter in our ears like great triumphers
In their applauding gates.
TIMON   Commend me to them
And tell them that, to ease them of their griefs,
Their fears of hostile strokes, their aches, losses,   230
Their pangs of love, with other incident throes
That nature's fragile vessel doth sustain
In life's uncertain voyage, I will some kindness do
    them.
I'll teach them to prevent wild Alcibiades' wrath.   235
FIRST SENATOR, ⌐*to Second Senator*⌐
I like this well. He will return again.
TIMON
I have a tree, which grows here in my close,
That mine own use invites me to cut down,
And shortly must I fell it. Tell my friends,
Tell Athens, in the sequence of degree   240
From high to low throughout, that whoso please
To stop affliction, let him take his haste,

245. **still:** always

248. **beachèd:** covered with the sand or pebbles of a beach; **verge:** margin, i.e., shore; **salt flood:** i.e., sea, ocean

249. **Who:** i.e., which; **his:** i.e., its; **embossèd:** foam-covered

252. **four:** i.e., a few

253. **mend:** rectify, put right

256. **unremovably:** irremovably

260. **dear:** dire, grievous

261. **foot:** movement

5.2 Athens learns that it will surely fall to Alcibiades. Its senators seek shelter behind its walls.

———————

1. **Thou . . . discovered:** perhaps, what you have learned (about Alcibiades' army) will turn out to be painful for us; or, perhaps, you have endured pain to learn what you have; **his files:** i.e., the ranks of his army

3. **spoke the least:** i.e., provided the most conservative estimate

4. **expedition:** speed, haste

5. **Present:** immediate

Come hither ere my tree hath felt the ax,
And hang himself. I pray you, do my greeting.
FLAVIUS, ⌐*to Senators*⌐
  Trouble him no further. Thus you still shall find him.   245
TIMON
  Come not to me again, but say to Athens,
  Timon hath made his everlasting mansion
  Upon the beachèd verge of the salt flood,
  Who once a day with his embossèd froth
  The turbulent surge shall cover. Thither come   250
  And let my gravestone be your oracle.
  Lips, let four words go by and language end.
  What is amiss, plague and infection mend.
  Graves only be men's works, and death their gain.
  Sun, hide thy beams. Timon hath done his reign.   255
                                         Timon exits.

FIRST SENATOR
  His discontents are unremovably
  Coupled to nature.
SECOND SENATOR
  Our hope in him is dead. Let us return
  And strain what other means is left unto us
  In our dear peril.   260
FIRST SENATOR   It requires swift foot.
                                         They exit.

⌐Scene 2⌐

Enter two other Senators, with a Messenger.

⌐THIRD⌐ SENATOR
  Thou hast painfully discovered. Are his files
  As full as thy report?
MESSENGER   I have spoke the least.
  Besides, his expedition promises
  Present approach.   5

6. **stand much:** i.e., remain at great

7–10. **I met ... friends:** The structure of this sentence changes before it concludes. **Whom,** referring to the **ancient friend,** also functions to indicate that he is the one on whom **our old love made a particular force.   one mine ancient friend:** i.e., a former or sometime **friend** of **mine   in general part:** i.e., in the main, in all important respects **particular:** personal, private, special

12. **imported:** (1) purported; (2) concerned, were related to

13. **His fellowship:** i.e., Timon's participation or sharing

14. **moved:** stirred up, commenced

17. **scouring:** swift hostile advance

5.3 One of Alcibiades' soldiers discovers Timon's tomb and, since he cannot read Timon's epitaph, he resolves to bring a wax impression of it to Alcibiades.

———

3. **span:** period of his life (Psalm 39.6, in the Prayer Book Psalter, reads: "Thou hast made my days as it were a **span** long." The Geneva Bible has "hand breadth" instead of **span.**)

6. **The character ... wax:** i.e., **I'll take** a **wax** impression of the **character** (inscription)

7. **figure:** i.e., kind of writing

⌜FOURTH⌝ SENATOR
  We stand much hazard if they bring not Timon.

MESSENGER
  I met a courier, one mine ancient friend,
  Whom, though in general part we were opposed,
  Yet our old love made a particular force
  And made us speak like friends. This man was riding   10
  From Alcibiades to Timon's cave
  With letters of entreaty which imported
  His fellowship i' th' cause against your city,
  In part for his sake moved.

Enter the other Senators.

⌜THIRD⌝ SENATOR   Here come our brothers.   15

⌜FIRST⌝ SENATOR
  No talk of Timon; nothing of him expect.
  The enemy's drum is heard, and fearful scouring
  Doth choke the air with dust. In, and prepare.
  Ours is the fall, I fear, our foe's the snare.

They exit.

⌜Scene 3⌝

Enter a Soldier in the woods, seeking Timon.

SOLDIER
  By all description this should be the place.
  Who's here? Speak, ho! No answer? What is this?
  ⌜*He reads an epitaph.*⌝
  Timon is dead, who hath out-stretched his span.
  Some beast read this; there does not live a man.
  Dead, sure, and this his grave. What's on this tomb   5
  I cannot read. The character I'll take with wax.
  Our captain hath in every figure skill,
  An aged interpreter, though young in days.

9. **set down:** encamped; **by this:** i.e., by now
10. **mark:** goal

5.4 A victorious Alcibiades listens to the apologies of the senators and agrees to the conditions they set. Athens then opens its gates to Alcibiades and his army. Presented with Timon's epitaph, Alcibiades reads it aloud and promises peace to Athens.

———

0 SD. **Powers:** army
1. **coward:** i.e., cowardly
2. **terrible:** terrifying
2 SD. **parley:** a trumpet call to initiate discussion between representatives of opposed forces
4. **all licentious measure:** i.e., all kinds of licentiousness
4–5. **making ... justice:** i.e., reducing **justice** to the attainment of your desires
7. **traversed arms: arms** crossed (rather than in an aggressive posture)
7–8. **breathed ... vainly:** i.e., spoke of our suffering in vain
8. **flush:** abundantly full, full to overflowing
9. **crouching marrow:** (1) vitality, which formerly cringed; or (2) vitality, now **crouching** to make a spring
10. **of itself:** on its own volition
12. **pursy:** fat; short-winded; **break his wind:** gasp for breath
15. **griefs:** grievances; **a mere conceit:** i.e., nothing but your own fancies
19. **their:** perhaps referring to **rages** (line 17), or, perhaps, to **griefs** (line 15)

Before proud Athens he's set down by this,
Whose fall the mark of his ambition is.   10

He exits.

⌜Scene 4⌝

Trumpets sound. Enter Alcibiades with his Powers
before Athens.

ALCIBIADES
Sound to this coward and lascivious town
Our terrible approach.   *Sounds a parley.*

The Senators appear upon the walls.

Till now you have gone on and filled the time
With all licentious measure, making your wills
The scope of justice. Till now myself and such   5
As slept within the shadow of your power
Have wandered with our traversed arms and breathed
Our sufferance vainly. Now the time is flush,
When crouching marrow in the bearer strong
Cries of itself "No more!" Now breathless wrong   10
Shall sit and pant in your great chairs of ease,
And pursy insolence shall break his wind
With fear and horrid flight.

FIRST SENATOR   Noble and young,
When thy first griefs were but a mere conceit,   15
Ere thou hadst power or we had cause of fear,
We sent to thee to give thy rages balm,
To wipe out our ingratitude with loves
Above their quantity.

SECOND SENATOR   So did we woo   20
Transformèd Timon to our city's love
By humble message and by promised means.
We were not all unkind, nor all deserve
The common stroke of war.

28. **trophies:** monuments, memorials; **schools:** public buildings

30. **them:** i.e., those **from whom / You have received your grief**

32. **motives . . . out:** i.e., instigators of your exile

33. **wanted:** lacked

36. **a tithèd death:** i.e., selecting one in ten to kill (the equivalent of the Latinate word **decimation**)

39. **die:** one of a pair of dice.

42. **square:** fair

43. **like lands:** i.e., unlike property

55. **rampired:** blocked-up

56. **So:** provided that

58. **Throw:** i.e., if you will **throw**

60. **That thou:** i.e., as a sign that you; **redress:** i.e., means of **redress** or reparation

FIRST SENATOR   These walls of ours   25
  Were not erected by their hands from whom
  You have received your grief, nor are they such
  That these great towers, trophies, and schools
      should fall
  For private faults in them.   30
SECOND SENATOR   Nor are they living
  Who were the motives that you first went out.
  Shame, that they wanted cunning, in excess
  Hath broke their hearts. March, noble lord,
  Into our city with thy banners spread.   35
  By decimation and a tithèd death,
  If thy revenges hunger for that food
  Which nature loathes, take thou the destined tenth
  And, by the hazard of the spotted die,
  Let die the spotted.   40
FIRST SENATOR   All have not offended.
  For those that were, it is not square to take,
  On those that are, revenge. Crimes, like lands,
  Are not inherited. Then, dear countryman,
  Bring in thy ranks but leave without thy rage.   45
  Spare thy Athenian cradle and those kin
  Which in the bluster of thy wrath must fall
  With those that have offended. Like a shepherd
  Approach the fold and cull th' infected forth,
  But kill not all together.   50
SECOND SENATOR   What thou wilt,
  Thou rather shalt enforce it with thy smile
  Than hew to 't with thy sword.
FIRST SENATOR   Set but thy foot
  Against our rampired gates and they shall ope,   55
  So thou wilt send thy gentle heart before
  To say thou'lt enter friendly.
SECOND SENATOR   Throw thy glove,
  Or any token of thine honor else,
  That thou wilt use the wars as thy redress   60

61. **our confusion:** i.e., a means for **our** ruin or destruction; **all thy powers:** your whole army

63. **sealed:** irrevocably ratified

65. **unchargèd ports:** unattacked gates

67. **set out:** expose

68. **atone:** reconcile

70. **pass his quarter:** leave his assigned place

72. **remedied:** i.e., subject for his wrong

73. **heaviest:** most severe

78. **insculpture:** inscription

81 SD. **epitaph:** Timon's **epitaph** combines two versions as they appear in Plutarch's *Life of Antony;* for yet another version, see picture below.

81. **corse:** corpse

83. **caitiffs:** wretches

89. **brains' flow, droplets:** i.e., tears

91. **conceit:** imagination

My wretched catife dayes,
expired now and paſt:
My carren corps intered here,
is faſt in grounde :
In waltring waues ,of ſwel-
lyng Sea ,by ſurges caſt,
My name if thou deſire,
The Goddes thee ,doe confounde.

Another version of Timon's epitaph. (5.4.81–86)
From William Painter, *The pallace of pleasure . . .* (1569).

And not as our confusion, all thy powers
Shall make their harbor in our town till we
Have sealed thy full desire.
ALCIBIADES   Then there's my glove.
⌜Descend⌝ and open your unchargèd ports.   65
Those enemies of Timon's and mine own
Whom you yourselves shall set out for reproof
Fall, and no more. And to atone your fears
With my more noble meaning, not a man
Shall pass his quarter or offend the stream   70
Of regular justice in your city's bounds
But shall be remedied to your public laws
At heaviest answer.
BOTH   'Tis most nobly spoken.
ALCIBIADES   Descend and keep your words.   75
                    ⌜*The Senators descend.*⌝

          Enter a ⌜*Soldier, with the wax tablet.*⌝

SOLDIER
My noble general, Timon is dead,
Entombed upon the very hem o' th' sea,
And on his gravestone this insculpture, which
With wax I brought away, whose soft impression
Interprets for my poor ignorance.   80
ALCIBIADES *reads the epitaph.*
Here lies a wretched corse, of wretched soul bereft.
Seek not my name. A plague consume you, wicked
     caitiffs left!
Here lie I, Timon, who, alive, all living men did hate.
Pass by and curse thy fill, but pass and stay not here   85
     thy gait.
These well express in thee thy latter spirits.
Though thou abhorred'st in us our human griefs,
Scorned'st our brains' flow and those our droplets
     which   90
From niggard nature fall, yet rich conceit

92. **Neptune:** i.e., the sea (literally, the Roman god of the sea); **aye:** ever

96. **olive:** i.e., **olive** branch, symbol of peace (See picture, below.)

97. **stint:** halt, check

99. **leech:** physician

Peace with olive branch and sword. (5.4.96)
From Gilles Corrozet, *Hecatongraphie . . .* (1543).

Taught thee to make vast Neptune weep for aye
On thy low grave, on faults forgiven. Dead
Is noble Timon, of whose memory
Hereafter more. Bring me into your city,   95
And I will use the olive with my sword,
Make war breed peace, make peace stint war, make
    each
Prescribe to other as each other's leech.
Let our drums strike.   100

                       ⌜*Drums.*⌝ *They exit.*

Longer Notes

1.1.57. wide sea of wax: This may be an allusion to the wax-covered writing tablet used in ancient times. The phrase is so unusual, however, that some editors change it to read "wide sea of tax," where *tax* has its meaning of "censure, accusation."

1.1.209–10. Till . . . honest: These lines are typical of Apemantus's speeches, which sometimes require considerable unpacking to tease out their sense. Their style is typical of satiric poetry of Shakespeare's time, when the genre of satire was associated, through false etymology, with the mythological figure of the satyr—half-man, half-goat, and notoriously rude and unmannerly. It was thus thought that the style of satire should be harsh and rough, riddling and compressed. Apemantus's first speech (1.1.209–10) features not only the coarse language of satire but also its great compression. An expansion and paraphrase of the speech might be "You can wait for me to say 'good morning' until I am courteous, and that time will not come until Timon is transformed into his **dog,** which will be the same time—i.e., never—that these villains become **honest** men."

1.1.231. dog: The Cynics were a sect of philosophers in ancient Greece, founded by Antisthenes, a pupil of Socrates. As a group, they openly displayed contempt for ease, wealth, and the enjoyments of life. The most famous was Diogenes, a pupil of Antisthenes, who carried the principles of the sect to an extreme of self-denial.

1.2.27. humor: In early usage, **humor** referred to the bodily fluids of blood, phlegm, black bile, and yellow bile; later, the term referred to the dispositions, character traits, or moods thought to be caused by those fluids, and then to moods or whims in general. Timon may be using the word in the more technical sense, or he may simply be alluding to Apemantus's disposition.

1.2.45. Methinks they should invite them without knives: According to the eighteenth-century antiquarian Joseph Ritson, "It was the custom in our author's [Shakespeare's] time for every guest to bring his own knife, which he occasionally whetted on a stone that hung behind the door. One of these whetstones may be seen in Parkinson's Museum. They were strangers, at that period, to the use of forks." Ritson is correct in saying that guests were expected to provide their own cutlery; it is also true that dinner forks were relatively unknown outside of Italy until well into the seventeenth century. Forks seem to have been introduced into England by Thomas Coryat, who brought one back from Italy and discussed dinner forks in his *Coryats Crudities* (1611).

1.2.134 SD. masque: Jacobean court masques were rehearsed spectacles in which performers appeared as mythological or allegorical figures. As in the present **"masque of Ladies as Amazons,"** the court masques ended with a dance that joined spectators and performers. In earlier times the **masque** had been a disguising or impromptu masquerade, in which the performers had worn masks and fancy clothes.

1.2.154. mine own device: These words have suggested to some editors that we are to think that Timon

himself devised the masque, including its prologue that is so flattering to him. More likely, however, Timon is merely flattering the performers by telling them that their masque could not have been more pleasing to him or more appropriate to the occasion if he had created it himself.

2.2.11. Varro: The character here addressed as **Varro** is actually "One Varro's servant," as he identifies himself at line 2.2.35. (At line 2.1.1 a character named Varro, along with a character named Isidore, is mentioned as one of Timon's creditors; neither Varro nor Isidore ever appears onstage—unless we imagine them among the undifferentiated lords, senators, and friends often called for in stage directions and generalized speech prefixes.) Here, the servants of Varro and of Isidore, who are referred to only by their masters' names both in their speech prefixes and in the dialogue, share the stage with another servant, Caphis, who is given speech prefixes in his own proper name. The play's use of a master's name to designate a servant, and the mixing within the same scene of such servants with those who have their own proper names, are some of *Timon's* oddest features. The problem becomes vexed in 3.4, in which stage directions and/or speech prefixes give names—Titus, Hortensius, and Philotus—to characters who are clearly servants. These three proper names appear nowhere else in the play. Thus it is quite impossible to determine whether the names are those of the servants (like "Caphis" in 2.2) or of the servants' masters (like "Varro" and "Isidore" in 2.2). Also in 3.4, as in 2.2, some of the other servants onstage are addressed only by their masters' names (e.g., "Lucius' Man"). Editors are divided in their representation of characters like the one called "Titus" in the

Folio, some calling him "Titus," others calling him
"Titus' Man" or "Titus' Servant." There is no knowing
which of these editorial choices is to be preferred. We
choose the former, because the simpler, treatment.

2.2.220. **even to the state's best health:** Editors are
divided about the meaning of this phrase. Some think
that it refers to the extent to which Timon believes the
state of Athens ought to contribute to his financial
recovery—namely, to the greatest possible extent, but
not so far as to imperil its prosperity (**best health**).
Others think that the phrase refers to the reason why
Timon believes the state of Athens ought to help him—
because in the past he has been responsible for main-
taining Athens in its **best health;** at 4.3.105–6,
Alcibiades speaks of Timon's "great deeds when neighbor states, / But for thy sword and fortune, [had] trod
upon" Athens.

3.5.2. **he should die:** There has been no previous
mention of the character who is sentenced to death by
senators in this scene or of the crime that he has been
convicted of committing. The sudden and prominent
reference to this character and to a murder midway
through the work has suggested to some scholars that
Timon of Athens cannot be a finished play; were it
complete, they argue, this scene would somehow have
been prepared for earlier. Directors have, of course,
found ways to stage the play so that this scene sur-
prises theatergoers less than it does readers. Some
directors, for example, have introduced a mute character into the first banquet scene (1.2) and have had
him exhibit violent behavior (though not murder)
there, and have then brought the same character
onstage in this scene (3.5) so that he is mutely present

at his sentencing. Thus directors are able to create continuity within their productions even where there is none in the play's text. (See "Alcibiades" and "The Athenian Senate" in "Historical Background," pages 205, 207.)

4.3.12–13. It is ... lean: These lines constitute a famous crux. The Folio reads "Pastour" where our text reads **pasture;** while "pastour" is an old spelling of *pasture*, it could also be modernized in other ways. The Folio also reads "leaue" where our text has **lean.** Most editors accept the emendation of "leaue" to "lean," but the editorial tradition also includes various emendations of the Folio's word "Brothers" (to, for example, "rother's" or "weather's [i.e., wether's]").

4.3.59. Misanthropos: In Thomas North's translation of Plutarch's *Lives of the Noble Grecians and Romanes* (1579), where Timon is discussed briefly, he is called in the marginal notes "Timon Misanthropos the Athenian."

4.3.122. planetary plague: In the cosmology of Shakespeare's day, which was still popularly based on the Ptolemaic image of the universe, planets and stars had direct influence over people's lives. (See picture, page xxxiv.) The position of the stars, moon, and planets at the moment of one's birth determined the course of one's life, and the heavenly bodies also had positive or malign influences over life on earth. In lines 122–24, **Jove** is pictured as using the planets to infect earth's **air** with a **poison** that causes epidemic illness. This image is a version of a belief, then popular, that God used visitations of the plague to punish wicked cities or nations.

4.3.137. **the throat shall cut:** Classical oracles were famous for giving ambiguous predictions of the future. Here Timon seems to be suggesting to Alcibiades that he should treat any **babe** he comes across as if the **oracle** had predicted that this infant would someday cut Alcibiades' throat—though, because the **oracle** pronounces **doubtfully,** the oracle's words might have meant instead merely that Alcibiades **shall cut the** babe's **throat.**

5.1.204. **take 't at worst:** Throughout this speech, Timon uses an ironically hostile tone toward Alcibiades while, at the same time, explicitly declaring his own utter indifference to the atrocities that the Athenian senators fear from Alcibiades.

Textual Notes

The reading of the present text appears to the left of the square bracket. Unless otherwise noted, the reading to the left of the bracket is from **F**, the First Folio text (upon which this edition is based). The earliest sources of readings not in **F** are indicated as follows: **F2** is the Second Folio of 1632; **F3** is the Third Folio of 1663–64; **F4** is the Fourth Folio of 1685; **Ed.** is an earlier editor of Shakespeare, beginning with Rowe in 1709. No sources are given for emendations of punctuation or for corrections of obvious typographical errors, like turned letters that produce no known word. **SD** means stage direction; **SP** means speech prefix; *uncorr.* means the first or uncorrected state of the First Folio; *corr.* means the second or corrected state of the First Folio; ~ stands in place of a word already quoted before the square bracket; ∧ indicates the omission of a punctuation mark.

1.1   0. SD *Enter Poet, Painter, Jeweler, and Merchant, at several doors.*] Ed.; *Enter . . . Ieweller, Merchant, and Mercer, at seuerall doores.* F
      27. gum which oozes] Ed.; *Gowne, which vses* F
      29. struck] F (*strooke*)
      50. Look, more] Looke∧ moe F
      85. scope.]~∧ F
     102. hands] F2; hand F
     102. slip] Ed.; sit F
     117. Ventidius. Well,] ~, ~: F

128 *and hereafter.* SP OLD MAN] F (*Oldm.* or *Old.*)

135. Lord] F (L.)

143. o'] F (a')

150. be,] ~∧ F

203. the] F (^e_y)

204. SD *2 lines earlier in* F

206. bear,] ~∧ F

224. thou'lt] F (thou't)

231. You're] F (Y'are)

236. thou'dst] F (thoud'st)

240. So∧] ~, F

244. cost] F3; cast F

255. feigned] fegin'd F

281. so, there!] so; their∧ F

290. depart] depatt F

291. SD *All . . . exit.*] *Exeunt.* F

292, 307. o'] F (a)

308. Come] Ed.; Comes F

1.2   28. to] F (too)

30. ever] Ed.; verie F

50, 148. 'T 'as] F ('Tas)

50. proved.] ~, F

53. notes.] ~, F

64. too] F (to)

104, 109. born] F (borne)

108. joy's∧] ioyes, F

110. methinks. . . . faults,] ~∧ . . . ~. F

117. Much! *Sound tucket.*] Ed.; Much. | *Sound Tucket. Enter the Maskers of Amazons, with Lutes in their hands, dauncing and playing.* F

118. SD *Enter Servant.*] *1/2 line later in* F

125. SD *Enter "Cupid."*] Ed.; *Enter Cupid with the Maske of Ladies.* F

129–30. touch,] ~∧ F
134. SP LUCIUS] *Luc.* F
134. SD *See nn. to lines 117 and 125.*
156. SP FIRST LADY] Ed.; *1 Lord.* F
161. SD *Cupid and Ladies exit.*] *Exeunt.* F
168. he'd] F (hee'ld)
173. SD *after line 183 in* F
175. lord] F (L.)
246. SD *All but Timon and Apemantus exit.*]
      Ed.; *Exeunt Lords* F

2.2   1 *and hereafter.* SP FLAVIUS] Ed.; *Stew.* F
4. resumes] Ed.; resume F
12 *and hereafter in this scene.* SP VARRO'S
      MAN] Ed.; *Var.* F
14 *and hereafter in this scene.* SP
      ISIDORE'S MAN] Ed.; *Isid.* F
58. SD *Timon . . . exit.*] *Exit.* F
91. SP PAGE] Ed.; *Boy.* F
98. thou'lt] F (thou't)
106. Ay. Would] Ed.; I would F
143. proposed] F2; propose F
152. found] F2; sound F
152. honesty.] ~, F
160. time.] ~, F
174. of] Ed.; or F
187. Lord] F (L.)
208. Flaminius] Ed.; *Flauius* F
209. SP SERVANTS] F (*Ser.*)
230. treasure] Treature F
260. SD *He exits.*] *Exeunt* F

3.1   0. SD *Enter Flaminius . . . Lucullus. . . .*
      Enter] Ed.; *Flaminius . . . a Lord . . .*
      enters F
11. bountiful] bouutifull F
53. SD *Lucullus*] F (*L.*)

54. that] F ($\frac{t}{y}$)

3.2 12, 24, 38. fifty] Ed.; so many F
28, 39, 64. SP LUCIUS] *Lucil.* F
50–51. Servilius,] ~. F
64. SD *Servilius exits.*] F (*Exit Seruil.*) *1 line earlier*

3.3 23. I] F2; *omit* F
3.4 0. SD *two Men*] *man* F
5 *and hereafter in this scene.* SP LUCIUS' MAN] Ed.; *Luci.* F
9. And, sir, Philotus'] And sir *Philotus* F
21. recoverable. I fear∧] ~, . . . , ~: F
39, 41. SP VARRO'S FIRST MAN] Ed.; *Varro* F
69. If 'twill] If 't 'twill F
99. SP HORTENSIUS] Ed.; *I Var.* F
124. Sempronius] *Sempronius Vllorxa* F

3.5 17. An] Ed.; And F
22. behave] Ed.; behooue F
30. born] F (borne)
51. felon] Ed.; fellow F
66. I] F2; *omit* F
66. has] F (ha's)
70. 'em] F2; him F
111. SD *Senators exit.*] F (*Exeunt.*)
124. 'Tis] ,Tis F

3.6 1 *and hereafter in this scene.* SPP FIRST FRIEND, SECOND FRIEND, THIRD FRIEND, FOURTH FRIEND] Ed.; *1, 2, 3, 4* F
19. here's] F (heares)
24. SD *1/2 line later in* F
35. awhile,] ~: F
47. SD *6 lines earlier in* F
55. SP FIRST AND SECOND FRIENDS] Ed.; *Both* F
63. Will 't . . . Will 't] F (Wilt . . . Wilt)

	82.	tag] Ed.; legge F
	94.	with your] Ed.; you with F
	112.	the] rhe F
	116.	naught] F (nought)
4.1	6.	steads! . . . filths∧] ~, . . . ~. F
	8.	fast!] ~∧ F
	13.	Son] F4; Some F
4.2	1.	Master] F (M.)
	17.	SD *1/2 line later in* F
	52.	has] F (ha's)
4.3	3.	Twinned] Ed.; Twin'd F
	12.	lards∧] ~, F
	12.	brother's] F (Brothers)
	13.	lean] F2; leaue F
	16.	say] fay F
	45.	at,] ~. F
	51.	Thou'lt] F (thou't)
	97.	tub-fast] Fubfast F

109, 149, 304, 350. thou] F (y̸)

	130.	window-bars] Ed.; window Barne F
	175.	scolds] Ed.; scold'st F
	179.	curled-pate] curld'pate F
	200.	SD *To . . . exit.*] *Exeunt.* F
	211.	thy] Ed.; the F
	211.	human] F (humane)
	221.	unctuous] F (Vnctious)

237, 392, 497, 587. has] F (ha's)

	241.	bade] F (bad)
	261.	e'er] F (ere)
	276.	Outlives∧] ~: F
	288.	command] Ed.; command'st F
	322.	my] Ed.; thy F
	411.	swoon] F (swoond)
	427.	son] F (Sunne)
	427.	sire] Ed.; fire F

429. everʌ] ~, F
436. slave, man,] ~-~ʌ F
446. SD *2 lines later in* F
448. them] Ed.; then F
448. SD *Apemantus*] F (*Apeman.*)
454. him.] ~, F
460. SP OTHERS] Ed.; *All.* F
487. villainy] Ed.; Villaine F
487. 't,] ~. F
488. workmen.] ~, F
507. us,] ~ʌ F
512. SD *Thieves exit.*] F (*Exit Theeues.*)
531. grant'st] Ed.; grunt'st F
535. I.] ~ʌ F
540. then.] ~ʌ F
545. that] F ($\frac{t}{y}$)
552. mild] Ed.; wilde F
569. A usuring] Ed.; If not a Vsuring kind-
       nesse F
601. SD *They exit.*] F (*Exit*)

5.1
   5–6. Phrynia and Timandra] Phrinica and
       Timandylo F
     9. has] F (Ha's)
    17. SD *13 lines later in* F
    53. worship] Ed.; worshipt F
    69. goʌ naked.] ~, ~ʌ F
    75. men] F2; man F
    82. therefor] F (therefore)
  131. SD *Timon . . . exits.*] *Exeunt.* F
  144. chance] F3; chanc'd F
  153. cauterizing] Cantherizing F
  170. sense] Ed.; since F
  208. reverend'st] F (reuerends)
  224. through] F (thorow)

5.2   1, 15. SP THIRD SENATOR] Ed.; I F

	6. SP FOURTH SENATOR] Ed.; 2 F
	16. SP FIRST SENATOR] Ed.; 3 F
	17. enemy's] F (Enemies)
	19. foe's] F (Foes)
5.4	26. their] rheir F
	33. Shame, that they wanted cunning,] ~∧ ~ . . . ~, ~∧ F
	35. spread.] ~, F
	36. death,] ~; F
	48. offended.] ~, F
	50. all together] F (altogether)
	57. thou'lt] F (thou't)
	65. Descend] F2; Defend F
	75. SD *Soldier*] Ed.; *Messenger* F
	76. SP SOLDIER] Ed.; *Mes.* F
	88. human] F (humane)
	89. brains'] F (Braines)

THE LIVES

OF THE NOBLE GRE-
CIANS AND ROMANES, COMPARED

together by that graue learned Philosopher and Historiogra-
pher, Plutarke of Chæronea:

Translated out of Greeke into French by IAMES AMYOT, Abbot of Bellozane,
Bishop of Auxerre, one of the Kings priuy counsel, and great Amner
of Fraunce, and out of French into Englishe, by

Thomas North.

A clerrk to writ

Imprinted at London by Thomas Vautroullier dvvelling
in the Blacke Friers by Ludgate.
1579.

Title page of the primary source for *Timon of Athens*.

Appendices

Historical Background

Like many tragedies written by Shakespeare and his contemporaries, *Timon of Athens* is grounded in history, though it departs widely from the history on which it is based. The characters of Alcibiades, Timon, Apemantus, and Timandra all figure in the work of classical historians. The most interesting nonhistorical element is the play's very prominent Athenian Senate.

Alcibiades (c. 450–404 BCE)

Of the historical characters presented in the play, Alcibiades is by far the most famous. His military and political career is detailed in the histories written by his Athenian contemporary Thucydides and by Xenophon (from the next generation) and in two orations by Isocrates, Xenophon's contemporary. However, it is the "Life of Alcibiades" by Plutarch (c. 46–120 CE), as translated into English by Sir Thomas North (1579), upon which *Timon of Athens* draws. There one finds several of the features that mark Alcibiades' character in the play: the eloquence he displays in 3.5 as he pleads for the life of his soldier; his licentiousness, represented in 4.3 by his appearing in the company of two concubines, Phrynia and Timandra (only one of whom, Timandra, is recorded in Plutarch); and Timon's devotion to Alcibiades (1.1, 1.2, 2.2), which Plutarch men-

tions in the course of a brief digression in his "Life of Marcus Antonius." In 3.5 *Timon*'s Alcibiades also refers to campaigns in Lacedaemon and Byzantium, campaigns that were conducted successfully by the historical Alcibiades in the last decade of his life when he was recalled to the service of Athens.

However, other events in the life of *Timon*'s Alcibiades have almost no connection to the career of the historical Alcibiades. There is nothing in history to match either Alcibiades' exile for insubordinate behavior or Alcibiades' campaign against Athens. The historical Alcibiades twice left the service of Athens, first when he was condemned to death in his absence while leading an expedition to Sicily and later, toward the end of his life, when he was relieved of his military command in Athens. Although neither of these departures technically constituted exile, Plutarch does write of him as "a banished man, a vagabond, and a fugitive," terms that may have inspired the writing of *Timon*'s 3.5 and later scenes with Alcibiades. And while the historical Alcibiades did have the opportunity, as Plutarch notes, to lead Athenian forces against the oligarchy that ruled Athens from 411 to 410 BCE, he declined to weaken Athens before its enemies by plunging it into civil war. For this restraint, Plutarch lavishes praise on Alcibiades, whose life he paralleled to that of Coriolanus, the Roman general who, after being banished from his native Rome, led an army against it. (His story is told in Shakespeare's *Coriolanus*.)

Timon

Unlike Alcibiades, Timon receives attention from few ancient writers, although more allude to him. The chief sources are Plutarch's *Lives*, cited above, and the fic-

tional *Dialogue of Timon* by Lucian of Samosata (c. 120–c. 200 CE). For the connection between Plutarch's Timon and the play's, see the entry under Geoffrey Bullough in "Further Reading."

The Athenian Senate

Athenian senators are among the play's prominent characters. They are Timon's false friends, and they exile Alcibiades. However, unlike Rome, Athens never had a senate. Its form of government underwent a number of changes in the late fifth century BCE, the temporal setting of the play, but certain features of its government remained fairly constant. Athens was governed by a popular assembly (*Ekklesia*). By the time the city-state's democratization was complete, all male citizens could, at least theoretically, take part in the Ekklesia, though the poorest are not likely to have exercised their rights. The agenda for the Ekklesia was set by a council (*Boule*) of five hundred of its members. This council had important executive functions, but it remained subordinate to the Ekklesia and never was a separate legislative body like a senate. The closest thing in Athenian history to the senators that sentence Alcibiades' soldier to death and Alcibiades to exile in 3.5 might be the *strategoi;* among the duties of these ten military leaders, elected annually, was to function as magistrates in military cases, bringing them to court and presiding over the trial. Alcibiades himself was a *strategos*. However, there is little reason to believe that *Timon of Athens* 3.5 is meant accurately to stage the workings of the *strategoi*.

The first three acts of the play create the strong impression that its fictional senate abuses its power: the senate refuses to help Timon, in spite of his crucial aid to the state in the past; the senators, according to

Alcibiades, are usurious and self-serving; and even those senators who address Alcibiades when he returns in 5.4 acknowledge the faults of their predecessors. It is tempting to compare this senate of the first three acts to the revolutionary oligarchic council known as the Four Hundred that suspended democracy in Athens between 411 and 410 BCE, murdered prominent democrats, and intimidated the Ekklesia. Oddly enough, although this oligarchy had originally been encouraged by the fugitive Alcibiades, its creation also led the Athenian fleet, loyal to the democrats, to appoint Alcibiades as their commander; after winning brilliant victories against Sparta, he was welcomed back to Athens in 407. However, it is very unlikely that the utterly unhistorical Athenian senate of *Timon of Athens* is to be understood as a representation of the Four Hundred.

Talents

a. *Timon of Athens* is the only Shakespeare play in which *talent* is used to refer to a particular sum of money. Historically, a talent was a vast sum. According to the most conservative reckoning, the Attic talent had a value equal to more than fifty pounds of silver. However, there are a number of indications both in *Timon of Athens* itself and in other contemporary plays that few if any dramatists of the time worked with a precise knowledge of the value of this sum.

b. In *Timon* there is an extremely wide range in the numbers of talents mentioned in the first three acts. Act 1 mentions only small numbers of talents: the **five talents** that Timon gives to free Ventidius (1.1.112) and the **three talents** that Timon gives Lucilius to make his

marriage (1.1.165), an amount that Timon must "strain a little," he says, to provide. Acts 2 and 3 regularly mention greater numbers of talents. Timon asks for **fifty talents** from each of his friends Lucius, Lucullus, and Sempronius (2.2.216), and he also plans to send to the senate of Athens a request for a **thousand talents** (2.2.222) before his steward, Flavius, persuades him that any request directed to the senate will be futile. Lucius is the character who mentions by far the largest sum in talents at 3.2.40: "He [i.e., Timon] cannot want [i.e., be without] fifty-five hundred talents." In order to make this line match the actual value of the talent a little more closely, many editors emend it to read "fifty—five hundred—talents," making Lucius refer to two different (but still vast) sums, instead of one unimaginably huge one. We do not emend, because it is possible to interpret the line as Lucius's (perhaps hyperbolic) tribute to what he believes to be Timon's inexhaustible wealth. Elsewhere Timon himself also reckons his wealth as virtually inexhaustible when he tells Flavius "To Lacedaemon did my land extend" (2.2.169). (Since Lacedaemon is in the southeastern part of the Greek mainland, Timon's land would have amounted to much if not most of eastern Greece south of Athens. See map, page xii.) Perhaps, then, we should regard the references to great numbers of talents as reliable indicators of Timon's wealth and his waste of it.

Against this possibility, however, we have to weigh other evidence suggesting that mention of sums of **fifty, a thousand,** and **fifty-five hundred talents** should not be read in any relation to the talent's historical value. This evidence is to be found in the appearance of Timon's servant Flaminius with an "empty box" in which he hopes to carry away fifty talents—in reality, well over a ton of silver (3.1.17). It would

seem, then, that by Act 3, if not before, the use of the
talent as a monetary sum in the fiction of the play—
however suggestive it may be of Timon's great expenditures and gifts—no longer bears any relation to the
talent's historical value. But the divergence between
these uses of "talent" may already have opened up
long before Flaminius alludes to his box. At the beginning of 1.2 Ventidius approaches Timon at the latter's
great banquet to "return those talents/ . . . from whose
help / I derived liberty" (6–8). If the **five talents** he is
returning had their historical value, Ventidius would
have brought with him almost three hundred pounds
of silver.

c. At three points in the Folio text of *Timon of Athens*
in the scene now designated as 3.2, we also find the
curious phrase "so many talents." When the Second
Stranger tells his story of Timon's request for money to
Lucullus, the Stranger says the request was "to borrow
so many Talents"; Lucius, who is listening to the story,
asserts that he "should ne're haue denied his [i.e.,
Timon's] Occasion so many Talents"; and when
Timon's servant Servilius announces Timon's request
to Lucius, the sum desired is "so many Talents" (line
numbers 991–92, 1003, and 1017 in the Folio text; line
numbers 3.2.12, 24, 38 in the current edition). As editors have long recognized, such imprecise language
cannot pass for adequate dialogue. Some editors have
proposed that the dramatist grew suspicious about the
accuracy of his understanding of the talent's value and
therefore used "so many" as a stopgap, to be replaced
with a number after he had correctly established what
the talent historically was worth. Against this argument is the evidence presented above that nowhere
does the play show any concern that the talent corre-

spond to its historical value. This same lack of concern is also evinced by other dramatists, as discussed below (see section d).

Other explanations of "so many" are possible. We know, for example, that the phrase could be used as a way of avoiding the repetition of a number already clearly provided. When, in Shakespeare's *All's Well That Ends Well*, Parolles is enumerating the strength of the companies in an army, naming each company by its leader's name, he says "Spurio a hundred and fifty, Sebastian so many, Corambus so many . . ." (4.3.172–74). In this speech "so many" means "a hundred and fifty." Thus "so many talents" in *Timon* may mean simply "fifty talents," the number that Timon has clearly announced to his servants that they are to request of both Lucullus and Lucius. Perhaps the dramatist used "so many" because he knew he had already made clear the number in question even though he may have forgotten just what the number was. In any case, as Shakespeare's earliest editors understood, an editor must substitute "fifty" for "so many" in order to provide intelligible dialogue. In 1709 Rowe emended Folio line 1017 (3.2.38) to read "fifty," and in 1733 Theobald introduced the same emendation into Folio lines 991–92 as well (3.2.12).

d. Several other plays written around Shakespeare's time give evidence of dramatists' ignorance of the talent's historical value. Of most relevance is an anonymous play—interestingly, another play about Timon of Athens—that exists only in manuscript and that appears to belong to the very early 1600s, thereby predating the Shakespeare play. In the manuscript *Timon*, four or five talents are characterized as "a little golden dust"; a character named Demeas, a mere orator, has

run up a debt of sixteen talents, for which he has been
arrested; and another character, Gelasimus, prays
to Fortune for "five or six talents [to] pour down suddenly / Into my hands or [to] hail . . . on my head." If
the wished-for talents were to come down in their historical value, they would break off Gelasimus's hands
and crush his head and him. The anonymous author
of *The Wars of Cyrus*, printed in 1594, seems equally
oblivious to the talent's actual worth. He rates five
hundred talents at approximately the same value as
"six hundred arming coats" or "three thousand Scythi-
ans' bows . . . finished with quivers." As one final
example of ahistorical representation of the talent in
plays, William Davenant's *The platonicke louers*, printed in 1636, represents Aristotle as having spent a thousand talents (historically, over twenty-five tons of
silver) on books.

Though dramatists of Shakespeare's time were not
acquainted with the precise historical value of the talent, they did recognize that it was worth considerably
more than other monetary units. Shakespeare's
Timon asks for fifty talents from his individual
wealthy friends, but when his requests are later
reported in terms of "pieces" (i.e., coins), he is said to
have asked for "a thousand pieces" (3.6.21). When
Timon's debts are reported in terms of crowns (five-
shilling coins), the number of crowns far exceeds the
number of talents he seeks to borrow: "three thousand crowns," "five thousand" (3.4.39–40). Such
appreciation of the high relative value of the talent is
also evident in other plays of the period. In one of the
Stonyhurst Pageants, written and performed in North
Lancashire sometime between 1610 and 1625, a character pairs "ten talents of white silver, and six thousand crowns in gold." All in all, in relation to the

drama of Shakespeare's time, there is nothing idiosyncratic or egregiously ignorant about the ahistorical use of the talent in *Timon*.

Timon's "Friends"

The group constituting Timon's friends is not precisely defined in the First Folio printing of the play. In the stage direction opening 1.2, those friends he has invited to dinner are named both generically (**States** [i.e., rulers], **Athenian Lords**) and specifically (e.g., **Ventidius**). (In the play's first scene, two of his guests were also named generically as *"two Lords"* [1.1.291 SD].) But the Folio stage direction opening 1.2 fails to include all the proper names that will be used later in the scene to designate speakers. It leaves out Alcibiades and the speaker whose speech is prefixed *"Luc."* in the Folio (line 134). Since among Timon's friends, as we learn later in the play, are both a Lucius and Lucullus, we cannot be sure precisely to whom this speech prefix *"Luc."* refers. We have converted *"Luc."* to the speech prefix "LUCIUS," but that choice is arbitrary. Otherwise, in 1.2, except for Alcibiades and *"Luc.,"* all Timon's friends are designated in speech prefixes generically as *"1. Lord," "2. Lord,"* and *"3. Lord."*

In Act 2, however, the play comes to focus on a number of particular friends of Timon, referring to them by their proper names: Lucius, Lucullus, Sempronius, and, again, Ventidius (2.2.211–13, 246–52). This tight focus on three or four of Timon's friends, all with proper names, continues throughout the first four scenes of Act 3, as Timon's servants visit Lucullus, Lucius, and Sempronius, and as we hear that Timon's

request for money has also been denied by Ventidius. In 3.4, when Timon orders that "all my friends again" be invited to a "feast," he names in particular "Lucius, Lucullus, and Sempronius" (123–25).

In spite of this focus on certain named individuals, the play does not, in Acts 2 and 3, abandon generic reference to Timon's friends. Among those friends to whom Timon hopes to turn in Act 2 are the senators of Athens (2.2.219–22). More important, the opening stage direction for 3.6, the second banquet scene, also contains only a generic reference: *"Enter divers Friends."* When these "Friends" reenter later in the scene, the stage direction again employs generic terms, albeit different ones: *"Enter the Senators, with other Lords"* (line 110 SD). This scene also ends with a stage direction phrased in generic terms: *"Exeunt the Senators."* In this scene, the only speech prefixes for the *"Friends"* are the bare numerals *"1," "2," "3,"* and *"4."* Editors have made various choices about expanding these Folio speech prefixes. Some have substituted the proper names of Timon's friends Lucius, Lucullus, Sempronius, and Ventidius for the Folio's numerals. Others have expanded the numerals to, for example, "FIRST LORD" or "FIRST SENATOR." We have chosen to follow the Folio as closely as possible, using its initial stage direction *"Enter divers Friends"* as a guide in expanding the Folio's numerals to read "FIRST FRIEND," etc.

The Folio's imprecision in designating Timon's friends has been used as evidence for two different theories about the origin of the play's text. The shifts in designation have been construed as signs of different authorial hands (see "Authorship of *Timon of Athens*," page liii). The lack of precision has also been used to support the theory that the play is by Shakespeare

alone, but that it remains unfinished (see longer note to 3.5.2, page 194, and the article by Una Mary Ellis-Fermor in "Further Reading"). Since, however, it is not possible to confirm either of these theories, a more useful approach might be to consider how the imprecision in designation functions in the play itself. It may be important, for example, that Timon's friends be thought of not as a handful of particular individuals (Lucius, Lucullus, etc.) but as representative of the whole of Athens and therefore, for Timon, of the whole of the human community. After all, when Timon becomes a misanthrope, it is all of Athens and all of humanity that he rejects. That rejection might seem silly if Timon were driven to it only because three or four individuals had disappointed him. Instead, by representing Timon's friends as a large and ill-defined group, the play may make his later repudiation of the human race somewhat more sympathetic. Directors will, of course, be inclined to use the same actors for the "Friends" that have been playing the parts of Lucius, Lucullus, and the others; such a choice both avoids adding cast members and adds coherence to the story.

THE LIFE OF TYMON
OF ATHENS.

Actus Primus. Scœna Prima.

Enter Poet, Painter, Ieweller, Merchant, and Mercer, at seuerall doores.

Poet.

Ood day Sir,
   Pain. I am glad y'are well.
   Poet. I haue not seene you long, how goes
the World?
   Pain. It weares sir, as it growes.
   Poet. I that's well knowne :
But what particular Rarity? What strange,
Which manifold record not matches : see
Magicke of Bounty, all these spirits thy power
Hath coniur'd to attend.
I know the Merchant.
   Pain. I know them both : th'other's a Ieweller.
   Mer. O 'tis a worthy Lord.
   Iew. Nay that's most fixt.
   Mer. A most incomparable man, breath'd as it were,
To an vntyreable and continuate goodnesse :
He passes.
   Iew. I haue a Iewell heere.
   Mer. O pray let's see't. For the Lord *Timon*, sir?
   Iewel. If he will touch the estimate. But for that—
   Poet. When we for recompence haue prais'd the vild,
It staines the glory in that happy Verse,
Which aptly sings the good.
   Mer. 'Tis a good forme.
   Iewel. And rich : heere is a Water looke ye.
   Pain. You are rapt sir, in some worke, some Dedication to the great Lord.
   Poet. A thing slipt idlely from me,
Our Poesie is as a Gowne, which vses
From whence 'tis nourisht : the fire i'th'Flint
Shewes not, till it be strooke : our gentle flame
Prouokes it selfe, and like the currant flyes
Each bound it chafes. What haue you there?
   Pain. A Picture sir : when comes your Booke forth?
   Poet. Vpon the heeles of my presentment sir.
Let's see your peece.
   Pain. 'Tis a good Peece.
   Poet. So 'tis, this comes off well, and excellent.
   Pain. Indifferent.
   Poet. Admirable: How this grace
Speakes his owne standing : what a mentall power
This eye shootes forth? How bigge imagination
Moues in this Lip, to th'dumbnesse of the gesture,

One might interpret.
   Pain. It is a pretty mocking of the life :
Heere is a touch : Is't good?
   Poet. I will say of it,
It Tutors Nature, Artificiall strife
Liues in these toutches, liuelier then life.

Enter certaine Senators.

   Pain. How this Lord is followed.
   Poet. The Senators of Athens, happy men.
   Pain. Looke moe.
   Po. You see this confluence, this great flood of visitors,
I haue in this rough worke, shap'd out a man
Whom this beneath world doth embrace and hugge
With amplest entertainment : My free drift
Halts not particularly, but moues it selfe
In a wide Sea of wax, no leuell'd malice
Infects one comma in the course I held,
But flies an Eagle flight, bold, and forth on,
Leauing no Tract behinde.
   Pain. How shall I vnderstand you?
   Poet. I will vnbolt to you.
You see how all Conditions, how all Mindes,
As well of glib and slipp'ry Creatures, as
Of Graue and austere qualitie, tender downe
Their seruices to Lord *Timon* : his large Fortune,
Vpon his good and gracious Nature hanging,
Subdues and properties to his loue and tendance
All sorts of hearts; yea, from the glasse-fac'd Flatterer
To *Apemantus*, that few things loues better
Then to abhorre himselfe; euen hee drops downe
The knee before him, and returnes in peace
Most rich in *Timons* nod.
   Pain. I saw them speake together.
   Poet. Sir, I haue vpon a high and pleasant hill
Feign'd Fortune to be thron'd,
The Base o'th'Mount
Is rank'd with all deserts, all kinde of Natures
That labour on the bosome of this Sphere,
To propagate their states : among'st them all,
Whose eyes are on this Soueraigne Lady fixt,
One do I personate of Lord *Timons* frame,
Whom Fortune with her Iuory hand wafts to her,
Whose present grace, to present slaues and seruants
Translates his Riuals.
   Pain. 'Tis conceyu'd, to scope
This Throne, this Fortune, and this Hill me thinkes

                            With

Timon of Athens:
A Modern Perspective
Coppélia Kahn

Timon of Athens is a curious play.[1] Many scholars have regarded it as unfinished, or at least unpolished, and some think Shakespeare wrote it in collaboration with Thomas Middleton, even though it shares themes and images with Shakespeare's *King Lear.* There is no contemporary mention of it, and we don't know if it was performed in Shakespeare's lifetime. Until the last twenty years or so, few scholars gave it much attention, and it was seldom performed. Like many of Shakespeare's plays, it doesn't fit neatly into a single generic category: some critics argue that its vituperative hero's harsh assessment of human nature brings it closer to satire than to tragedy. Its structure, moreover, is strikingly bipolar: Timon's lavish, frenetic displays of generosity and declarations of altruistic love in the first three acts stand in mordant contrast to his hatred of all humankind and withdrawal from society in the final two. Most mysterious of all, perhaps, is the hero's character: should we see him as a wastrel who perversely brings on his own ruin, or as a noble idealist whose downfall accords him insight into fundamental human failings?

Recently, though, important changes in literary criticism have opened new windows onto *Timon.* Intense interest in early modern social practices and behaviors as the matrix rather than merely the context or back-

ground of literary production has enabled critics to posit a certain logic underlying Timon's obsessive generosity and subsequent misanthropy, a logic both social and emotional. In addition, Shakespeare criticism has rejected the narrow, time-bound standards by which it formerly judged certain works to be "bad" Shakespeare or even not Shakespeare at all. Finally, the play's perspective on the power of money to configure—perhaps to determine—human relations resonates with a twenty-first-century sense of capitalism and credit finance as global forces that can create or destroy social stability. In this era of junk bonds, leveraged buyouts, and credit card debt, *Timon* has something to say to us.

The play begins as those who seek Timon's favor gather for an opulent banquet at his house. The Poet, describing the work he will offer to Timon, presents the play's central fable in a vision that describes Timon's rise and, in effect, predicts his fall (1.1.51–110). The goddess Fortune, a colossal, maternal presence, is portrayed as if from an infant's or child's perspective, a "sovereign lady" looming above the mass of men who "labor . . . / To propagate their states" on her bosom. She singles out one man for her favors while "translat[ing] his rivals" to "slaves and servants"; he then takes her place, her worshippers now becoming his dependents, who "through him / Drink the free air." In the play's early scenes, Timon's bounty is similarly grandiose and magical: he acts as though his wealth cannot be depleted, needs no replenishment, and has no limits. In the final movement of the Poet's description, however, "Fortune in her shift and change of mood / Spurns down her late beloved," while his dependents rise above him, "[t]he foot above the head." Similarly, Timon will experience the loss of his fortune

(about which his steward Flavius often warns him) and of the friends he wins through lavish gifts and hospitality (whose hypocrisy the Cynic philosopher Apemantus frequently points out) as a sudden, brutal, and unmerited betrayal that transforms his world.

Upon his entrance, Timon frees a debtor from prison and confers on a servingman a fortune and the bride he seeks, as easily as Fortune wafts her hand. As Flavius remarks, "Who is not Timon's?" (2.2.186): all flock to him, hang on him, fix their hopes on his generosity. But his openhandedness has another side, revealed when he rejects any attempt to reciprocate his gifts, declaring that "there's none / Can truly say he gives if he receives" (1.2.11–12). Timon will brook no competitors in philanthropy: he demands that he stay on top, the phoenix of generosity in Athens, his lavishness holding all comers in awe. Thus he treats gifts not as a medium of exchange but rather as tokens in a competition for prestige, as though he is engaged in a perpetual potlatch. Yet at the same time, he thinks of his gifts as creating "true friendship" (1.2.19) that makes donor and recipient "brothers" who command each other's fortunes (1.2.107–8). At his banquet, he delivers a long paean to friendship (1.2.90–110) in which he explains its quasi-fraternal bonds first as based on mutual help ("I shall have much help from you. How had you been my friends else?"), then on mutual need ("what need we have any friends if we should ne'er have need of 'em?"). He concludes with the idea that friends "were the most needless creatures living, should we ne'er have use for 'em." This modulation from "help" to "need" to "use" suggests an increasingly prominent element of self-interest at odds with the frankly sentimental tone of the speech, which Timon finishes in tears.

In Shakespeare's time, *use* was a virtual synonym for

usury, widely practiced but also widely condemned as unethical. Thus Timon's paean evokes two conflicting registers of social exchange coexisting at the same cultural moment. Timon first describes an ethos of nobly disinterested friendship, represented for the Renaissance in the writings of Cicero and Seneca and characterized by informal reciprocity among peers. Then the speech slides toward the discourse of usury, profit-oriented and based on legal contracts that turned friends into creditors and debtors with fixed obligations who were liable to penalties for forfeit. Cicero's _De Amicitia_ explicitly states that in friendship, we "indeed make no usury of our pleasures . . . because all the fruit thereof resteth in very love [it]self."[2] In fact, friendship and usury are in conflict from the very first scene, where a lord describes gifts to Timon as money lent at interest, repaid with profit when Timon reciprocates with gifts of larger value: "No gift to him / But breeds the giver a return exceeding / All use of quittance" (1.1.313–15). Later, a senator, preparing to call in his loans to Timon because the senator sees the great man's credit beginning to fail, refers to the gifts he made Timon as investments: "If I want gold, steal but a beggar's dog / And give it Timon, why, the dog coins gold" (2.1.5–6). Timon's friends, then, are making "use" of him all along as a sort of investment banker, while he, captive to a fantasy of magical bounty—endless supply, endless outgo—that removes him from the realm of need, remains oblivious to their practices. As the churlish Apemantus aptly remarks at the opening banquet, "[W]hat a number of men eats Timon, and he sees 'em not!" (1.2.40–41).

What we see as a conflict between altruistic friendship and making loans for profit might have been understood in Shakespeare's day in the somewhat (but

not completely) different terms of royal patronage. The Tudor dynasty, beginning with Elizabeth's grandfather Henry VII, centralized power in the sovereign, but had no paid bureaucracy to run the state and no standing army to defend it. Like her forebears, Elizabeth used gifts to entice talented nobles and gentry into serving her government, and James followed the same custom. By handing out titles that conferred prestige on the holder, paid offices ranging from embassies to clerkships, landed estates, lucrative financial favors such as monopolies and leases, and presents such as money or jewels, the monarch created a governing class to do his or her bidding, while confirming the loyalties of that class. There were costs, however, on both sides. Those seeking such favors had to attend the sovereign at court and maintain a costly, ostentatious style of life that usually entailed going into debt; on their side, Elizabeth and James had to support the expensive "magnificence"—a combination of display and hospitality—traditionally expected of monarchs while keeping up the flow of gifts to courtiers on which the social order depended. In the process, Elizabeth and James also went into debt—ironically, like Timon, often to the same courtiers to whom they had dispensed patronage. As in Shakespeare's play, this system was predicated on a fiction: that the giver, whether monarch or courtier, gave "freely," expecting no return. (We might compare such practices to today's ongoing controversy in the United States about the implicit connections between large donations to presidential campaigns and invitations to White House social events, or positions bestowed by successful candidates on campaign supporters.)

Though Elizabeth maintained her court in the style expected of her, she was notoriously sparing in patron-

age. James, in contrast, resembled Timon in his compulsive need to give freely without regard to the actual contents of his treasury. Between 1603 and 1625, he gave the peerage alone more than one million pounds in lands and rents, while keeping a far more lavish court than Elizabeth had; as a result, he went deeply into debt. Numerous letters and contemporary accounts document not only the magnitude of his gifts but also, Timon-like, his failure to heed frequent warnings of the consequences. When Parliament debated whether to grant James a yearly subsidy of £200,000 to resolve his financial crisis, one member urged the House of Commons not "to draw a silver stream out of the country into the royal cistern." This metaphor resembles Flavius's imagery of "drunken spilth" and riotous flow. Because Shakespeare wrote *Timon of Athens* during the period in which the king's finances became an urgent public issue known to a fairly wide audience (1605–10), it is possible that Shakespeare's portrait of a man who literally gives away his fortune was inspired or at least influenced by the improvident James.[3] Yet the play's relevance to its times need not depend on seeing Timon's bounty as resembling James's, for lending money at interest was then a widespread and well-established practice despite religious prohibitions. Not just the wealthy and well-born but also ordinary people who had saved a little money might loan it at interest to friends and neighbors in order to eke out a slender income, and it is easy to imagine a confusion between friendship and usury resembling that which is dramatized in the play. Timon gave as a friend and expects to borrow as a friend, but when his money finally gives out, his "friends" treat him like any debtor—bound not by ties of love but by the conditions of a legal contract—and he is ruined.

Women are conspicuously absent from Timon's reception rooms, except for the virtually wordless "Ladies as Amazons" who dance in the masque of the first act, and the only women Timon encounters in the wilderness are Alcibiades' concubines (4.3). Athenian society seems to be purely homosocial; that is, it consists only of male social equals who imitate and emulate one another. But in another sense, the action as a whole is driven by a fantasy of woman: specifically, the fickle woman Fortune who arbitrarily rewards, then spurns, her suitors. At least that is Timon's point of view. Thus the structures of desire in this play skirt the problematics of sexual desire and sexual difference. The one difference that matters is enjoying Fortune's maternal—and material—bounty or being deprived of it: identification with the mother as opposed to alienation from her, both of which are projected onto the entire dramatic landscape. Timon acts out the difference between the two in an anti-banquet he stages after his ruin (3.6). At first he plays the bountiful host as always, welcoming his guests effusively. Once they are seated, however, he delivers a caustic grace, praying "For these my present friends, as they are to me nothing, so in nothing bless them, and to nothing are they welcome," then with a flourish invites them to eat: "Uncover, dogs, and lap" (83–87). The elegant dishes hold nothing but stones and warm water, which he throws in their faces. Thus Fortune's bounty is replaced by nothingness, and Timon abandons all-embracing love for totalizing hatred.

Yet no sooner has he stepped outside the city walls into the wilderness than he rhetorically re-creates Athenian society through a sequence of scathing apostrophes (4.1, 4.3). In this figure of speech, the speaker addresses a dead, absent, or inanimate being who is

thereby animated and made present.[4] Apostrophe in
Timon dramatizes what one might call the central
polarity of the play: altruistic fusion of the ego with the
other as opposed to egocentric negation of the other.
Timon's first apostrophe calls on social types emblem-
atic of Athenian society: on matrons, slaves and fools,
bankrupts and bound servants (4.1.1–12); then on values, such as piety and fear or customs and laws, that
Athens has flaunted (15–21); and finally on the plagues,
fevers, lust, and liberty (21–30) that he hopes will
destroy the city. He thus animates Athens only as a
mode of obliterating it, just as he gave only to prevent
others from reciprocating so that he might stand alone.
As Karen Newman remarks, in these apostrophes
"Timon's impossible imperatives pre-empt the place of
the *you* in the I/Thou structure of direct address and
thereby enact what the lines demand—the annihilation
of the *you*, the Athenians whom Timon so abhors."[5]

Having verbally annihilated Athens, in a pastoral
gesture Timon turns to the earth for primitive suste-
nance uncorrupted by humanity: he digs for roots.
Ironically, he finds gold instead. Addressing the earth
in a final apostrophe as "Thou common whore of
mankind," he vows to use the all-corrupting metal not
to obliterate Athens but rather to turn it upside down,
making "Black white, foul fair, wrong right," in effect
replicating the reversal he suffered at Fortune's hands
(4.3.1–49). For Timon, there is no escape from the core
fantasy of an all-powerful woman whose bounty is
equaled only by her treachery, a woman who can give,
take away, and give again.

Timon's exile is dramatized through a series of con-
versations with characters similarly excluded from or
disappointed by society: the banished general Alcibi-

ades and the Cynic philosopher Apemantus, followed by bandits who have heard rumors that Timon still has gold, and, finally, his faithful steward Flavius. Alcibiades remains a sketchy character, and the subplot centering on him, which might have helped articulate the play's stark polarities, is too rough and undeveloped to serve that purpose. His brief appearance in the first act sets him apart from pleasure-seeking Athens as a soldier happier at a battle than a banquet. He reappears much later (3.5), pleading with senators to spare the life of an unnamed friend condemned to death for murder. First relying on strained and unconvincing arguments for leniency, he then turns to his own merits, urging the senators to spare his friend because he himself has served the state in war.

The scene works mainly to establish a parallel between Timon and Alcibiades: both turn against Athens in the belief that, given over to the pursuit of profit and luxury, it has rewarded their conspicuous virtue only with meanness. Shakespeare seems to aim at a certain critique of Timon's extremism, however, when Alcibiades, having brought Athens to its knees, relents. Whereas Timon refuses to allow even Flavius's loyalty and love to soften his misanthropy, the general is persuaded by arguments that "All have not offended. . . . Crimes, like lands, / Are not inherited" (5.4.41–44). He agrees to punish only Timon's enemies and his own, in contrast to Timon's hatred of "the whole race of mankind, high and low" (4.1.40). Unfortunately, Alcibiades' gesture comes too late and is too summary to compete in dramatic impact with the bite and swing of Timon's unrelenting negativity.

Timon's peppery dialogue with Apemantus also seems intended to deepen the rationale underlying the hero's misanthropy. The Cynic philosopher, character-

istically skeptical, at first charges "Thou dost affect my
manners and dost use them" (4.3.225). He thinks
Timon's transformation amounts only to sour grapes
("Thou'dst courtier be again / Wert thou not beggar"
[274–75]) and lacks the coherence of his own comprehensive critique of society. Timon counters that he had
the world as his "confectionary" and lost it in an
instant, a much greater moral shock than Apemantus's
long-term alienation. "Why shouldst thou hate men? /
They never flattered thee," he asks (294, 304–6). This
exchange degenerates, however, into a slinging match,
which ends in rhetorical collapse ("A plague on thee!
Thou art too bad to curse," declares Apemantus [403]).
Actually, from the moment Timon turned his back on
Athens, he began to sound like Apemantus, anatomiz-
ing human greed and hypocrisy in scathing catalogues
and often using the philosopher's favorite epithet,
"dog."

In misanthropy as in what he called friendship,
Timon has no intimate relations with others: he dies as
solitary as he lived. And yet the curious circumstances
of his death (he sets up his own tomb and apparently
buries himself) suggest another dimension of his isolation. Timon is Shakespeare's last narcissist: his predecessors are the young man of the sonnets and the hero
of the early narrative poem *Venus and Adonis*. The
young man of the sonnets, who prefers "traffic with
[him]self alone," would consume himself in single life
(sonnet 4), becoming "the tomb of his self-love" (sonnet 3). Timon's tomb, described four times and then
shown onstage, is located "upon the very hem o' th'
sea" (5.4.77). Its meaning and poetic appeal derive
from its site, as Timon describes it, "Upon the beachèd
verge of the salt flood, / Who once a day with his
embossèd froth / The turbulent surge shall cover"

(5.1.248–50). Here Shakespeare envisions for Timon a quasi-maternal embrace, as the ocean sweeps over him daily. The impersonal but rhythmically repeated caress of the sea recalls Venus perpetually embracing Adonis, who has been metamorphosed into a flower that she places in her bosom: "My throbbing heart shall rock thee day and night," she says; "There shall not be one minute in an hour / Wherein I will not kiss my sweet love's flow'r" (1186–88).

Timon parallels *King Lear* in its theme of ingratitude and in its hero's rages against the hypocrisy and selfishness of mankind. However, *Timon* focuses not on the intensity and intimacy of family ties, as *Lear* does, but rather on the paradox of the narcissist, who withdraws from others to an imaginary realm of the self in search of the kind of boundless, constant love that he has failed to find in the world, a love that can exist only in the womb before the separation of self from world. Timon's stony, solitary tomb suggests his emotional isolation, whether as paragon of generosity in Athens or misanthrope in the wilderness, while the sea foam washing over it daily evokes a fusion of self with other—like the fusion Timon sought through giving—that can be imaged in mother and child but never realized in life.

---

1. Parts of this introduction have been adapted from my essay " 'Magic of bounty': *Timon of Athens*, Jacobean Patronage, and Maternal Power," *Shakespeare Quarterly* 38 (1987): 34–57.

2. M. Tullius Cicero, *De Amicitia*, trans. John Harington (1550), in *John Harington of Stepney, Tudor Gentleman: His Life and Works*, ed. Ruth Hughey (Columbus: Ohio State University Press, 1971), pp. 164, 172.

3. See David Bevington and David L. Smith, "James I and *Timon of Athens*," *Comparative Drama* 33 (1999): 56–87.

4. See Karen Newman, "Cultural Capital's Gold Standard: Shakespeare and the Critical Apostrophe in Renaissance Studies," in *Discontinuities: New Essays on Renaissance Literature and Criticism*, ed. Viviana Comensoli and Paul Stevens (Toronto: University of Toronto Press, 1998), pp. 96–113.

5. Newman, "Cultural Capital's Gold Standard," p. 105.

Further Reading

Timon of Athens

Bullough, Geoffrey, ed. "Timon of Athens." In Narrative and Dramatic Sources of Shakespeare, vol. 6, pp. 225–345. 1966. Reprint, London: Routledge and Kegan Paul; New York: Columbia University Press, 1975.

Bullough reprints excerpts from two primary sources—"The Life of Marcus Antonius" and "The Life of Alcibiades" in Sir Thomas North's 1579 translation of Plutarch's Lives of the Noble Grecians and Romanes; two possible sources—Lucian's "Dialogue of Timon" (translated from N. da Lonigo's 1536 Italian version) and John Lyly's Campaspe (1584); and several analogues—M. M. Boiardo's 1487 Timone, William Painter's 1566 Palace of Pleasure, the 1581 edition of P. Boaistuau's Theatrum Mundi (translated by John Alday), and an anonymous Timon manuscript play intended for an academic performance sometime after 1601. Plutarch provided Shakespeare with "the general statement of misanthropy," Timon's relationships with Alcibiades and Apemantus, the anecdote of the fig tree (5.1.237–44), and Timon's two epitaphs (5.4.81–86). Most of Shakespeare's material came, however, from Lucian, who developed the Timon legend into "a tale of excessive liberality, base ingratitude, disillusionment, withdrawal and revenge." Bullough speculates that the protagonist's "extreme misanthropy and ... self-severance from humanity" led Shakespeare to abandon the Timon story for that

of Coriolanus, a narrative that would "give a richer opportunity for a tragedy of wrath and ingratitude."

Cartelli, Thomas. "The Unaccommodating Text: The Critical Situation of *Timon of Athens*." In *Text, Interpretation, Theory*, ed. James M. Heath and Michael Payne, pp. 81–105. Lewisburg, Pa.: Bucknell University Press; London: Associated University Presses, 1985.

To fault *Timon of Athens* (as many have done) for its single-minded commitment to a protagonist with a "stubbornly inflexible point of view" and for its failure to generate "unresolvable conflicts" is to impose on the play an aesthetic that privileges complementarity, compromise, and mediation of tensions and conflicting pressures. When the play's own "peculiar dramatic aims and organization" are accepted rather than resisted, *Timon* emerges as a "radical experiment in the psychology of theatrical experience . . . [one] that requires its audience both to identify and to engage in a critical dialogue with a character who is at once its bane and its ideal, its representative and its accuser, the anatomizer and embodiment of its own values and assumptions." Cartelli claims that Shakespeare deliberately denies both the protagonist and the audience "recourse to strategies" designed to accommodate the consolation and "outlines of reconciliation" typically associated with tragic closure. "[W]hat finally distinguishes *Timon* from Shakespeare's other tragedies is not its failure but its refusal to be complementary."

Elam, Keir. " 'I'll plague thee for that word': Language, Performance, and Communicable Disease." *Shakespeare Survey* 50 (1997): 19–27.

In an essay that further develops his earlier analysis of the language of pestilence (see the entry below), the

author explores the "three-way pathogenic dialectic" of speech act, performance, and epidemic in *Timon of Athens, Venus and Adonis, The Rape of Lucrece,* and *Love's Labor's Lost.* Elam reads *Timon* against the backdrop of King James's patent creating the company of the King's Servants (19 May 1603). The document contains three royal speech acts: two performative rites of nomination—the naming of an acting company and of the epidemic ("plague") that upstaged the king's triumphal entry into London—and one rite of suspension that directly linked the first two by postponing theatrical performances until less infectious times. Focusing on Timon's illocutionary signature, "the contagious curse," Elam argues that the play provides "an altogether darker and less reassuring version of the epidemic-creating performative power of language than James's decrees." The protagonist's "plaguey imprecations translate the epidemic into the epideictic, giving rise to a series of formidable oratorical performances, ironically replete with a contagious theatricality of their own." Ultimately, however, Timon's identification of speech with infection leads to his own destruction when his language "implodes" and he is "done in by [words]."

Elam, Keir. " 'In what chapter of his bosom?': Reading Shakespeare's Bodies." In *Alternative Shakespeares, 2,* ed. Terence Hawkes, pp. 140–63. London: Routledge, 1996.

In answer to the question "Whatever happened to semiotics?"—the systematic study of how signs function in signification and/or communication—Elam observes that current critical movements (new historicism, cultural materialism, and feminist criticism) have appropriated the terminology and methods of semiotic analysis for their own ideological ends. The notable shift in the study of Renaissance drama from language

to a concern with the body as the principal object of
inquiry or analytic desire—specifically the "split, suffering, diseased, tortured and transgressive body"—leads
Elam to propose a performance-based "post(humous)
semiotics" of Shakespeare's plays in which the "medical-
ized" body is recognized not as signifier but as symptom, and the stage body as "the material bearer of the
symptom." With its "veritable outbreak" of plague references and its misanthropic protagonist who continually
bequeaths disease to both his on- and offstage audiences, *Timon of Athens* (probably written after a 1603
visitation of the plague) illustrates a "pestilential poetics" that objectifies the Puritan "anti-aesthetic . . . of
drama as pathology." The Poet's talk of secretion
(1.1.27–28) figures dramatic poetry itself as bubonic
plague or venereal disease. As an example of "drama's
capacity in performance to transform the symptomatic
into the signifying," Elam discusses Peter Brook's 1974
"stripped-down colloquial French" *Timon*, in which the
director emphasized a "shifting . . . spatial semiotics . . .
of vicinity and distance" and used the bodies and different accents of his multiethnic group of actors to "disrupt
automatic cultural categories."

Ellis-Fermor, Una Mary. *"Timon of Athens." Review of
English Studies* 18 (1942): 270–83. Reprinted in *Shakespeare the Dramatist and Other Papers*, ed. Kenneth
Muir, pp. 158–76. London: Methuen, 1961.
  In this frequently cited essay, Ellis-Fermor attributes
the play's failure to achieve critical favor to its being
"unfinished," both textually and conceptually. In addition to the "uneven" act construction, the author discusses the weak introduction of Apemantus, prosodic
irregularities, the "patch-work effect" of even the best
speeches, the "inexplicable appearance of the fool" in

2.2, and the unanticipated and disconnected (although powerful) trial scene in 3.5. The greatest problem, however, is Timon himself; lacking a family, a past, and a personality, he is too isolated and detached from his society and circumstances and thus proves "inadequate" to the play's theme: the "hollowness of society and its relations." Since Shakespeare never links Timon's fate to that of the other characters, the play's "resultant action" lacks tragic inevitability. Its faults notwithstanding, Ellis-Fermor finds marks of Shakespeare's mature power in the imagery and prosody of the opening passages and in the first three scenes of Act 3: Timon is "a play such as a great artist might leave behind him, roughed out, worked over in part and then abandoned."

Empson, William. "Timon's Dog." In *The Structure of Complex Words*, pp. 175–84. 3rd ed. London: Chatto and Windus, 1979. [First published in 1951.]

In this study of metaphoric language, Empson examines the ambiguity of the iterative dog imagery in *Timon of Athens*. The double meaning of *dog* as a symbol of fawning flattery and snarling, envious cynicism functions as an index to the paradoxical nature of the self-contempt and misanthropy linking Apemantus and Timon, the former eventually moving from cynic to flatterer while the latter reverses that trajectory. Most of the metaphors suggest hatred of dogs, but the curious thing about *Timon* is that it also praises dogs, for the fawning spaniel can be affectionate and loyal, and the cynic is often a "disappointed idealist" who values honesty and tells the truth. The puzzle is that the "rival pregnancies" of the metaphor remain separate, its conflicting judgments both presented and refused: *dog* never manages to become a symbol inclusive of

cynicism and flattery, honesty and affection, "so as to imply a view of their proper relations." For Empson, "the striking thing . . . is that the dog symbolism could be worked out so far and yet remain somehow useless."

Fly, Richard D. "Confounding Contraries: The Unmediated World of *Timon of Athens*." In *Shakespeare's Mediated World*, pp. 117–42. Amherst: University of Massachusetts Press, 1976.

What Apemantus says of the play's "radically disjunct" protagonist—"The middle of humanity thou never knewest, but the extremity of both ends" (4.3.341–42)—is equally true of the unmediated discontinuities and polarizing opposites that control *Timon of Athens*'s overall dramatic design, suggesting that "Shakespeare's determination to avoid the middle ground of compromise and moderation extends far beyond the schizoid personality of his protagonist." *Timon*, in fact, represents "an explosive climax [in] Shakespeare's progression towards a play composed with 'no midway.' " The discontinuities of the action, the central character's absolute failure to enter into relationship with his Athenian society, the atomistic imagery and syntax, the "strangely bifurcated conclusion," and the play's difficulty in engaging the audience's emotional involvement reveal that "every element of [*Timon*'s] organization reflects the nonparticipatory stance of the misanthrope." Having created a play that "stubbornly resists all formal tendencies towards synthesis," and having pushed the dramatic medium itself to its breaking point in Timon's "suicidal silence," Shakespeare suddenly pulls back to suggest a return to mediation and balance in the redeeming figure of Alcibiades, who promises, by "us[ing] the olive with [his] sword," to make war and peace "prescribe" to each other (5.4.96–99). In doing so,

the dramatist may have sensed the metadramatic implications of his experiment in "confounding" rather than mediating "contraries."

Fulton, Robert C., III. "Timon, Cupid, and the Amazons." *Shakespeare Studies* 9 (1976): 283–99.
Like other mythological representations, Cupid and the Amazons possessed double meaning for the Renaissance: the blindfolded or "hoodwinked" Cupid held lethal as well as erotic potential, and the Amazons symbolized both heroic virtue and unconstrained passion and ferocity. This doubleness mirrors the "radically broken world" of Timon's Athens, in which splendor gives way to barrenness, friendship "dissipates in hypocrisy," and the invectives in Acts 4 and 5 counterpoint the "sweet airs" of Act 1. Apemantus's acerbic commentary on the masque underscores the show's ambiguity, rendering the whole entertainment "suspect"; for when the moral implications of Cupid and the Amazons are understood, what appears on the surface to be a "celebration of love and social harmony" becomes a banquet of the senses and carnality. When Timon, the "metaphorical whore and bawd of Athens," confronts two literal prostitutes in 4.3, his charge to them to infect the city with venereal disease "provides a crucial metaphoric reversal which fuses the play's broken halves": whereas Timon had been the food for Athens in the first three acts, now he will eat Athens. As visual suggestions of the "mastic and whoring" imagery central to the relationship between Timon and his city, Cupid and the Amazons "incarnate a unifying imagery within the play's polar movement."

Handelman, Susan. "*Timon of Athens:* The Rage of Disillusion." *American Imago* 36 (1979): 45–68.

In this feminist-psychoanalytic study, Handelman interprets *Timon of Athens* as "a demonstration of the rage which refuses to accept loss." Substituting male money for female milk and seeking "a male fantasy of exclusive brotherhood, based on an identity which needs to destroy the other," the protagonist refuses to mourn the primal loss of union with the nurturing mother; to desire such a "gratifying union" would destroy his "illusion of narcissistic omnipotence." For Handelman, the virtual exclusion of women from the play explains Timon's misanthropy, since "accepting woman means accepting loss." A world without the possibility of a Cordelia, the idealized embodiment of love and goodness, "splits itself apart," thereby precluding the integration of self and other. Justice and a semblance of order may be restored at the end of the play, but without the mediating presence of women and their capacity for making sense of pain and loss, transforming those ills "into life-affirming energies," no balancing order of love, mercy, and art is possible.

Jackson, Ken. " 'One Wish' or the Possibility of the Impossible: Derrida, the Gift, and God in *Timon of Athens*." *Shakespeare Quarterly* 52 (2001): 34–66.

Jackson uses Jacques Derrida's recent work on the "gift" (*Given Time: 1. Counterfeit Money* and *The Gift of Death*) to illuminate Shakespeare's "profound exploration of religion" in *Timon of Athens*. In contrast to Marcel Mauss, who emphasizes the principle of reciprocity (see Kahn below), Derrida calls "the gift, the impossible" because it demands something totally selfless, with no thought given to receiving something in exchange for one's generosity. Timon's passionately religious search for the gift that exists outside the circular economy of exchange "produces the critical crux"

at the heart of the play's scholarship—i.e., the central character's sudden shift from a generous noble to a mad misanthrope. Only in the faithful steward Flavius's offer of money to his former master (4.3.547–49) and wish that Timon "had power and wealth / To requite me by making rich yourself" (582–83) do we find a flash of the "gift": that "pure obligation or ethics toward the other . . . not grounded on any economy of exchange, but grounded on itself alone: a religion without religion." While "negotiating" the work of Derrida, Jackson frequently references G. Wilson Knight's "The Pilgrimage of Hate: An Essay on *Timon of Athens*," in *The Wheel of Fire: Interpretations of Shakespearean Tragedy with Three New Essays* (1930), calling his own essay a " 'postmodern' mutation" of Knight's "modernist classic."

Kahn, Coppélia. " 'Magic of bounty': *Timon of Athens*, Jacobean Patronage, and Maternal Power." *Shakespeare Quarterly* 38 (1987): 34–57. Reprinted in *Shakespearean Tragedy and Gender*, ed. Shirley Nelson Garner and Madelon Sprengnether, pp. 135–67. Bloomington: Indiana University Press, 1996.

Combining elements of feminist, psychoanalytic, and new historicist criticism, Kahn argues that "a deeply felt fantasy of woman and of power animates [*Timon of Athens*] and provides a paradigm for its strikingly bifurcated action." The "core fantasy" linking Timon's initial liberality with his later misanthropy is that of the child who is both attracted to and fearful of union with "a seductively maternal female presence," in this play figured as the goddess Fortuna, who generously gives and cruelly takes away. In the first two acts, Timon's aggressive generosity reflects his identification with the bountiful mother; the way he gives, however—

making the recipients of his bounty feel overwhelmingly indebted—leads to a "total disidentification" with the mother that takes "the form of an undiscriminating hostility toward all things human." To make this fantasy of "maternal bounty and maternal betrayal . . . dramatically intelligible," Shakespeare turned to the gift-giving practices and credit finance through which power was brokered at the court of James I. Under a patronage system that encouraged both king and courtiers alike to give and spend beyond their means, the ambiguities underlying gifts and loans often proved "lethal." *Timon's* concern with the social and psychological anxieties "resulting when bounty leads to indebtedness" renders it "a doubly topical play, linked to both the economic world and fantasy world of the Jacobean court." Central to Kahn's reading is Marcel Mauss's *The Gift: Forms and Functions of Exchange in Archaic Societies,* translated by Ian Cunnison (1925; reprint, New York: Norton, 1967). Mauss emphasizes the principle of reciprocity and the power relations involved in a gift exchange, especially those present when a "Big Man's" extravagant giving makes him so superior to the recipient that reciprocity becomes impossible.

Newman, Karen. "Cultural Capital's Gold Standard: Shakespeare and the Critical Apostrophe in Renaissance Studies." In *Discontinuities: New Essays on Renaissance Literature and Criticism,* ed. Viviana Comensoli and Paul Stevens, pp. 96–113. Toronto: University of Toronto Press, 1998.

Newman draws on John Guillory's work relating to "cultural capital" and "literary canon formation" in order to examine "what constitutes 'cultural capital' in the late twentieth-century United States academy."

She contends that mass cultural forms—television, contemporary movies, musical forms like rap, and cultural icons like Elvis—are "fast superseding 'literature' as cultural capital"; in the process, they are reducing the traditional canon to a "synecdoche"—Shakespeare and a handful of his plays "deemed properly Shakespearean." Justifying Shakespeare's centrality to contemporary cultural poetics, Newman makes *Timon of Athens*, the most "canonically problematic" of Shakespeare's plays, her prime example to demonstrate that "canonicity is always a question of rereading [in terms of contemporary cultural interests], that it is produced, not ontological, natural, innate." Her discussion of apostrophe and homoerotic relations in the play (a slightly revised version of her argument in the essay annotated below) deliberately inflates *Timon*'s canonical value in today's academy, apostrophizing (i.e., reanimating) the play "by reading it as a chapter in the history of early modern sexuality."

Newman, Karen. "Rereading Shakespeare's *Timon of Athens* at the fin de siècle." In *Shakespeare and the Twentieth Century: The Selected Proceedings of the International Shakespeare Association World Congress, Los Angeles, 1996*, ed. Jonathan Bate, Jill L. Levenson, and Dieter Mehl, pp. 378–89. Newark: University of Delaware Press; London: Associated University Presses, 1998.

Newman reads *Timon of Athens* "not in terms of what would recuperate it to contemporary normative historicist or psychoanalytic protocols in Renaissance studies, but instead by way of different economies of figure and address." Central to her argument is the figure of apostrophe, which involves directly addressing an absent, dead, or inanimate being. Troping not on

the meaning of a word but on its "circuit of communication" (i.e., its indirect manipulation of the "I/You"
relationship in direct address), apostrophe functions
as a figure of reciprocity and giving, thus animating
and bestowing agency; however, it may also compli-
cate that process by raising questions about the very
identity of the addressee. Apostrophe is, therefore,
"a preeminently suitable trope for Timon; it is the
'gold' of the play in its powers of performance and
address." Among the examples Newman cites are the
poet's "periphrastic apostrophe" that introduces
Timon as "seemingly infinite, even supernatural . . .
'bounty' " (1.1.8–9), the apostrophized walls of Athens
(4.1.1–21), and Timon's apostrophe of gold when digging for roots (4.3.28–53, 425–38). This last example
leads Newman to privilege the influence of Plutarch
over Lucian in an "act of critical apostrophe" that animates a different *Timon of Athens*, one insistently
homoerotic. Plutarch's characterization of Alcibiades,
in particular, encourages a reading open to the play's
"sodomitical economy." Applying Jacques Lacan's
"equivalence function of the phallus" to Timon's apos-
trophed gold, Newman argues that Timon sets a
"phallic standard" of male love and passionate friendship that "adumbrates another view of Jacobean gift
giving."

Walker, Lewis. "*Timon of Athens* and the Morality Tradition." *Shakespeare Studies* 12 (1979): 159–77.
   In sharp contrast to the standard negative assessment of *Timon of Athens*, Walker finds the work to be
unified and coherent, largely as a result of its indebtedness to the medieval morality play tradition. Going
beyond those who have simply noted the play's fable-
like qualities and the allegorical nature of its charac-

ters, Walker discusses specific features linking *Timon* to the earlier type of drama: e.g., the protagonist's relationship to the generic Mankind figure (especially in his worldly phase); Apemantus's choric function and the role of Mankind's good and bad advisers; the symbolic use of music to register earthly power and "ironically to undercut that power"; the introduction of the masque, which recalls the role of the five senses in the morality conception of Mankind's bondage to the world; the introduction of the Fool in 2.2 as a nexus between greed and lust that draws on the morality play's linking of those two vices; and the portrayal of a corrupt Athenian society that reflects the fragmentation of the generic Mankind figure into representatives of different social classes and professions, all linked through the vice of greed, a pervasive theme of late-sixteenth-century morality drama.

Shakespeare's Language

Abbott, E. A. *A Shakespearian Grammar.* New York: Haskell House, 1972.
    This compact reference book, first published in 1870, helps with many difficulties in Shakespeare's language. It systematically accounts for a host of differences between Shakespeare's usage and sentence structure and our own.

Blake, Norman. *Shakespeare's Language: An Introduction.* New York: St. Martin's Press, 1983.
    This general introduction to Elizabethan English discusses various aspects of the language of Shakespeare and his contemporaries, offering possible meanings for hundreds of ambiguous constructions.

Dobson, E. J. *English Pronunciation, 1500–1700*. 2 vols. Oxford: Clarendon Press, 1968.

This long and technical work includes chapters on spelling (and its reformation), phonetics, stressed vowels, and consonants in early modern English.

Houston, John. *Shakespearean Sentences: A Study in Style and Syntax*. Baton Rouge: Louisiana State University Press, 1988.

Houston studies Shakespeare's stylistic choices, considering matters such as sentence length and the relative positions of subject, verb, and direct object. Examining plays throughout the canon in a roughly chronological, developmental order, he analyzes how sentence structure is used in setting tone, in characterization, and for other dramatic purposes.

Onions, C. T. *A Shakespeare Glossary*. Oxford: Clarendon Press, 1986.

This revised edition updates Onions's standard, selective glossary of words and phrases in Shakespeare's plays that are now obsolete, archaic, or obscure.

Robinson, Randal. *Unlocking Shakespeare's Language: Help for the Teacher and Student*. Urbana, Ill.: National Council of Teachers of English and the ERIC Clearinghouse on Reading and Communication Skills, 1989.

Specifically designed for the high-school and undergraduate college teacher and student, Robinson's book addresses the problems that most often hinder present-day readers of Shakespeare. Through work with his own students, Robinson found that many readers today are particularly puzzled by such stylistic devices as subject-verb inversion, interrupted structures, and compression. He shows how our own colloquial language

contains comparable structures, and thus helps students recognize such structures when they find them in Shakespeare's plays. This book supplies worksheets—with examples from major plays—to illuminate and remedy such problems as unusual sequences of words and the separation of related parts of sentences.

Williams, Gordon. *A Dictionary of Sexual Language and Imagery in Shakespearean and Stuart Literature.* 3 vols. London: Athlone Press, 1994.
  Williams provides a comprehensive list of the words to which Shakespeare, his contemporaries, and later Stuart writers gave sexual meanings. He supports his identification of these meanings by extensive quotations.

Shakespeare's Life

Baldwin, T. W. *William Shakspere's Petty School.* Urbana: University of Illinois Press, 1943.
  Baldwin here investigates the theory and practice of the petty school, the first level of education in Elizabethan England. He focuses on that educational system primarily as it is reflected in Shakespeare's art.

Baldwin, T. W. *William Shakspere's Small Latine and Lesse Greeke.* 2 vols. Urbana: University of Illinois Press, 1944.
  Baldwin attacks the view that Shakespeare was an uneducated genius—a view that had been dominant among Shakespeareans since the eighteenth century. Instead, Baldwin shows, the educational system of Shakespeare's time would have given the playwright a strong background in the classics, and there is much in

the plays that shows how Shakespeare benefited from such an education.

Beier, A. L., and Roger Finlay, eds. *London 1500–1700: The Making of the Metropolis.* New York: Longman, 1986.
Focusing on the economic and social history of early modern London, these collected essays probe aspects of metropolitan life, including "Population and Disease," "Commerce and Manufacture," and "Society and Change."

Bentley, G. E. *Shakespeare's Life: A Biographical Handbook.* New Haven: Yale University Press, 1961.
This "just-the-facts" account presents the surviving documents of Shakespeare's life against an Elizabethan background.

Chambers, E. K. *William Shakespeare: A Study of Facts and Problems.* 2 vols. Oxford: Clarendon Press, 1930.
Analyzing in great detail the scant historical data, Chambers's complex, scholarly study considers the nature of the texts in which Shakespeare's work is preserved.

Cressy, David. *Education in Tudor and Stuart England.* London: Edward Arnold, 1975.
This volume collects sixteenth-, seventeenth-, and early-eighteenth-century documents detailing aspects of formal education in England, such as the curriculum, the control and organization of education, and the education of women.

De Grazia, Margreta. *Shakespeare Verbatim: The Reproduction of Authenticity and the 1790 Apparatus.* Oxford: Clarendon Press, 1991.

De Grazia traces and discusses the development of such editorial criteria as authenticity, historical periodization, factual biography, chronological development, and close reading, locating as the point of origin Edmond Malone's 1790 edition of Shakespeare's works. There are interesting chapters on the First Folio and on the "legendary" versus the "documented" Shakespeare.

Dutton, Richard. *William Shakespeare: A Literary Life.* New York: St. Martin's Press, 1989.

Not a biography in the traditional sense, Dutton's very readable work nevertheless "follows the contours of Shakespeare's life" as he examines Shakespeare's career as playwright and poet, with consideration of his patrons, theatrical associations, and audience.

Fraser, Russell. *Young Shakespeare.* New York: Columbia University Press, 1988.

Fraser focuses on Shakespeare's first thirty years, paying attention simultaneously to his life and art.

Schoenbaum, S. *William Shakespeare: A Compact Documentary Life.* New York: Oxford University Press, 1977.

This standard biography economically presents the essential documents from Shakespeare's time in an accessible narrative account of the playwright's life.

Shakespeare's Theater

Bentley, G. E. *The Profession of Player in Shakespeare's Time, 1590–1642.* Princeton: Princeton University Press, 1984.

Bentley readably sets forth a wealth of evidence about performance in Shakespeare's time, with special attention to the relations between player and company, and the business of casting, managing, and touring.

Berry, Herbert. *Shakespeare's Playhouses*. New York: AMS Press, 1987.
Berry's six essays collected here discuss (with illustrations) varying aspects of the four playhouses in which Shakespeare had a financial stake: the Theatre in Shoreditch, the Blackfriars, and the first and second Globe.

Cook, Ann Jennalie. *The Privileged Playgoers of Shakespeare's London*. Princeton: Princeton University Press, 1981.
Cook's work argues, on the basis of sociological, economic, and documentary evidence, that Shakespeare's audience—and the audience for English Renaissance drama generally—consisted mainly of the "privileged."

Greg, W. W. *Dramatic Documents from the Elizabethan Playhouses*. 2 vols. Oxford: Clarendon Press, 1931.
Greg itemizes and briefly describes many of the play manuscripts that survive from the period 1590 to around 1660, including, among other things, players' parts. His second volume offers facsimiles of selected manuscripts.

Gurr, Andrew. *Playgoing in Shakespeare's London*. Cambridge: Cambridge University Press, 1987.
Gurr charts how the theatrical enterprise developed from its modest beginnings in the late 1560s to become a thriving institution in the 1600s. He argues that there were important changes over the period 1567–1644 in the playhouses, the audience, and the plays.

Harbage, Alfred. *Shakespeare's Audience*. New York: Columbia University Press, 1941.

Harbage investigates the fragmentary surviving evidence to interpret the size, composition, and behavior of Shakespeare's audience.

Hattaway, Michael. *Elizabethan Popular Theatre: Plays in Performance*. London: Routledge and Kegan Paul, 1982.

Beginning with a study of the popular drama of the late Elizabethan age—a description of the stages, performance conditions, and acting of the period—this volume concludes with an analysis of five well-known plays of the 1590s, one of them (*Titus Andronicus*) by Shakespeare.

Shapiro, Michael. *Children of the Revels: The Boy Companies of Shakespeare's Time and Their Plays*. New York: Columbia University Press, 1977.

Shapiro chronicles the history of the amateur and quasi-professional child companies that flourished in London at the end of Elizabeth's reign and the beginning of James's.

The Publication of Shakespeare's Plays

Blayney, Peter W. M. *The First Folio of Shakespeare*. Hanover, Md.: Folger, 1991.

Blayney's accessible account of the printing and later life of the First Folio—an amply illustrated catalog to a 1991 Folger Shakespeare Library exhibition—analyzes the mechanical production of the First Folio, describing how the Folio was made, by whom and for whom, how much it cost, and its ups

and downs (or, rather, downs and ups) since its printing in 1623.

Hinman, Charlton. *The Norton Facsimile: The First Folio of Shakespeare*. 2nd ed. New York: W. W. Norton, 1996.

This facsimile presents a photographic reproduction of an "ideal" copy of the First Folio of Shakespeare; Hinman attempts to represent each page in its most fully corrected state. The second edition includes an important new introduction by Peter W. M. Blayney.

Hinman, Charlton. *The Printing and Proof-Reading of the First Folio of Shakespeare*. 2 vols. Oxford: Clarendon Press, 1963.

In the most arduous study of a single book ever undertaken, Hinman attempts to reconstruct how the Shakespeare First Folio of 1623 was set into type and run off the press, sheet by sheet. He also provides almost all the known variations in readings from copy to copy.

Key to
Famous Lines and Phrases

'Tis not enough to help the feeble up,
But to support him after.

[Timon—1.1.125–26]

Here's that which is too weak to be a sinner,
Honest water, which ne'er left man i' th' mire.

[Apemantus—1.2.61–62]

Men shut their doors against a setting sun.

[Apemantus—1.2.149]

Happier is he that has no friend to feed
Than such that do e'en enemies exceed.

[Flavius—1.2.214–15]

When every feather sticks in his own wing
Lord Timon will be left a naked gull.

[Senator—2.1.31–32]

. . . pity is the virtue of the law,
And none but tyrants use it cruelly.

[Alcibiades—3.5.8–9]

    . . . his poor self,
A dedicated beggar to the air,
With his disease of all-shunned poverty,
Walks, like contempt, alone.

[Second Servant—4.2.14–17]

"We have seen better days."

[*Flavius*—4.2.31]

Timon hath made his everlasting mansion
Upon the beachèd verge of the salt flood.

[*Timon*—5.1.247–48]